Learning from E
Principles and Practice i

For Jo and Jessie,
youthful and energetic critics,
who have always ensured that whatever I think I know
will be called into question . . .

Learning from Experience: Principles and Practice in Action-Research

by
Richard Winter

with contributions from
Susan Burroughs, David Crosson,
Ann Leontovitsch, Helen Thorne

The Falmer Press
(A member of the Taylor & Francis Group)
London • New York • Philadelphia

UK   The Falmer Press, Falmer House, Barcombe, Lewes,
East Sussex, BN8 5DL

USA   The Falmer Press, Taylor & Francis Inc., 242 Cherry Street,
Philadelphia, PA 19106-1906

© Richard Winter 1989

First published 1989

British Library Cataloguing in Publication Data

Winter, Richard, 1943–
Learning from experience: principles and practice in action-research.
1. Action research. Methodology
I. Title
300'.72

ISBN 1-85000-610-5
ISBN 1-85000-61113   pbk

Library of Congress Cataloguing in Publication Data

Winter, Richard, 1943-
Learning from experience: principles and practice in action-
research/by Richard Winter with Susan Burroughs... [et al].
    p. cm.
Bibliography: p.
Includes index.
ISBN 1-85000-610-5. — ISBN 1-85000-611-3   (pbk.)
1. Action research in education. 2. Action research in education-
Great Britain. I. Title
   LB1028.24.W55 1989
   370'.7'8—dc20

Jacket design by Caroline Archer
Drawing by Jessica Jackson–Winter, aged 11 years

*Typeset in 10½/12 points in California by
Chapterhouse, The Cloisters, Formby L37 3PX
Printed in Great Britain by Taylor & Francis (Printers) Ltd, Basingstoke*

9. 24. 90

Contents

Preface

Some years ago, I received a rather irritating birthday card. On the front was a cartoon picture of a perspiring, red-faced driver trying to manoeuvre his (much dented) car into a very tight parking space. Inside was the motto: 'A fool learns from his own mistakes; a wise man learns from the mistakes of others — Confucius'. This book is written to present the counter-argument: that the process of understanding must start from reflection upon one's own experience, and that the sort of 'wisdom' derived entirely from the experience of others is at best impoverished, and at worst illusory.

This is particularly the case where one is concerned, not with driving a car (where perhaps indeed 'learning from experience' can be rather expensive) but with attempts to understand professional work involving decisions about and for other people, for example, education, nursing, social work, management. The fundamental purpose of the book is to provide encouragement and advice for practitioners in such professions about the process of action-research as a method of professional learning. It is addressed particularly to those who sense that they would *like* to base the next step of their professional development upon an *investigation* into the work with which they are involved, but are deterred by warnings that practitioners cannot fully understand their own practice without the benefit of all the books on the subject based on what 'wise men' have observed to be the case. Refutations of such warnings are part of the argument of the book. Action-research work is sometimes criticized for lacking rigour and general significance in comparison with conventional research, and one of my central themes is that such attacks are misguided, and rest on simplistic notions about the nature of validity in social science.

In an important sense, the book is also about the nature of the *learning* process, about the link between practice and reflection, about the process of attempting to have 'new' thoughts about familiar experiences, and about the relationship between particular experiences and general ideas. 'Action-research' here is used as a way of referring to ways of investigating professional experience which link practice and the analysis of practice into a single productive and continuously developing sequence, and which link researchers and researched into a single community of interested colleagues.

The book has arisen out of my experience of action-research in educational contexts, both as a practitioner investigating aspects of my own work and as a tutor on In-service courses where the 'students' are teachers and lecturers carrying out their own developmental projects. Consequently, the examples given throughout the book refer to the profession of education. But all the underlying ideas and methods are equally applicable to other 'people-oriented' professions, and I therefore hope that they too will find it of interest. My main hope is that after reading the book practitioners (teachers, lecturers, educational advisers, and even managers, nurses or social workers) will think: 'Well, yes, it seems do-able: complex, but nothing mysterious or impossibly time-consuming about it. And I can think of a problem in my work where it might be a useful approach.'

The first part of the book presents *methods* for action-research. It starts with a summary of some quite familiar methods (chapter two), and goes on to argue (in chapter three) that certain aspects of those methods, particularly concerning the process of 'reflection' — the *analysis* of experience — need clarification. Finally, chapter four presents a revised set of principles for practitioner action-research. These are presented in a practical form, with general principles illustrated by concrete examples; the theoretical arguments and the academic tradition on which they are based are to be found in the author's earlier book, *Action-Research and the Nature of Social Inquiry*, published in 1987.

Part two presents examples of work carried out in the light of the methods described in chapter four, and also discusses issues and processes involved in writing appropriate research reports for this kind of work (chapters five and eight). Part three deals with the question of deciding 'what to investigate', of finding the links between institutional priorities and one's own individual interests. The link between the approaches advocated in this book and the controversial question of 'ideology' is discussed in a postscript.

The book was written specifically for teachers on In-service courses, which increasingly are based on professional investigation and development; and I should like to acknowledge the help and inspiration I have received over the past few years from all the 'students' on the Anglia part-time MEd in Educational Research and Evaluation, at Brentwood, Essex. For their dedication, determination, subtlety, and resourcefulness in the face of every obstacle, I have unbounded admiration; they were my immediate audience, to whom, in imagination I was speaking as I wrote.

I must also acknowledge the enormous debt which this book owes to Susan Hart. Her criticism and advice, based on her experience as Head of Special Needs in a London comprehensive school, as a support teacher in primary schools, and as a researcher at Thames Polytechnic (together with her own substantial experience as a writer on education) have at every stage of the work been invaluable; and the faults which nevertheless remain are due to my inability to learn sufficiently from our conversations.

Richard Winter
February 1989
Anglia Higher Education College
Sawyers Hall Lane
Brentwood
Essex

PART ONE: METHOD

'The Opposition are twisting the facts'

Dr Otto Hasler,
Leader of the Lichtenstein Government Party
(Reported on BBC Radio 4 News, 4 March, 1989)

Chapter 1

Introduction to Part One: Action-Research — Opportunities and Method

---

Action-Research as a Professional Ideal

The main part of this book will be concerned, in one way or another, with methods. But in order to provide a proper context for the discussion of methods, it is important to consider (first) the ideas which lie behind the use of the term 'action-research', and (second) the nature of the contribution which action-research can make to current professional issues in education.

For a long time now, professional educators have been claiming the value and the possibility of research as an activity which could and should be an integral part of professional work, as opposed to a separate activity carried out by specialist academics *upon* professional workers.

> The general organization of research is that one set of people (researchers) carry out research on another set of people (for example, teachers) . . . . There are a number of reasons why the chances of such research having practical outcomes are small. (Bartholomew, 1972)

> A specialist research profession will always be a poor substitute for a self-monitoring educational community. (MacDonald and Walker, 1975)

The specific form of research which is adapted to this purpose is summed up in the phrase 'action-research':

> Action-research might be defined as: the study of a social situation with a view to improving the quality of action within it . . . (The) total process — review, diagnosis, planning, implementation, monitoring effects — provides the necessary link between self-evaluation and professional development. (Elliott, 1982, p.ii, p.1)

The overall claim for the value of action-research by practitioners has a number of aspects. Firstly, professional workers are in a position to avoid the split between theoretical and practical understanding which bedevils the institutional role of the academic social scientist; hence the use of the term 'action-research', indicating the basic unity of theoretical and practical knowledge. Professional workers are not, therefore, to be thought of as the 'objects' of research into professional practice but always (at least) as collaborating research workers and (ideally) as well placed to initiate and carry out the investigation and development of the practices and understandings in which they are involved. (This is not to deny the possibility that outsiders of different kinds may make valuable contributions as facilitators, expert consultants, etc.) Hence the complete phrase which describes the activity is 'practitioner action-research'.

This phrase ('practitioner action-research') describes both a viable mode of organizing educational 'research', and also an ideal which is already inherent within the role of 'professional' worker. Practitioner action-research is thus part of the general ideal of professionalism, an *extension* of professional work, not an *addition* to it. It thus points to a form of learning which is an intrinsic outcome of professional *experience*, and to a form of involvement with practical experience which is intrinsically *educational*.

This is a way of asserting the real value of small-scale research and development projects carried out by practitioners on a part-time basis, concurrently with their professional work. The development of understanding and the initiation of innovative practice are therefore not to be thought of as the prerogative of an *elite* of academics or managers, but a possibility and even a responsibility for professional workers *in general*. Hence the assertion of the viability of practitioner action-research is the assertion of a democratic social and political ideal, the ideal of a creative and involved citizenry, in opposition to the image of a passive populace awaiting instruction from above. The significance of this argument is strengthened by the ever-increasing number of workers of different categories who claim that they too are 'professional' workers, and are thus entitled to the consideration appropriate to their expertise and their responsibilities.

A substantial body of writing elaborates these claims and describes methods and examples of work; see for example: Elliott *et al*, 1974; Nixon (Ed), 1981; Kemmis *et al*, 1982; Elliott, 1982; Walker, 1985; Carr and Kemmis, 1986; Winter, 1987; and above all the series of *Classroom Action Research Network* Bulletins, Nos 1–9, 1978–1989. The practitioner action-research tradition thus has available principles, methods and examples of work. The range of procedures is varied and powerful enough to enable practitioners to respond constructively to the rapidly changing series of issues which structure professional work, as a result of historical changes and government policies. Indeed, the speed of these changes, and the speed with which new policy directives are produced 'on high' are going to require precisely the form of creative, innovative professionalism evoked by the practitioner action-research ideal. This is especially important if we as teachers are to retain any sort of significant control over our working lives, and if the current series of managerial directives is to generate anything other than a combination of massive organizational confusion, plummeting morale, and a sequence of vacuous policy documents gathering dust on various shelves and notice-boards. Let us then consider briefly some of the current opportunities and challenges which make the development of these methods an urgent priority for our profession.

Action-Research and Current Educational Issues

Practitioner action-research is equally relevant to work in schools, colleges of further education, institutions of higher education, LEA administrative and advisory staff, and (indeed) to many other professional contexts, but I will restrict this account to schools, colleges and HE institutions.

Schools

As a result of recent initiatives, headteachers are going to have to explore ways of introducing staff appraisal processes, ways of implementing equal opportunities on the basis of gender, ethnicity, and class, ways of negotiating the effectiveness of staff meetings (now that they are to be in teachers' *directed* time), ways of relating to the newly enhanced powers of governors (and hence ways of socializing newly appointed governors into attitudes compatible with the educational philosophy of the school), and ways of negotiating the utilization of school-based INSET days in relation to staff concerns and perceptions of their professional needs. Class teachers are faced with the complex tasks of negotiating common ground between (on the one hand) the generalized demands both of national curriculum documents and of formal test criteria, and (on the other hand) the specific and variable emotional and intellectual characteristics of the children they are teaching. The requirements of children with 'special' educational needs will require careful analysis of the curriculum provision for the whole class of which such children are a part. And the emphasis on the need for relevant and concrete links between secondary curricula and work experience is going to require the development of new forms of assignment, new methods of assessment, and the negotiation of relationships with staff working in different institutions with different values and assumptions. None of these are matters where simple rules could be prescribed and applied, even supposing that someone somewhere knew what such rules ought to be: on the contrary, each school and class and pupil presents unique demands, which must be carefully analyzed if the correspondingly unique opportunities are to be grasped. Each new process as it is negotiated for the first time will only be incompletely successful, and will thus need continuous evaluation and development.

Colleges of Further Education

Here the need for enhanced professional flexibility and innovativeness is not only due to political directives concerning specific administrative arrangements but also to long-term historical factors. The introduction of effective birth-control in the sixties means that the size of age cohorts entering work is now even more of a social than a natural phenomenon, and thus much more unpredictable. This in turn creates a further instability in the relationship between an age-group and its employment possibilities, in addition to the instabilities created by the economic cycle of booms and slumps. Periods of massive youth unemployment will thus continue to alternate dramatically with periods of massive skill shortage, and the role of the FE college will thus be subject to frequent corresponding convulsions, as it operates in a *market* for vocational training opportunities which will be continuously affected by powerful economic forces. Staff will thus find their work is both shifting and varied. No longer will former craft workers simply be able to transmit their skills to youngsters whose needs can be assumed to resemble those of the lecturers' own earlier selves. Instead the FE lecturer must become involved as a tutor, as a course marketeer and entrepreneur, as a provider of distance learning materials and tutorial counsellor for home- or work-based students, and as a placement organizer, evaluator, and liaison worker. In each respect, staff will find themselves working in new and unpredictable environments, needing to negotiate new and varied relationships, and thus requiring continuously to analyze their effectiveness and to develop innovative practices, at the level of organization, student selection, curriculum provision, and assessment. Careers are likely to involve periodic work placements for 'updating', and subsequent analysis of the relevance of that new learning for further phases of work in course provision. FE lecturers, then, are going to need to become not only experts in their 'trade', but also experts in the skills of innovation and experts at learning from their own varied experiences.

Higher Education

Many of the same factors and developments apply as in further education. The modularization of courses will give students greater power to opt in or out of particular course elements, requiring lecturing staff to be more concerned than has traditionally been the case for the relationship between the 'demands' of academic disciplines and students' perceived interests. Staff will thus need to monitor and evaluate responses to their teaching and to consider their own proper response to student feed-back. Furthermore, the provision of access courses in FE colleges and the introduction of procedures for giving academic credit for students' prior learning experience (at work and elsewhere) will combine to widen the range of students in HE. This will require HE staff to adapt to the needs and styles of student groups who will *not* all have been socialized by 'A' levels into compliance with academic modes. This in turn will throw open a whole range of questions as to admissions procedures. It will also, again, require HE lecturing staff to reconsider their teaching methods and the relevance of their course content. However, these reconsiderations will be less and less likely to produce new definitive solutions: increasingly, HE staff, like lecturers in further education colleges and in school, will find that they cannot simply transmit a corpus of knowledge but must teach in ways which continuously draw on the experiences of their students, through processes of concurrent negotiation and subsequent evaluation. The reduction of funding for full-time courses will create demands for the provision of distance learning materials, for courses based on intermittent day-release punctuating work on individual projects. As a result, the HE staff member will become less of a lecturer (a 'Don' — figure of knowledge-based power) and more of a consultant (a resource and a guide). The same is true of research activity, which financial pressures will render less autonomous and more responsive, creating greater need for processes of negotiating accountability to clients.

All this means that HE staff will be faced with questions of how to innovate in response to continuously shifting demands and how to evaluate in order to learn from the experience of those demands. Consequently, all the decisions about course content and teaching methods which lecturers have tended to make 'instinctively' (on the basis that their 'real' qualifications for the job lie in their subject expertise) are now clearly on the agenda for professional educators facing the *challenge* of satisfying the complex and varying demands of highly competent adults. The newly harsh 'competitive market' environment for HE means that there will be a choice between effective responsiveness in relation to these matters and empty classrooms, threatening disaster.

The underlying argument of this section is that the skills of practitioner action-research are highly (and increasingly) relevant to current problems in the role of educators (and indeed of other professionals) in all types of institution. The type of institution does not matter: in general terms 'methods' are 'the same', except in the very important sense that every practitioner and every investigative project must at one level improvise appropriate methods afresh on every occasion. The essence of action-research is that, being responsive to and inseparable from the practices and situations it seeks to develop, its methods can be given as a set of general principles and as a set of illustrative examples, but *not* as a set of precise prescriptions. Deciding what exactly to do in one's own situation, (given one's particular resources and purposes) is in itself both a necessary task and the origin of much of the resultant learning. This returns us to the methodological theme of the book.

Action-Research and 'Methods'

If one of the characteristics of practitioner action-research is that it denies the necessity for expert social scientists to carry out the investigation of professional work, then there has to be at least a potential irony about an emphasis on methods. If the process is an inherent part of the professional ideal anyway, are specific methods necessary? The point is clearly made by Bridget Somekh (1989), coordinator of the Classroom Action Research Network, in her opening address to the 1988 conference:

> I am concerned that the definition of action research has some-
> how narrowed....I find myself wondering how we have come to
> see it as something complicated. By some perverse process we
> seem to have built an ivory tower around it and turned it into
> something exclusive....I want to reaffirm action research as
> belonging to teachers (p. 1).

I sympathize entirely with the spirit of these words, but I do not think that they necessarily suggest that practitioner action-research has no need of methods, because although it should certainly not be exclusive, this does not mean that it is easy. 'Experience' is not quite the same as *'learning* from experience'. We have all heard the witticism directed at a colleague who is supposed to have had 'ten years' experience': 'No,' comes the reply, 'They've had *one* year's experience repeated *ten* times over.' The point is that when we learn *significantly* from our experience, we use skills (which can be improved) and methods (which can be described). Thus I would argue, judging from my own and others' experience, that although action-research need *not* be exclusive (given a minimum of support and guidance, anyone can do it), nevertheless it *is* complex — and that is part of its value. Furthermore, without guidance concerning the processes involved, there is a real danger that many of those who begin quite optimistically may become dispirited when they wonder 'how much' of an apparently endless mountain of data they 'need', and 'where to start' interpreting it. The danger is that action-research then really does become exclusive — to a small proportion of exceptional people who combine enormous vocational devotion, a natural inclination towards self-analysis, academic qualifications in social science, minimal domestic commitments, and (preferably also) fairly severe workaholism!

Thus, I am not wishing to 'narrow the definition' of action-research. What I wish to do, rather, is to clarify some of the difficulties which will be encountered, so that practitioner action-researchers can have confidence in the basis for their decision-making. In other words, my concern to describe specific methods arises from a desire to ensure that the process of successfully engaging in an action-research project is fully available to all, and also from my own experience of the practical difficulties involved.

The plan of part one of the book is as follows. Chapter two provides a summary of the essential starting points for an understanding of action-research methods, in the widely influential work of John Elliott and Stephen Kemmis. Chapter three suggests that some of the methods described in chapter two leave unanswered certain key theoretical and practical questions, largely because they tacitly borrow from research methods devised by and for full-time academic researchers. These methods therefore require more time and data than are available to a practising professional worker, and this can lead to a sense of inadequacy on the part of the would-be action-researcher. This also helps the opponents of practitioner action-research, (for example, academic researchers who would prefer to preserve their monopoly of the production of new understanding, and unsophisticated managers who think their problems might be solved if they could persuade professional workers to adopt the role of obedient employees) by enabling them to dismiss practitioner action-research as but a weak and amateurish imitation of 'real research'. Chapter four then describes a series of six basic methodological principles which provide a consistent (and thus easily defended) set of practical procedures (which are illustrated by a series of specific examples in part two).

The six principles are the outcome of a theoretical study (Winter, 1987), and anyone who is interested in the theoretical basis which underlies the practical principles outlined in chapter four is referred to this work. However, the origin of that study was itself wholly practical: I was engaged in trying to carry out an action-research investigation of an aspect of my own work as a teacher (of college students), and found that I did not know how to set about making fundamental practical decisions, for example, how to select from a mass of data, how to set about 'interpreting' my colleagues' opinions, etc (see Winter, 1980, 1982). I am writing therefore as a practitioner action-researcher. What I wish to argue is that practitioners are *potentially* well placed to originate investigations of practice, innovations in practice, and new understandings of practice; but that when they do so, they are likely to find, as I did, that difficulties occur when they attempt to use the methods and principles devised for research as an activity to be carried out by academics in the role of outside observers. What, therefore, is needed is a set of methodological principles designed specifically for the opportunities and limitations of being *both* a practitioner *and* an investigator of practice. It is the purpose of this book to provide such a set of usable methodological guidelines.

Chapter 2

Action-Research: The Basic Process

As an introduction to action-research methods, this chapter presents a descriptive summary of the basic process, derived mainly from two well-known texts — *The Action-Research Planner* (1982), by Kemmis *et al*, and Elliott's (1982) working paper: 'Action-Research: A Framework for Self-Evaluation in Schools'. The chapter begins with some general proposals, gives summaries of a number of actual projects by way of illustration, and finally lists some details of the methods and procedures involved.

The Practitioner is the Researcher

Elliott (1982) describes action-research as 'the study of a social situation, with a view to improving the quality of action within it' (p.1). The broadness of this definition is useful at this stage, since it allows in principle for a wide range of approaches and methods, while indicating the guiding ideal of an intrinsic link between theory and practice, and hence between the role of the practitioner and the role of the researcher. It is useful to bear in mind the broadness of this definition, so that the more precise descriptions of procedures and methods in the latter half of the chapter may be seen as examples, rather than as prescriptions.

Earlier, Elliott emphasizes that action-research 'provides the necessary link between self-evaluation and professional development' (*ibid*, p.ii). There are two important points in this phrase. The first is that the process involves *reflection*, i.e., the development of understanding (signalled in Elliott's use of the word 'evaluation'); the second is that the process involves changes in *practice*, as indicated in the term 'professional development'. One of the fundamental claims of action-research is that although these two aims can be separated conceptually, they are best achieved *together*, i.e., by one person or one group of people working 'together'. Hence:

> A distinguishing feature of action-research is that those affected
> by planned changes have the primary responsibility for deciding
> on courses of action which seem likely to lead to improvement,

and for evaluating the results of strategies tried out in practice. (Kemmis *et al*, 1982, p.6).

Therefore, since the evaluators are also the practitioners — and vice versa — evaluation within an action-research process will have elements of 'self-evaluation', although this will often involve a mutual, collaborative process between two or more people and may also include seeking outsider perspectives as a check or a stimulus. Thus, the agenda for the evaluation is not determined by an outside agency (an 'academic' researcher or an institutional superior) but by those whose practices are to change as a result of the evaluation.

A slightly different emphasis in the argument, that action-research also involves increasing one's factual knowledge about the situation, is added in the following statement by Elliott (1980):

> Basically classroom action-research relates to any teacher who is concerned with his own teaching; the teacher who is prepared to question his own approaches in order to improve its quality. Therefore the teacher is involved in looking at what is actually going on in the classroom . . . it is implicit in the idea of *action* research that there should be some practical effect or end product to the research; but based on an increased awareness of what actually happens in the classroom. (p.36)

The Action-Research Cycle

The other way in which action-research seeks to unite its two central concerns — improvement in practice and increased knowledge and understanding — is by linking them into an integrated *cycle* of activities, in which each phase learns from the previous one and shapes the next. This idea is usually associated with the work of Lewin (1946, p.38). Kemmis *et al* (1982) describe it as follows:

> In practice, the process begins with a general idea that some kind of improvement or change is desirable. In deciding just where to begin in making improvements, one decides on a field of action — where the battle (not the whole war) should be fought. It is a decision on where it is possible to have an impact. The general idea prompts a reconnaissance of the circumstances of the field, and fact-finding about them. Having decided on the field and made a preliminary reconnaissance, the action researcher decides on a general plan of action. Breaking the general plan down into achievable steps, the action researcher settles on the first action step, a change in strategy which aims not only at improvement, but a greater understanding about what it will be possible to

Figure 1: The action-research cycle, as interpreted by Elliott (1982, p. ii, p. 3) and by Kemmis et al (1982, p. 7)

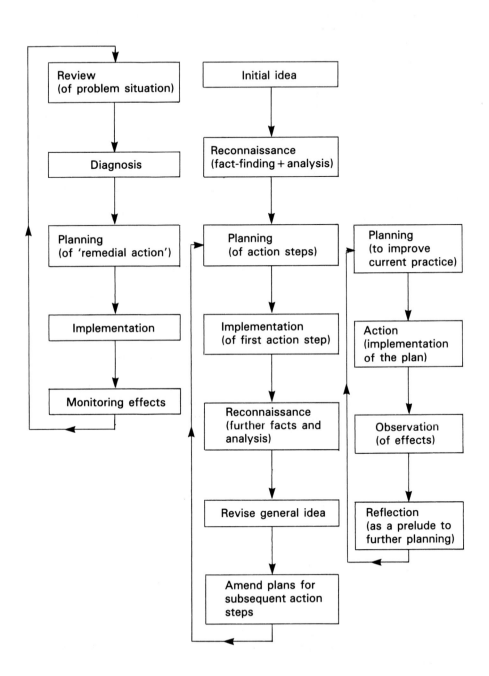

achieve later as well. Before taking this first step, the action researcher becomes more circumspect and devises a way of monitoring the effects of the first action step, the circumstances in which it occurs, and what the strategy begins to look like in practice. When it is possible to maintain the fact-finding by monitoring the action, the first step is taken. As the step is implemented, new data starts coming in and the circumstances, action, and effects can be described and evaluated. This evaluation stage amounts to a fresh reconnaissance which can prepare the way for new planning. (pp. 6–7)

Kemmis and Elliott present this repeating sequence of activities in broadly similar terms, as set out in figure 1, which makes it clear that the action-research process is conceived as a 'spiralling' relationship between the analysis of practice (leading to proposed changes) and the implementation of changed practices (leading to increased understanding). As Elliott (1982) says: 'In action-research "theories" are not validated independently and then applied to practice. They are validated through practice' (p. 1).

One possible question then is: does it matter which comes first? Do you *start* by implementing a change? Or do you start by analyzing current practice in order to formulate a desirable change? Elliott's emphasis on 'self-evaluation' tends to suggest the latter, but Brown *et al* (1982) seem quite precise in their recommendation that it should be the former:

Action-research . . . has as its central feature the use of *changes in practice* as a way of inducing improvements in the practice itself, the situation in which it occurs, the rationale for the work, and in the understanding of all these. Action-research uses strategic action as a probe for improvement and understanding. In fact the action-researcher selects a particular variation of practice with these two criteria uppermost. (p. 2)

Although this emphasis serves to differentiate action-research quite clearly from other forms of inquiry, it could seem rather difficult to implement. It might lead us to feel that we could not investigate an aspect of our practice without starting by changing it, one important reason for wishing to investigate something is an uncertainty as to what to change and how. It is important to notice, therefore, that Brown *et al* stress that the changes are introduced with a 'strategy' for development in mind. This seems to imply that a major part of the intellectual effort should go into the formulation of this strategy, which might thus be similar to Elliott's first phase of gathering and analyzing data, as part of the initial 'planning' — see figure 1.
see figure 1.

Hopkins (1985), in contrast to Brown *et al*, presents the following sequence, where changes in practice are clearly an outcome rather than a method of inquiry:

1 Data collection and the generating of hypotheses;
2 Validation of hypotheses (the checking of hypotheses against further data;
3 Interpretation;
4 Action (adapted from Hopkins, 1985, p.114).

Hopkins is concerned to define his approach as *not* action-research, ostensibly because the sequences of activities given by Elliott and Kemmis are too complex and prescriptive (Hopkins, 1985, pp. 39–40) but more importantly because he wishes to insist upon a conventional social science rationale for the collection and interpretation of data (see pp. 42–3, and pp. 110–3). The problems which this approach gives rise to are discussed in detail in the next two chapters. However, even at this stage we can see that Hopkins' sequence must be incomplete, for the simple reason that 'data-gathering' cannot begin without a perceived problem to give it relevance and direction. We can also be fairly sure that the 'validation' of hypotheses and the adequacy of interpretations will be further tested by the action phase, that the 'action' will be a practical response to the initial problem in the light of the inquiry undertaken, and that the action decided upon as a result of the inquiry will inevitably generate further professional problems, which could well be the topic of further inquiry.

This last point (a fairly obvious one, since no-one would wish to equate professional improvement with the sudden attainment of perfection) would complete the similarity between Hopkins' sequence and those of Elliott and Kemmis, by reintroducing the cyclical format which is — as we have seen — a characteristic of action-research. This in turn suggests why the cyclical format is important. It is not so much part of a specific technical method (to which Hopkins would object) as a general recognition that any phase of data-gathering and interpretation can only be one tentative step forward, *not* a final answer, In this way, action-research expresses two general ideals to which Hopkins would also subscribe: firstly the professional ideal of continuing openness to the development of practice, and secondly the 'scientific' ideal of the continuing growth of understanding through critique and revision.

Action and Evaluation: Some Illustrations

In order to give some idea of the range of topics and approaches covered by the general outline offered above, the following section presents brief summaries of a number of actual projects.

Lee Enright (1981): Social Studies and Science in a Middle School

Enright's initial concern was 'the way in which children use ideas to solve problems for themselves, how these ideas might be shared through more effective group discussion, and how the teacher might collaborate with the pupils in the learning that goes on in the classroom' (Enright, 1981, p. 37). Recognizing the very broad scope of her concerns, she adopted three basic approaches. The first was to keep a daily diary throughout the first seven weeks of the summer term, recording 'as much detail as (she) could remember' (p. 37). At the end of this her interests had focused on 'the part played by talk and discussion in learning' (p. 37) and so she repeated her diary-keeping the following year. The deputy head, who also taught the class, read the diaries and added her comments. Secondly, Enright began to tape-record the discussions among the pupils, partly to find out the details of their interaction, but also as part of a strategy to 'bring order' into their discussions. Thirdly, she joined groups of children working together during team-teaching sessions, when the sessions were being led by another teacher. Enright reports a number of insights as a result of this work, including: increased appreciation of the children's abilities (p. 41), the value of allowing children to make their own decisions (p.41), and the danger of a teacher being led by her own enthusiasm into dominating pupil discussion (p. 44). Practical outcomes of the work included: 'greater success in discussion work' (p. 45), and 'increased ability to gear (her) teaching to the needs of individual children' (p. 51).

David Jackson (1981): English in a Secondary School

Jackson wanted to increase his understanding of what was 'going on' during his teaching of a second year English class. Apart from keeping a journal (together with a retrospective commentary), he also gave his pupils the opportunity to write evaluative responses to his introduction of a different teaching method that involved them in more discussion and decision-making. He suggests that this not only created valuable information for him as the teacher, but increased the children's understanding of 'the classroom experience' (p. 60). His final comment suggests that the work of analysis brings about increased personal confidence, due to the sense that 'you are . . . really taking control of and caring about the quality of what is going on in your classroom' (p. 60).

John Wilkinson (1982): The Role of the Primary School Head

Unlike the two previous examples, which are largely based on a self-evaluation process, Wilkinson's work is much closer to the notion of learning through the initiation of 'strategic action' suggested by Brown *et al* (see p. 13 above).

Wilkinson's main purpose was to provide an INSET experience for his staff, in order to increase their willingness to look self-critically at their own teaching. But he approached this indirectly: he used some innovatory science curriculum materials with a class of children and involved two key staff (including the children's usual teacher) in observing him teach and encouraging them to adopt a critical stance towards his work. He documents the development of the staff responses, from an initial wary politeness, through criticism of his teaching, towards a recognition that they too perpetrated similar errors to those they criticized in him.

Ostensibly he carried out a self-evaluation of himself as a teacher. At another level he demonstrated to his staff, by his own example, a route to self-evaluation which they could follow. But at a third level, the switch in his activity — from manager to teacher — enabled him to develop his function as a head: by engaging with his staff in the practice of teaching and the evaluation of his teaching, he developed a more realistic understanding of his staff (p. 49). Consequently, 'by being accepted as a peer (i.e., as a teacher — RW) the Headteacher/Researcher was able to help his staff to become change agents working as a team, cooperating in efforts to improve the setting and themselves' (p. 51). In this way, Wilkinson's project shows how a collaborative action-research structure can, by setting up complementary roles within the project, enable the members of the project to progress in their own different directions at the same time.

Thea Prisk (1987): Unsupervised Group Talk in an Infant School

Prisk's work illustrates very clearly Elliott's (1982) definition of action-research as 'the study of a social situation with a view to improving the quality of action within it' (p. 1). She introduces her report as follows:

> Our language policy placed considerable emphasis on the value of discussion; we believed that talking to, and with, children was a way of evaluating their understanding. However, as Head-teacher, I was worried that the emphasis on adult-led group talk and the involvement of parents in the implementation of the policies, decreased the opportunities available to the children for experimentation on their own. In discussing this, the teachers felt that, if it was intended to extend opportunities for unsupervised talk, they needed to have more knowledge of its educational value in order to feel justified in encouraging it....Studying the language of discussions undertaken by children we knew might enable us to make more accurate judgments about the educational outcomes. (pp. 88–9)

Transcripts were made of tape-recorded discussions among the children, and the details of these were carefully analyzed. This led the teachers to a positive evaluation of the children's unsupervised talk, and to a general re-thinking of intervention strategies, as part of a greater understanding of the nature of the children's verbal and intellectual skills. Prisk concludes:

> There is no doubt that the project had beneficial outcomes for the school. The discussions which arose from the implications of the results had considerable effect on staff perceptions. What had started as an attempt to evaluate a small part of the language curriculum had effect upon all areas of the school's activity. Class-rooms were reorganized to facilitate group work; group problem-solving was seen as a valuable method of tackling mathematical, scientific, and creative topics. (p. 101)

Barbara Zamorski (1987): Individual Work on the Effects of Racial Tension in a Junior School

This study concerns a socially isolated Asian boy, apparently suffering from a problem of low self-esteem connected with racial tensions in the school and its community. The sequence of strategies is described which gradually enabled the boy to join in the general life of the classroom. Zamorski care-fully observed his behaviour with other children, experimented with small group games with varying groups of children, and examined patterns of linguistic interaction during the work. She also intervened to counteract racist comments by some children, and negotiated changes in partners for classwork and seating arrangements. The study documents the progress of an individual 'therapy', and analyzes the effect of each successive strategy in the light of a developing theory as to the origin and the structure of the problem. The work illustrates clearly the nature of the links between attempts to *solve* the problem (the isolation of the boy) and attempts to *understand* the problem (the patterned effects of institutionalized racism).

Julie Payne (1988): Continuity between Primary and Secondary School Mathematics

This project combined work at a number of different levels: participation in an LEA working party drawing up general policies, an evaluative study based on questionnaires and interviews with groups of secondary children, and liaison work from a secondary school to its various feeder-schools. This last element involved day visits by the primary children, return visits by first year secondary pupils to their former primary school, and staff exchanges. The results of the study suggested that the problems of discontinuity were less than had been assumed, but one of the outcomes was an increased willingness on the part of Payne's colleagues in the secondary school to experiment with types of work which were characteristic of the primary schools. The detailed work by Payne in one group of schools was fed into the general work of the LEA working party of which she was a member, and at the same time the arrangements and terms of reference of the working party structured (without – in the end – constraining) the detailed evaluation study. The relationship between the various elements was complex, and not always easy, but the study as a whole shows an interesting degree of collaborative flexibility, and illustrates how an action-research project can operate at levels other than that of the individual class-room.

Joe Haves (1988): Attitudes towards Staff Appraisal in a Secondary School

Haves' study is based upon the interpretation of a questionnaire survey and a sequence of interviews with a cross-section of staff, in order to elicit their attitudes concerning staff appraisal (preferences, worries, issues raised, etc). The purposes of this were: a) generally to guide senior management in the future implementation of an appraisal scheme, and b) 'to enable effective appraisal to occur, yet embody safeguards to retain the confidence of staff' (p.3).

There is another dimension to the study, however. Haves begins by presenting the following concern:

> Staff appraisal had become an issue that would ultimately affect every member of the teaching profession, and if the government reassurance on consultation (with teachers) was to be meaningful, then teachers had to acquire informed opinion on the subject. My fear . . . was that many staff were ill-informed about appraisal and would therefore be at a grave disadvantage if appraisal schemes were implemented in their schools. (p. 2)

In other words, Haves is using the *investigation* of staff attitudes as a way of raising staff consciousness through increased understanding. Consequently, an important purpose (and effect) of the work seems to have been to reduce suspicion of appraisal and thereby to make it easier to introduce a pilot scheme (pp. 83–4).

Heather Crouch (1988): School Experience for College Tutors — Higher Education

Crouch summarizes her work as follows:

The Government White Paper 'Teaching Quality' and the subsequent DES Circular 3/84 spelt out to institutions concerned with teacher training that their staff 'should have enjoyed success as teachers in schools and their school experience should be recent, substantial, and relevant'.

This case study is a piece of action research which serves to illuminate how the concept of school experience has been variously interpreted and experienced at the Anglia Higher Education College (AHEC).

A literature review pertaining to staff development within colleges of higher education was undertaken. Focus then shifted to the staff development policy at AHEC and how the new school experience scheme fitted into this. Several issues and problems were revealed by this investigation.

Semi-structured interviews with all AHEC college tutors engaged in school experience during the academic years 1986–88 were recorded, as were those with the Head of School and the County Primary Inspector. From a study of these transcripts and those from two staff seminars, key issues and some surprises began to emerge. Continued data analysis led to an ideal-type model for school experience being drawn up. A questionnaire, based on the main issues which arose from the interviews, was given to the class teachers and Headteachers involved in the AHEC School Experience scheme, as part of the triangulation process. Analysis of all this qualitative data gave strong direction to arrangements for my own school experience, which in turn was evaluated as an aspect of my own staff development, by analyzing it in terms of the ideal-type model.

Throughout the research there was a progressive focusing upon themes and dilemmas arising from a cumulative understanding of the nature of school experience. By systematically reviewing, describing, interpreting, and evaluating the data, a concept of professional self-review with me as 'tutor-as-class-teacher-as-researcher' emerged.

The case study provides some provisional knowledge, open to public debate and scrutiny, which is founded upon experience and analysis, and an attempt has been made, via the model, to provide a theoretical framework for future practice in arranging school experience for college tutors.

Methods

It is clear from this list of examples that behind the variety of topics there is a specific range of working methods. In this section I wish to summarize the explicit proposals on methods of inquiry which have been put forward. Again, what follows is based largely on the work of Kemmis and Elliott, used earlier in this chapter.

Planning

The first aspect of the process which is described in detail by Kemmis and Elliott is the formulation of the general plan. Kemmis recommends using a preliminary checklist of questions in order to develop a *description* of the situation, such as: What is happening already? What is the rationale for this? What am I trying to change? What are the possibilities? Who is affected? With whom must I negotiate? etc. (See Kemmis *et al*, 1982, pp. 21–2 for the full lists from which this selection has been adapted.)

Elliott divides the planning process into sub-phases, consisting of:

a identifying and clarifying a 'general idea' — which can shift as the work progresses;
b describing the facts of the situation;
c explaining the facts of the situation by generating hypotheses (for example, by means of brainstorming sessions);
d testing the hypotheses (adapted from Elliott, 1982, pp. 4–6).

This last phase (hypothesis-testing) could perhaps be seen as the first move away from the general plan into what Kemmis *et al* (1982) call the first 'strategic action step' (p. 23), whereas the activities listed under (b) and (c) correspond to what Kemmis *et al* call setting out a 'working description' of the 'field of action' (p. 22).

Data Gathering

Considerable attention is given by both Kemmis and Elliott to methods of gathering 'data' in order to 'monitor' the professional practice which has been placed at the centre of the inquiry. The purpose, then, is to gather information about the situation so that preliminary interpretations can be checked. This means gathering information that will tell us more than, as practitioners, we usually know; for example: making systematic records where usually we are content with our spontaneous impressions, making permanent records, where usually we are content to rely on our memories, and collecting detailed statements from people whose general opinions we usually take for granted. More specifically, this may involve a combination of the following procedures.

1 *Keeping a detailed diary* of anecdotes, of subjective impressions, of intriguing comments, of descriptive accounts of meetings and lessons

observed. At first the aim will be comprehensive description, but later on criteria for selectivity will arise, so that one can concentrate on aspects which confirm an important but tentative interpretation, or on what is unexpected and surprising.

2   *Collections of documents relating to a situation*; for example, a collection of work produced in response to a particular teaching strategy; a collection of all the work produced by one or two contrasted learners — covering a range of subjects for a week, or from just one subject during a term or even a year; collections of staff meeting minutes, of letters sent home to parents . . . etc, etc.

3   *Observation notes* of lessons, meetings, etc. As with diary entries, these may begin with general impressions and comprehensive description, and may take the form of what Elliott (1982) calls 'a running commentary' (p. 16). Later they may become more specific in orientation, using *checklists* of relevant phenomena (derived from earlier analyses) and schedules of how frequently and in relation to whom they occurred. *Schedules* may be based on standard categories (for example, open/closed questions, initiatives/responses, task-oriented/control-oriented talk) or on improvised categories related to the specific purposes of the work.

4   *Questionnaire surveys* of staff or pupil attitudes, preferences, experiences. These may use an *open* format — invitations to respondents to give their ideas in response to general questions, generally used when the work is *exploring* a situation in order to expand a range of possible interpretations. In contrast, when the purpose is to *check* an interpretation or to choose between interpretations, a *closed* format may be used — requiring the respondent to tick one of a number of predetermined responses or to arrange them in a rank order.

5   *Interviews* — with colleagues, with pupils' parents, with groups of pupils, etc. The sustained interaction allows the many subtle nuances of an unfamiliar perspective to be explored in detail and gradually clarified. Again, depending on the stage and purposes of the work, interviewees may be asked to respond to a set of predetermined questions or invited to explore a topic in their own way with minimal prompting.

6   *Shadow studies*. An individual pupil or teacher or other participant in a situation may be followed by an observer over a lengthy period of time and a 'running commentary' made. This might be particularly revealing in a setting where the activities are divided into separate categories (for example, lessons) such that one set of participants (for example, teachers) are relatively unaware of the overall experience undergone by the other set (for example, pupils). Shadow studies can thus dismantle the conventional time boundaries of institutional life and disclose unnoticed patterns which cut across those boundaries (for example, a surprising degree of repetition or of discontinuity between different lessons).

7   *Tape-recording*. Interviews and teachers' talk can be tape-recorded quite readily. Children's contributions can usually only be tape-recorded

during small group interaction. Tape-recordings provide an objective record, which can be listened to repeatedly and/or transcribed, so that patterns of interaction or 'revealing' comments that go unnoticed at the time can be noted for detailed commentary. Of course, some people feel that their behaviour will be inhibited or distorted by the very presence of a tape-recorder, although this is a problem which can 'wear off' after a few minutes have passed and the interaction itself begins to be of sufficient interest for the presence of the tape-recorder to be forgotten.

8   *Negotiating a set of notes.* If the presence of a tape-recorder is not acceptable for some reason, or if one wishes to avoid the time-consuming business of transcription, interview notes can be made with the direct participation of the interviewee. The process of checking back may either become built into the structure of the conversation ('So what you're saying, then, is this: . . . ') or alternatively one can write up one's jotted notes into a fairly elaborate account immediately afterwards, and send it to the interviewee for amendment.

9   *Video-recording.* Classroom or other activity may be video-recorded, so that other observable dimensions may be monitored, as well as the verbal interactions. Again, this enables repeated viewing, to allow one to notice 'surprising' features of the situation which one initially glossed over under the influence of a general impression of familiarity. But it is also important to note that a video camera operated from within a room does not record the whole of the situation in that room: it has to be *pointed*, selectively, at certain activities, while other activities have to remain unrecorded, beyond the camera angle. Furthermore, a video camera is an obviously intrusive element in a situation, and harder to forget than a microphone, so it must always be assumed that it is having a distorting effect on what is being recorded.

10   *Still photographs and slides.* These may be made fairly unobtrusively, but they nevertheless require an outsider as photographer (unless a teacher is photographing children at work). As visual reminders of an experience, they can trigger detailed memories, and can thus form a very useful starting point for retrospective discussion among participants.

11   *Triangulation.* The creation of a variety of types of data — as indicated above — is important for small-scale research. It means that a situation can be investigated using a number of different methods, each of which can partly transcend its own limitations by functioning as a point of comparison with another. Several different methods may thus seem to 'converge' on one interpretation, thereby giving grounds for preferring it to another interpretation which is only suggested by one method of investigation. Normally at least three methods or points of view are needed for the comparisons and contrasts to be illuminating, and to allow conclusions to be drawn. This is because three-way comparisons are less likely to lead to simple polarized oppositions which merely move back and forth without allowing for resolution. Hence: 'triangulation'. (Alternatively one

might think of a 'triangle' being constructed when a comparison between the different points of view of two different participants yields an emergent *third* interpretation which reconciles the other two.)

Managing the Interpersonal Ethics of Investigation

It is clear that the data-gathering methods such as those outlined above involved the professional practitioner in new sets of relations with colleagues and clients. Ethical guidelines for the process are therefore proposed by writers on action-research in order to ensure that the activities of inquiry are compatible with other professional responsibilities, i.e., that the investigative process is not at any point consciously exploitative or destructive. This is the familiar issue as to whether 'the end justifies the means'. Is a teacher at liberty to teach a class badly in order to test an educational hypothesis? The answer must be, No: teachers are required ethically to give their prior professional responsibility to the effectiveness of learning. The necessity for an agreed ethical basis for practitioner action-research is thus urgent, complex, and wholly practical, since those involved will have to work together after the inquiry phase is over and professional practices are resumed under the usual auspices. This presents an interesting challenge, which outside researchers do not *necessarily* have to face (although most would agree that they ought to). There are well-known rumours of academic researchers who made a reputation with a book but who dare not show their faces back in the institution where the data was gathered, because of the resentment they caused, and of schools who felt so abused by the activities of previous researchers that further research there had become impossible. (See Midwinter, 1972, p. 47; MacDonald, 1980, p. 37.)

Some might wish to claim that this line of argument suggests that practitioner action-research must be inhibited from telling 'the whole truth', whereas an outsiders is 'free' to do so. But this is to presuppose that outsiders' views are unbiased, rather than being biased in their own, different way. Only on this assumption is there any value in the 'freedom' of the outsider from an insider's responsibilities. In any case, an equally strong argument could be made to the effect that the freedom of the outsider (even if it is not an illusion) may well be a form of self-indulgence, leading to superficiality. In contrast, one might argue, the practical necessity for practitioner action-researchers to work in such a way that they preserve their own professional role constitutes a rigorous intellectual discipline, ensuring that the conclusions of the work are broadly based, balanced, and comprehensively grounded in the perceptions of a variety of others. The outcomes of the work are thus 'objective' and 'truthful' in the sense that Habermas (1972) proposes as the aim of interpretive inquiry:

> The understanding of meaning is directed in its very structure towards the attainment of possible consensus among actors (an understanding which is both) mutual and action-orienting. (p. 310)

The ethical procedures which will be required by practitioner action-researchers are introduced by Kemmis *et al* (1982) as follows:

> Action researchers must pay attention to the ethical principles guiding their work. Their actions are deeply embedded in an existing social organization and the failure to work within the general procedures of that organization may not only jeopardize the process of improvement but existing valuable work. Principles of procedure for action research accordingly go beyond the usual concerns for confidentiality and respect for the persons who are the subjects of enquiry and define in addition, appropriate ways of working with other participants in the social organization . . . (p. 43)

The following summary indicates the sort of principles proposed:

Make sure that 'the relevant persons, committees and authorities' have been consulted.

All participants must be allowed to influence the work, and the wishes of those who do not wish to participate must be respected.

The development of the work must remain 'visible . . . and open to suggestions' from others.

Permission must be obtained before making observations or examining documents produced for other institutional purposes.

Descriptions of others' work and points of view must be negotiated with those concerned before being published.

The researcher must 'accept responsibility for maintaining confidentiality'.

The principles guiding the work must be accepted in advance by all involved. (adapted from Kemmis *et al*, 1982, pp.43–4)

Methods for Reflection and Analysis

The other central issue of methodology which arises out of the data-gathering phase is: what do the data 'mean'? (Kemmis *et al*, 1982, p. 35) Hence: what methods of analysis (Elliott's preferred word) does one use in order to make them mean something useful?

It is interesting that far less detailed advice is given on this phase of the cycle of activities. Elliott (1982) describes the process of analysis as 'explaining' effects and 'any failure to implement' the action steps (p. 3). Kemmis's (1982) main emphasis is on the need to write a report, even if it will not be distributed, in order to 'crystallize your thoughts' and 'provide you with useful insights for future action which cannot be gained any other way' (p. 35). Kemmis and Elliott agree on their specification for the contents of the report — a 'case study' — which, they say, should follow a chronological, historical narrative; beginning with 'how one's "General Idea" evolved over time', through 'what action steps were undertaken', 'the extent to which proposed actions were implemented', and 'the intended and unintended effects of one's actions', to 'any ethical problems which arose' (extracts from Elliott, 1982, p. 20).

Conclusion

This has been a very brief introduction to the basic process of action-research, and readers are urged to read the texts by Kemmis and Elliott, for a wealth of valuable practical advice and clarification. But one crucial problem emerges from this review, and that is the very cursory treatment given to the process of reflection in two key texts on action-research which provide considerable detail on other aspects. This leads on to the theme of the next chapter. 'Reflection' refers to the crucial process by means of which we make sense of evidence — whether from specific data-gathering procedures or from our practical experience as it occurs. In order to ensure that we *learn* from experience, then, it seems reasonable to suggest that the process of reflection upon evidence is just as worthy of careful thought as the process of gathering evidence. The fact that the process of reflection is largely taken for granted in these two texts (as in most writing on action-research) suggests that reflection is tacitly assumed to be a straightforward familiar process, or one where the comprehensiveness of the data automatically guarantees the validity of the interpretation, or one which action-research can simply *borrow* from elsewhere, i.e., from 'common sense' or from conventional research methods.

I think all of these assumptions are seriously misleading, for reasons which the next two chapters will elaborate. Let us end this introduction by considering a statement by David Hopkins, which will serve to introduce the nature of the problems which have now surfaced. Hopkins (1985) writes:

> The four stages of classroom research, although based on sociological research methods, are, in fact, only organized common sense. (p. 114)

Now, if practitioners researching their own work context are armed only with the methods of 'organized common sense', how are they able to go beyond what they already know and do — which is also based on 'organized common sense'? Or rather: what *special* form of 'organization' of one's thinking is required? Conversely, how can practitioners researching their own work contexts with a view to improving their practice use the same methods as 'sociology', given that the methods of sociology were devised for specialist academic theorists operating on principle as outsiders, with relatively vast time resources and *no* direct commitment to improving the qualtiy of the practices under investigation? At the very least these are large and awkward questions, to which we now turn.

Chapter 3

Action-Research and the Problems of Positivism

The General Issue of Positivism

This chapter is concerned with the problem of why practitioner action-research cannot simply use the research methods of conventional social science, and suggests that previous work on action-research methods, indispensable though it is as a starting point, still leaves unanswered certain key questions, as indicated at the end of the previous chapter. We need to start by considering the general relationship between professional work and professional knowledge, especially in those professions where 'work' consists of taking complex decisions about human affairs (teaching, social work, nursing, management, etc). This in turn will require us to consider the crucial differences between natural and social science. These differences are sometimes minimized by conventional social research, but for action-research they are part of its fundamental rationale. Very briefly: conventional social research can attempt to use the so-called 'positivist' methods of the natural sciences (the term is explained below), since its fundamental stance is that of the 'unbiased outside observer'. Action-research, being in an important sense the study of a *changing* situation *from the inside*, must ensure that its methods do not depend on 'positivist' assumptions; otherwise it will be open to attack as being *like* conventional research, but incompetent ('biased', 'anecdotal', etc).

Let us begin, then, with 'professional knowledge'. Professional work may be thought of as work which is carried out by practitioners who are defined as having a specific expertise, and the conscious possession of this expertise creates a sense of responsibility to the clients on whose behalf it is exercised: professionals feel an implicit obligation to exercise their expertise in such a way as to 'get it right' — to make the decision which really is in the client's interest. But many forms of professional work involve responsibilities where the available body of knowledge is not authoritatively established but is continually open to question, so that 'getting it right' is never an outcome one can be sure of in advance. In this sense, engineers' knowledge of the behaviour of physical materials and physical

27

structures offers a clear contrast to educators' knowledge of the behaviour of human minds and institutional structures. Engineers can be fairly confident that they can satisfy their clients, by designing a bridge which will withstand a given stress, whereas educators can never be so sure that a curriculum they have designed is going to 'work' as far as their clients (their students, or even the future employers of their students) are concerned. Even bridge builders are, of course, prone to error, but we can see that there is an important difference in the degree of uncertainty involved. Architects and doctors occupy intermediate positions on this scale of professional uncertainty, but teachers and other professional 'people-workers' are clearly towards one extreme — where the exercise of their professional expertise can never even seem to be the routine application of established general rules, but will always entail self-conscious analysis and development, as a necessary part of the interpretation of that expertise in each specific instance. In education, as in other professions dealing with people, the authority derived from expertise is therefore always open to question, and thus professional work must entail a continual process of reflection, evaluation, and innovation. Hence the substantial body of work which argues for the value (and necessity) of professional workers' involvement in action-research, as part of their 'extended professionalism'. (See previous chapters.)

However, it is clear that we have missed out a step in the argument. The fact that our knowledge of educational phenomena is not well established might lead us to conclude that we need a lot more research into classrooms, schools, etc., carried out by specialist educational research workers in roughly the same way that research departments in universities and polytechnics continue to develop new techniques for use by practising engineers. Where does practitioner action-research enter the argument? The explanation is quite clear, and of very general importance, since it concerns the special relationship between the researcher and the object of research when the object of research is another human being.

What is special, in this case, is that while the researcher is observing and interpreting the actions of the human 'object' that same human object is also observing and interpreting the actions of the researcher, and *deciding* how to respond. Social scientists are divided into two camps on this matter. Some say that it doesn't matter very much, that with careful experimental design and cunning disguise of the observer's intentions, human beings can be studied in ways that are not fundamentally different from the methods of natural science, that if only enough situations can be studied with enough care and objectivity, we will in the end be able to generalize about the behaviour of people in the same way as we do about the behaviour of, say, malarial mosquitoes or of concrete structures under stress. According to this point of view, social science research (like natural science research) requires large amounts of carefully observed data, accurate descriptions which genuinely correspond to external phenomena, and interpretations which can be replicated with other bodies of data, and can thus claim to be 'generalizable'.

This view of our knowledge of human beings is often labelled 'positivist', following the term originally used by Auguste Comte.[1] What is 'positive' about it may be thought of as follows. Firstly, it suggests that knowledge is ('positively') certain: it really has been established; it is not mere speculative interpretation or value judgment, so we will not find tomorrow that we wish (or need) to change it. Secondly, it therefore gradually accumulates, so that we can, with 'positive' optimism, look forward to greater and greater certainty in our understanding.

The other view of social science knowledge is that the special 'double-ended' relationship (between the researcher and the human actor who is being researched) changes *everything*. According to this view there is an inescapable liberty and privacy about consciousness which means that it cannot be predicted nor accurately described. This means that the development of our understanding of human beings has a quite different form from the development of natural science: it does *not* accumulate, because it is not a series of observations (*by* one person *of* others) but takes place within an interaction between mutually observing individuals. (A single observation, being a static instant, can in principle form a stable starting point from which to build, but an interaction is in principle a continuously shifting process, and thus provides no such stable starting point.) Hence, positivist researchers' desire for detachment, for large data samples, and for interpretations with the status of general laws, must be seen as fundamentally misplaced — as a combination of naivety and arrogance — because they can never explain how they themselves (as researchers) are freely creating new understandings through their activities, whereas the people they are observing can apparently be interpreted as merely behaving according to general rules, which the researchers hope to be able to specify as their findings. In other words, positivist social science researchers can always only *assume* (and can *never* be sure) that they are not being misunderstood, taken for a ride, sent up, manipulated, or otherwise misled by those whose activities they claim to be able to 'describe'.

It is this latter view which underlies the movement towards practitioner action-research as the basis for the development of professional knowledge. The argument is that (in principle) the sort of knowledge of educational phenomena created by specialist educational researchers is inevitably of dubious 'validity' (especially as far as teachers themselves are concerned), in comparison with the analytical, critical, developmental work of teachers themselves. The reason for this is that most significant knowledge of educational processes cannot be of a law-like, general nature, but will always be intimately related to specific contexts, that it can never be based on 'pure' observation, but will always be bound up with contextual, here-and-now judgments (concerning the interpretation of

29

particular data), and that it can never be established, finalized, and codified in abstract theories, because it will always be developing alongside and within professional practice. Action-research, then, is an attempt to reject the claims of, and to surmount the limitations of, social science positivism.[2]

However, this is easier said than done. In the above argument I have intentionally tried to make the positivist version of social science seem rather obviously questionable. But we *live* in what has been called a 'culture of positivism' (Whitty, 1974, p. 120). There are two senses to this statement. Firstly, the achievements of the natural science model of research are all about us. Technology confronts us as the one clear dimension of human progress: we can certainly travel faster and lift heavier weights more quickly than our ancestors, so what more natural than for us secretly to nurse the hope that such important activities as those involving justice, morality, social care, and education can be improved in an analogous fashion? And what more natural than for this secret hope to be subconsciously converted into a belief? In other words, our images of professional expertise have a generalized yearning towards the stereotype of the white-coated laboratory scientist. We wish that our expertise could have the authority of natural science, and this wish is perhaps especially acute in those areas where our doubts about our expertise are greatest, as part of a more widespread yearning for a supposedly 'lost' authority and certainty. Secondly, positivism seems comfortingly to echo very obvious features of commonsense existence. We experience an external world, which we report upon in the form of objective data ('I saw a plum-coloured pair of jeans in Marks and Spencers yesterday') and upon which we can erect generalizations ('Yes, they had them in Littlewoods too: it's probably this year's fashion colour'). So, although elaborate arguments against positivism in social science have been made it is extremely difficult to avoid slipping back into positivist lines of argument: there is a sort of ideological undertow in that direction.

Nevertheless, in presenting a strong argument for the claims of practitioner action-research, I do not wish to deny the value of other forms of social research. For example, it is clearly of importance that evidence be gathered by various administrative agencies in order to inform the policy-making process within those agencies. Typical examples might be: the monitoring of rates of unemployment among school-leavers in terms of their ethnic background, or the gender and race of staff appointed to senior management positions. This sort of work may be thought of as an interface between large-scale management and social statistics, and has its own purposes, methods, and methodology, which can broadly be termed 'positivism'. What makes these methods appropriate for such purposes is that the investigation can take for granted the relevance and the nature of the basic categories ('gender', 'ethnicity', 'employment') and can focus on the problems concerning their correlation. What I wish to argue, in contrast, is that where investigations deal with the detailed understanding of educational practices, in ways which can inform their development, it is precisely the nature and relevance of the central categories which are at stake. And for this type of work the appropriate methodology is *not* that of positivism (although there are certainly examples where this has been tried[3]) but of practitioner action-research. In general terms, the principles of this methodology (as outlined below in chapter four) can certainly be adapted for use by researchers who are not full-time practitioners at the time of the research (the arguments for this are presented in Winter, 1987). However, the reverse argument does not hold: if practitioner action-researchers attempt simply to borrow the methods of positivism, which are justifiable at the level of macro-management, their work will appear to be deficient as well as different, for reasons which will be presented in the next section. In order to avoid this appearance of deficiency, therefore, it must utilize a different, but equally coherent (equally 'valid') set of methodological principles to guide *its* work. The theoretical basis for this argument also is presented at length in Winter, 1987; the practical reasons which make it necessary are presented in the next two sections.

Positivist Echoes within Action-Research

As the previous chapter indicated, one of the most influential ways of conceiving of the action-research process is derived from Lewin's (1946) cycle of planning, action, and 'fact-gathering'. The following diagram, taken from figure 1 in the previous chapter, is based on the well-known formulations of the process by Elliott (1982) and by Kemmis *et al* in *The Action Research Planner* (1982), which have already been discussed. The positivist echoes here lie in the central role given to the collection of facts, i.e., to 'observation', 'diagnosis', and the 'monitoring of effects'.[4]

Planning	→Action	→Observation	→Reflection
Planning	→Implementation	→Review	→Diagnosis
Review and Diagnosis	→Planning	→Implementation	→Monitoring Effects

Let us start our discussion by noting that this process could be interpreted on three different scales.

1   On the smallest scale: it describes the process of informed and thoughtful decision-making which routinely characterizes professional work. For example, I organize a teaching session for a group of learners whose needs I have considered, I put it into practice, and in the light of what happens, I spend some time considering what to do in the next session. On this scale there is no problem: the diagram indicates the pattern of any sensible individual's everyday purposeful action.

2   On the largest scale: it might be taken as describing how, say, a government department might monitor the outcomes of its administrative decisions (for example, to pay an incentive bonus to physics teachers) by commissioning a survey of a national sample (for example, of the numbers of physics teachers on training courses in three successive years) and drawing conclusions as to whether the decisions might need changing (for example, whether or not the number of physics teachers in training rose in the years after the incentive had been introduced). On this scale also there is no problem: the diagram indicates an important phase of any sensible management process.

3   But the scale of action-research comes in between 1 and 2, and this is where problems start to arise. It has to be more elaborate than scale 1 (observation will be more extensive, and reflection will be both more systematic and more speculative) since its purpose is not merely to maintain a pattern of action but to change it, not merely to draw on an existing level of understanding but to develop it in new directions. On the other hand it has to be *less* elaborate than scale 2 because of the limitations of resources. This means that the number of observations will be too small to be able to claim that they are based on a representative sample, and this in turn threatens to undermine the value of any conclusions.

Let us pursue the nature of the problem by considering what might be meant by 'reflection'. If observations are based on a representative sample, then reflections on these observations can tentatively claim to be generalizations, and so the results of observation can be fed back into the planning and action phases with every confidence that action will, now, be 'soundly' based. In contrast, if (given the resource constraints of practitioner action-research) observation is *not* based on a representative sample, then it is not at all clear on what principle reflection should proceed: if we cannot aim at generalizable interpretation (because our data are not adequately representative) what *are* the aims of reflection?

We can elaborate the significance of this question by going back to the terms of the original diagram. Firstly, what is a 're-view'? How can we know that our new series of observations will not simple confirm our old 'view'? Notice that if they do, we cannot then say that our old view is thereby justified as 'correct', since (as we have already admitted) these new observations are no more representative than the old ones. However, if we cannot aim at correctness, can we perhaps aim at 'value'? If a review is to be *valuable* the crucial thing is that it must open up previously neglected possibilities; otherwise it is, in retrospect, 'unnecessary'. So the question now becomes: what specific forms of observation and reflection would be relatively more likely to achieve this 'opening up' function, and *less* likely merely to confirm what is already known. (Within the terms of this argument, the problem about confirming what is already known is not that it is erroneous but that it is superfluous — a poor return for the expenditure of precious time.)

Secondly, what form of reflection upon observation is 'diagnosis'? 'Diagnosis' carries impressive and comforting connotations of certainty, derived from professional contexts where positivism seems to 'work'. The normal habitats of diagnosis are, for example, the hospital and the garage, where the observed results of *tests* are reflected upon by being submitted to the scrutiny of 'science and technology', where diagnosing the problem is followed by prescribing the remedy, i.e., curing the disease, repairing the fault. Thus, one of the problems of 'diagnosis' in the context of practitioner action-research simply returns us to the unrepresentative and questionable nature of the available data: action-research projects are too wide-ranging, too exploratory, to restrict themselves entirely to the evidence of 'tests', and even if we do try to restrict reflection to 'diagnosis', limited time always means limited data, and thus our diagnosis may seem to be dubious or premature, lacking in scientific authority because based on incomplete evidence. Admittedly, the notion of diagnosis helpfully suggests that reflection is to do with deciding on a practical course of action in a particular case (rather than with attempting to create general law-like statements, for example) but it does not suggest what form of reflection would be appropriate in cases where evidence is necessarily incomplete. We need a model for the process of reflection which is clearly *different* from the logic of natural science (based on the experimental testing of variables); otherwise action-research projects will merely seem to be incompetent versions of 'real science'. And yet we need a model for reflection which is clearly different from the logic of everyday action (based merely on an awareness that our practices have consequences and need justifications); otherwise action-research projects will merely seem to be rather time-consuming versions of 'what we already do anyway'. What form of 'reflection' this might be is an important theme of the next chapter.

Thirdly, what of 'implementation'? 'Implementation' suggests that the relationship between theory and practice takes the form of what could be termed a 'prescriptive sequence': theory is derived from the 'correct' observation of one situation, and this theory is then taken to be a prescription for action in another situation; in other words, research *firstly* produces 'findings' which *subsequently* are to be 'implemented'. But this model of theory and practice is derived from the conventional hierarchical division between those who find out (researchers) and those who receive findings (practitioners), and this is exactly what practitioner action-research wants to get away from. One of the reasons why it wishes to do so is that a widespread reaction to prescription is rejection: 'Research says X, Y, and Z, but it's all very well for them: they don't have to teach *my* class day in, day out; I *know* that in practice, for me, it wouldn't work.' How then can we avoid the *problem* of 'implementation'? How can we go about 'finding out' in ways which are, from the outset, closely bound up with practice itself, so that we are concerned with *one* process rather than a sequence of two?

These then are some of the questions which arise out of the contradictions within current formulations of the action-research process. Notice that the arguments above do not represent a *disagreement* with the diagram from which they started. They merely suggest that the diagram does not explain enough: the arrows which link the terms leave us with a series of questions as to the nature of the processes they seem to be referring to. I have also tried to suggest that these questions have been ignored because action-research has tried to *borrow* certain aspects of the positivist model of investigation, while at the same time trying to create a quite different model of the relationship between theory and practice, between research and action. (This argument is presented more fully in Winter, 1987.) The next chapter presents a series of general principles which aim to remove the positivist elements from the action-research process, to enable action-researchers to engage in clearly specified procedures with their own coherent, self-consistent forms of adequacy, independent of the natural science model of inquiry. But first, in the last section of this chapter, I should like to draw together four crucial practical problems which arise when we try to enact an action-research process within a set of procedures which still depend on positivist assumptions. These four problems indicate the *practical necessity* for the principles described in chapter four.

Four Practical Problems

We have already hinted at the nature of the first problem, that of *time*. One important reason for the existence of a division of labour within professional work, between practitioners who do it and researchers who investigate it, is that most 'people-processing' institutions (for example, schools, welfare agencies, hospitals) are notoriously underfunded, and consequently most professional workers are notoriously overworked: after the work itself has been accomplished, one feels as though one has little time or energy left over for investigation, evaluation, or innovation, even though one might agree in principle that these elements ought to be an integral part of the professional role. It would therefore seem quite plausible to argue that full-time research workers are needed who have enough time to investigate professional practice in ways that can claim to be 'valid'. What, then, is the link between time and 'validity'? In a word: data. In positivist social science, methods of research involve using large amounts of data, so that interpretations can claim to be generalizable because they are based on a large sample, or because many different examples have been exhaustively cross-checked against each other. If data are gathered by interviewing or observing, then large amounts of time are needed to gather the data in the first place, and then even more time is needed to analyze them. Further, if interviews are tape-recorded, then analysis is difficult unless the material is transcribed, and this is another enormous consumer of time. So the problem of time is as follows: can we formulate a method of work which is sufficiently *economical* (as regards the amount of data gathering and data processing) for a practitioner to undertake it alongside a normal workload over a limited timescale?

We have also already hinted at the second problem: how can a small-scale investigation by a practitioner lead to genuinely *new* insights? Only if it does so can the time and energy spent on it be justified. Experienced practitioners approach their work with a vast and complex array of concepts, theoretical models, provisional explanations, typical scenarios, anticipations of likely alternatives, etc. These are developed 'naturally' in the course of professional practice, since professional work is essentially complex, consisting as it does of subtle interpersonal interactions requiring the continuous exercise of interpretive skill and flexibility. A 'research' process must demonstrably offer something over and above this pre-existing level of understanding. We need therefore to establish a clear *difference* of procedure between action-research's form of gathering and analyzing the data generated through professional practice, and the procedures of professional practice itself. Otherwise the outcomes of practitioners' action-research may well meet such taunts as: 'We knew that already', 'We're doing that already', or, more precisely: 'Is *that* all action-research is? Gathering and analyzing data? We do *that* every day of our lives.' In a word: action-research procedures need to be *specific*. We have already seen that positivist procedures characterize everyday decision-making as well as the methods of large scale social science surveys. Unless action-research can be differentiated from both these activities, it will risk being confused with one or the other, and attacked as *either* too minimal to be valid as a form of investigation, *or* too elaborate to be feasible as a form of practice.

However, we then run up against the third problem, because it is important that we do not specify the action-research approach in such a way that it appears to require prior possession of, say, a social science degree. Methods for an investigative stance must be clearly differentiated from methods for practice, and yet they must be readily available to anyone who wishes to adopt them. They must build upon the competences which practitioners already possess; they cannot be 'different' merely in the sense of requiring practitioners to reinterpret their experiences in the light of an academic corpus of knowledge (for example, sociology, psychology, curriculum theory, management theory, sociolinguistics, etc). If the 'difference' of the action-research stance were to take this academic form, then we would at the very least return to the problem of the lack of *time* (in which to master the body of academic knowledge), and thus we would in effect reintroduce the hierarchical division of labour (between theorists and practitioners). As we have already noted, it is this division which action-research specifically wishes to oppose, putting forward instead an ideal of the reflective, innovative professional whose theoretical awareness develops in and through practice itself. Action-research procedures, then, need to be *accessible*.

But there is a final practical question, namely: why bother? Having agreed that practitioners already possess a great fund of expertise, in the form of their normal competences, and having also agreed that time and energy are scarce, we need to be able to argue convincingly that action-research can contribute a *genuine improvement* of understanding and skill, beyond that prior competence, in return for the time and energy expended. Action-research needs, in other words, some sound basis for claiming 'validity'. But here precisely is one of action-research's fundamental problems: limited in data, lacking an external, 'uninvolved' observer, its theorizing enmeshed in its practical interests, in what sense can action-research claim to be objective or valid? Surely (we are entitled to insist), at the end of a lengthy investigation we cannot simply admit that the validity of our findings is 'merely subjective' ('It's my honest opinion') or pragmatic ('It works, doesn't it?'). Put another way, as practitioners we inevitably rely upon opinions, beliefs, assumptions, and various forms of ideology, but if action-research is to be worth the effort then we must have a way of arguing that the procedures of action-research help us to 'go beyond' (to check, question, 'test') our opinions, beliefs, assumptions, and ideologies, so that at the end our understanding and our practices are more securely based (and in that sense 'more valid') than when we set out. Unless it can claim improved validity for its outcomes, why should anyone do action-research, and why should anyone else take it seriously?

But 'validity' is a dangerous word. Unless we are continuously alert we are likely to slip into its positivist sense, meaning that our understanding is either generalizable, or replicable, or a correct representation of an external world. Even supposing, for a second, that such claims could plausibly be made about positivist research findings, we have already seen that limitations of time and data preclude practitioner action-researchers from formulating their claims along these lines. To avoid misunderstanding, therefore, let us say that the practical problem is not so much: 'How can we ensure that our findings are valid?' but rather: 'How can we ensure that our procedures are rigorous?' In making this shift, the action-researcher avoids the unanswerable question as to whether an interpretation 'coincides with reality' — unanswerable for the simple reason that we can never perceive reality except by means of one interpretation or another — and adopts instead the cautious attitude of the doctor, the lawyer, and the priest, who do not guarantee a successful outcome, but offer an assurance that well established principles will be carefully applied. Indeed, many of the more thoughtful commentators on the methodology of the natural sciences would not be willing to press their claims much further than this. So, if action-research procedures are systematically grounded in justifiable and coherent principles (i.e., if they are 'rigorous') then we shall have grounds for thinking that the conclusions we come to will be more than the result of personalities, emotions, or expediency. In conclusion, to be worth the effort, action-research needs to have a *more* rigorous process for the investigation of affairs than that which characterizes the everyday practices of professional life, and a *different* conception of 'rigour' than that which characterizes positivist research.

Here then are four crucial practical questions. Without borrowing from positivist assumptions and methods:

1   How can action-research procedures be *economical*?
2   How can action-research procedures be *specific*?
3   How can action-research procedures be *accessible*?
4   How can action-research procedures be *rigorous*?

The next chapter sets out a series of principles which attempt to formulate action-research in such a way that the questions raised in this chapter can, tentatively at least, be answered.

Notes

1   An extract from Auguste Comte's work is conveniently reprinted in Thompson and Tunstall (1971).
2   For accounts of action-research as a critique of positivism, see Carr and Kemmis (1986), Winter (1987), and (1990).
3   One well-known example is that of Bennett (1976) *Teaching Styles and Pupil Progress* which generated enormous controversy (because it appeared to offer 'factual evidence' for both sides in a politically topical ideological argument) but — in the end — little insight into either the nature of teaching styles or of pupils' educational progress. See Bennett (1976) and subsequent articles by Bennett (1978) and by Kitwood and Macey (1976).
4   Lewin himself uses the term 'reconnaissance', explicitly based on the analogy with wartime flights by aircraft to gather facts so that subsequent bombing raids could accurately 'target' their 'objectives' — an image whose extraordinary inappropriateness for action-research is quite relevant to the argument presented in this section.

Chapter 4

Six Principles for the Conduct of Action-Research

Introduction

In the previous chapter it was suggested that practitioner action-researchers need to redefine the key processes of observation, reflection, and implementation. Otherwise they will not be able to refute the criticisms of those who cast doubt upon the value of small-scale inquiry carried out with minimal resources by people actively engaged in the situations they are investigating. Redefinitions are needed in order to free action-research from its reliance on positivist criteria and concepts, since it is this continued reliance on positivism which produces inconsistency, and even confusion, concerning the nature and status of action-research outcomes. It is to this end that the following six principles are presented.

In the presentation below, each principle is introduced by an indication of the sort of major methodological problem to which that particular principle is addressed. The first two principles, Reflexive and Dialectical Critique, suggest ways of redefining the processes of observation and reflection; together they give general and objective grounds for selecting among the many lines of argument and interpretation that may seem potentially interesting in relation to given data. They present an approach which is specific and rigorous, and yet at the same time accessible (i.e., not requiring a body of specialist theoretical knowledge) and economical (not requiring massive amounts of data). Each of these two principles is preceded by a brief explanation of the underlying general arguments on which it depends. The redefinition of the processes of observation and reflection implies a redefinition of the relationship between the initiator of an investigation and the other members of the situation being investigated. This is the topic of the next three principles: Collaborative Resource, Risk, and Plural Structure. The final principle — Theory, Practice, Transformation — draws together the previous arguments into a redefinition of the process of implementation, i.e., of the relationship between reflection and action, between analysis and practice. These six principles are not independent of each other; on the contrary, precisely because they form a coherent overall approach, each one implies and requires the others. In this way they provide for practitioner action-research a coherent general alternative to positivism.

Reflexivity — An Explanatory Summary

The problem. As professionals, our working lives are a never-ending sequence of *judgments*: what is 'appropriate'? what is 'worthwhile'? what is 'interesting'? whose work is 'better' than someone else's? what is 'the reason' why something happened, and what is 'the best' thing to do about it? We know that all such judgments are open to 'question', but how can we analyze the process of making judgments, without simply imposing a further set of judgments? It is here that the principle of 'reflexivity' is relevant.

Suppose that, as a teacher, I wish to make a judgment about an external reality, for example, 'Martin and Rosie in my class know the rules for multiplication'. We can begin by dividing the statement into two parts. First there is the phrase 'Martin and Rosie in my class'. Language here seems to work as a system of labels with which I, as a language user, can identify phenomena which are external both to me and to you, (the receiver of my utterance) so that you can identify those phenomena too — two particular children out of several hundred in the school. But consider the remainder of the sentence: '. . . know the rules for multiplication'. Here there are immediately a number of questions: what do I mean by 'the rules', and what do I mean by 'know'? What experiences (of Martin's and Rosie's work) have I had which lead me to feel able to make such a judgment? Have I checked that: (1) they have not copied from their friends, (2) the rules they are using are the conventional ones and not idiosyncratic procedures which happen, so far, to work, (3) they could carry out these operations with respect to *any* numbers and not just the examples I have set, etc, etc? When I make this part of the statement I am not using language as a set of labels; instead I am taking part in a highly complex structure of shared assumptions; that you and I know 'the sort of thing' I am referring to, even though I have not made it absolutely explicit; that if you said it I would be able to make sense of your words in the same way that I hope you can make sense of mine. Thus, in order to make the statement I must first imagine myself in your shoes, and make the further judgment that if you said it to me I would make the same interpretations (as to what experiences lie 'behind' the statement) as I am expecting you to make. In other words, in trying to communicate with you I must first construct my meaning for myself. Only then, having done so, may I reasonably hope that you will construct (from my words) a 'similar' meaning. In this sense 'Martin and Rosie in my class know the rules for multiplication' only *appears* to be a description of an external reality. At another level it is a 'reflexive' communication, i.e., 'bent back' (see figure 2) into my own experiences, and thus refers largely to my own interpretations, assumptions, and concerns.

Now, positivism claims that, given an effort to 'define our terms', all statements can be converted into a system of specific lables for external phenomena (like 'Martin and Rosie in my class'). The thesis of reflexivity, in contrast, argues that most statements which are of any interest are not of the simple 'Martin and Rosie' type, but, like the remainder of the sentence, reliant on complex interpersonally negotiated processes of interpretation. Individual words only have effective meaning because of the vast array of knowledge (of other words and *their* meanings) brought to bear, by speaker and hearer, writer and reader, to *make* the process of communication work. Thus, whereas positivism imagines a single individual using words to label an external reality as he or she perceives it, the thesis of reflexivity suggests that this is quite misleading: using language is not a *private* act, whereby an individual represents what he or she perceives. Furthermore, since there is no way of grasping what it is that we perceive *except* (partly at least) through language itself, language structures our consciousness and, at the same time, our relationships with others.

The thesis of reflexivity has an academic tradition[1] but this does not mean that there is anything fundamentally unfamiliar in the idea. Admittedly, we live in a 'culture of positivism' which suggests that words exist as labels which can be used to present our experience directly, as a world of observable facts. However, we are also aware of what might be termed a 'counterculture of reflexivity', in which we continually remind ourselves that we live within language, as a complex set of meanings, so that our attempts to grasp the significance of our experience are an endless struggle with the possibilities and limitations of the meanings of words. Hence, for example, when we wish to make a complex statement that we wish others to take seriously we typically try to support its plausibility by showing that we are aware of the problems involved in making the statement. This may be expressed quite directly, by saying, for example: 'I find this hard to put into words, BUT . . . '. More generally, we live within a vast culture of jokes, comic understatements, distortions, and exaggerations, puns, crosswords, and quiz games, which celebrate our awareness that words have many simultaneous meanings and references, which we habitually play with (for our entertainment) and make use of (for our creative, innovative thought).[2]

This in turn reminds us that the words in which we present one experience (for example, 'Martin's mother helps him with his reading') will always refer at the same time to other experiences (for example, my feelings about my own mother, about my own current reading of a novel or a policy document, or about 'helping' as a moral value). Thus, in making a statement about Martin I am also evoking a whole range of other aspects of my life which are, apparently, 'nothing to do with' Martin, but which the

Figure 2: How reflexive judgments create the illusion of being objective descriptions

For example, the judgment: 'Martin knows the rules for multiplication'

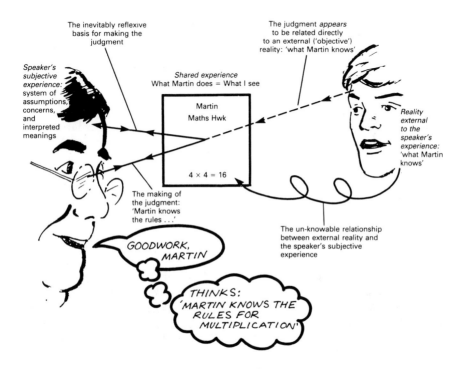

Explanation

'Re-flexive' means, literally, 'bent back'. A reflexive judgment is inevitably bent back (↘) into the speaker's subjective system of meanings, but creates an illusory straight line (─◄─ ─) which suggests that the judgment is an objective description of a reality external to the speaker. The actual relationship between what Martin knows and my experience of what he does must ultimately remain un-knowable (～).

Note the analogy with the creation of a 'virtual image' in a mirror.

words themselves begin to link and, possibly, to mingle. Again, this is a common theme. In a number of TV series, where one of the central characters with whom we identify is investigating some sort of problem (usually a crime), the point of the episode — or even of the whole series — is frequently that a similar problem to the one they are investigating emerges as significant for their own private lives: in recreating the external order of things (in solving the crime) they are also — reflexively — formulating their *internal* order (coming to terms with an aspect of their own lives). (*Cagney and Lacey, Lou Grant*, and *Quincy* are largely based on this principle.)

The thesis of the inescapable reflexivity of judgments does not in any way mean that we must abandon all sense that there are criteria for judging more and less 'valid' statements. To begin with, it is important to remind ourselves that positivism's claim that judgments can be converted into unambiguously defined descriptions of external events, although it may *appeal* to our subconscious yearnings for final certainties, does not accord with our experience. The 'findings' of research into, say, the effect of comprehensive schools on educational standards are notoriously ambiguous and disputable, even where they *are* based on crude labels such as exam marks, and where the analysis is based on apparently objective statistical procedures. Thus, social statistics are commonly both revered (as the *only* sort of evidence we can take seriously) *and* lampooned ('lies, damned lies, and statistics').

In contrast, the thesis of reflexivity begins by insisting upon *modest* claims: making judgments depends on *examples* from various personal experiences (not on representative samples of universally agreed categories). These examples can be analyzed, but no analysis will be complete or final, because inquiry will take the form of questioning claims rather than making claims. The result of inquiry will thus take the form of a dialogue between writers and readers concerning *possible* interpretations of experience, rather than a *single* interpretation thrust upon a passive reader by a writer whose enquiry has resulted in certainty. It is this process of questioning claims which is itself a dimension of validity — not the only one, but an important one. It works in the following way.

The reflexivity of judgments may be inescapable, but within the normal pressures of our professional lives we are forced to forget it. As a teacher with a class of twenty-seven, I am prepared to say, 'Martin and Rosie know the rules for multiplication, but Damion doesn't', and to give out the worksheets accordingly: woe betide any damn-fool would-be action-researcher who comes in just before the bell goes, and invites me to acknowledge the reflexive basis on which such judgments depend, and to question the various claims they imply. In practical life reflexivity *must* go unnoticed, so that the complex skills of communication can be managed. But for that very reason, the recognition and analysis of the reflexivity of a statement (through the *questioning* process of a *research* stance) is a way of appraising it, of increasing its validity by showing more fully its foundations.

There is another step also. By showing that a statement is grounded in reflexive interpretive judgments, rather than in external facts, I make it possible to review other possible interpretive judgments concerning that statement, and thus to envisage modifying it. Thus, although I might never agree that in making the claim that Martin and Rosie know the rules I am wrong about 'the facts', I might well be prepared to reconsider more carefully what I am implying by making the claim. (How do I know they are not copying? What are and were my own experiences of learning rules and applying them? What rules do *they* see themselves as using? etc, etc.) In this way, by questioning my claim, I may increase its validity by relating it more closely to the experiences in which it is grounded. This is what is meant by 'reflexive critique'.

Principle No. 1: Reflexive Critique

The basic procedure will have three steps. (1) Accounts will be collected, such as observation notes, interview transcripts, written statements from participants, or official documents. (2) The reflexive basis of these accounts will be made explicit, so that (3) claims may be transformed into questions, and a range of possible alternatives will be suggested, where previously particular interpretations have been taken for granted.

The accounts we collect from the various sources mentioned above will all make reference to the observed 'facts' of the situation, and these facts will be presented as illustrating well established patterns of what is taken to be normal in such situations, and what are expected anomalies (which are known to crop up from time to time). The accounts will also suggest a number of motives or causes which 'probably' explain these facts, and what range of other matters is relevant to this situation even though not immediately part of it. In different ways, therefore, accounts will be making implicit claims to be authoritative, to be firmly embedded in a competence to *understand* the situation, and thus to make judgments as to normality, relevance, and causation. Some of the accounts we collect will rest on claims to a professional authority, namely an expertise based on full and proper training, up-to-date reading, and long practice. Other claims to make authoritative interpretations (e.g., those made by pupils, parents, governors, or helpers) will rest upon competences which have arisen through the informal processes of everyday experience, of having 'been around', of 'knowing the score'. The authoritative claim made by an account is twofold. Firstly it implies that it accords with 'the facts', and secondly it implies that it is generally true, i.e., that anyone else would have come up with the same account if they had been there to observe. In contrast to these two claims, the thesis of reflexivity enables us, firstly, to question the claim of any statement simply to label a factual state of affairs (without, of course, involving any claim that the statement is 'wrong'). And secondly it enables us to question any claim to generality, by noting the string of particular assumptions and judgments on which any interpretation must always depend.

Thus, having begun with an account which claims to be a series of descriptions and authoritative judgments (whether of expert professional knowledge or of competent common sense knowledge), our critique will begin by making explicit its reflexive basis in the personal interpretive systems of those concerned. We thereby establish that the basis of the account is *not* simply factual (and thus indisputable) *nor* a universal law derived from an agreed body of knowledge (and thus necessarily true). This in turn establishes that, concerning the situation of which the account has been given, a number of alternative accounts *could* be relevant and important. Reflexive critique in this way *open up* lines of argument and discussion.

The following example is taken from data collected for an empirical study of the process of deciding between applicants for an in-service course based on an individually chosen project.

An Account

The following extract is from the transcript of a discussion about a number of application forms. My colleague, F, is giving reasons in favour of one applicant:

> . . . Because there's a continuity in what she wants to do. I mean, what she wants to do follows from what she's *been* doing. With other people I've looked and I've seen they've done a bit of this and a bit of that, and then something on computing, and then the area they think they'll work on is art-and-craft or something. That worries me, whereas someone like this, I can see there's a kind of progression.

Making the Reflexive Basis Explicit

(Questioning what is taken-for-granted by recollecting neglected possibilities)

(a) F claims, tentatively, that 'continuity' is a descriptive fact of this applicant's career. But continuity and discontinuity are judgments (and inescapably reflexive judgments), which do not simply describe aspects of the applicant's career, but also necessarily involve F's own theories and his concerns about the continuity and coherence of his own activities. Thus we can ask: what, for F, is 'continuity', and what isn't? What is 'discontinuous' in the relation between computing and art-and-craft? What forms of 'continuity' might — on the contrary — link them?

(b) F uses 'progression' as an evaluative criterion indicating that one thing builds on another in a series of logical stages. This criterion is very widely used by examination boards in evaluating curriculum proposals, and is thus backed up by an authoritative body of expertise. However, it is clear that other models for professional career development could have been invoked, because F has used a term from *curriculum* structure to evaluate a *career* pattern. F's argument therefore relies on a *metaphorical* comparison, so that we can ask what other metaphors could have been used, what other comparisons made between careers and curricula, and what *different* judgments might they have led to?

Recollecting Excluded Possibilities

(In carrying out the analysis, the questions and the possibilities seem to spring to mind almost simultaneously; they are separated here merely for ease of presentation.)

(a) Possible career continuities underlying computing and art-and-craft: an interest in creativity; an interest in developing curriculum opportunities for children with language difficulties; an interest in Computer-Aided-Design as a curriculum area.

(b) Alternative acceptable career patterns, other than 'progression': diversification to avoid narrow specialization; diversification to prepare for a future post involving general responsibilities.

(c) An alternative analogy between careers and curricula, other than 'progression': the analogy with a *modular* curriculum based on flexible structure and individual choice might lead one to see a highly *varied* career as indicating (positively) an applicant's independence and breadth of concern rather than (negatively) a *lack* of *focus*.

Commentary

In no sense am I disagreeing with F, nor even preferring the possibilities raised by the critique to F's original account. The question of whether I agree or disagree with F's judgments, which is a key issue within the practical professional interaction, is postponed, interrupted, by the process of the critique. By making a reflexive critique of F's account I am able to use its details more fully and more explicitly, in order to become more explicitly aware of the relevance of a number of practical possibilities concerning our procedures, as follows:

1 Applicants' careers *could* be classified in various ways, but is the

information on the application forms a sufficient basis for doing so?

2   Members of the admissions panel will have various beliefs, values, and ideologies concerning more and less desirable types of career, but could (or should) a workable consensus be agreed among us?

3   Could the requirements of the course itself be analyzed in order to establish more and less desirable types of prior career?

In this way the procedure of reflexive critique moves from the account (which arose within the practical interaction) towards a set of theoretical possibilities, and then back to the practical issues where the theoretical possibilities have relevance.

Dialectics — An Explanatory Summary

The problem. Normally, the various situations, people, and events of our professional lives present themselves to us in terms of a familiar vocabulary of explanatory concepts, each dovetailing with the rest to create a stable world of meanings. And yet we also know that this stability is only provisional: given the right frame of mind, we can step back from this familiar system of concepts and notice how it is incomplete, simplified, and inaccurate. However, when we do step back from our familiar set of meanings (as when we wish to adopt a 'research' stance, in order to 'reflect' upon 'possible' reinterpretations) we can easily feel overwhelmed by a sense that 'theoretically' *anything* could be suggested as 'possible'. Dialectics is proposed here, therefore, as a method of analysis which genuinely prises apart our familar ideologies, without suggesting that we have available an *infinite* choice of alternative interpretations. It helps us decide what is 'significant'.

'Dialectics' is a general theory of the nature of reality and of the process of understanding reality, yet its original Greek meaning is 'the art of discussion' (or more literally: 'through or by means of words'). The combination of ideas echoes one aspect of the thesis of reflexivity — that we can experience reality only by means of our competent participation in the complex structures of language. Consider a tree. The only way I could have direct sensory experience of a tree without 'going through' the structures of language would be if I were suddenly to overbalance backwards and hit the back of my head on a tree which I had previoulsy been unaware of. The rarity of this combination of circumstances helps to emphasize that in all other circumstances I experience a tree in terms a set of meanings which are available to me through the language which I have come to know. For example I know that it is 'hard', not 'soft' (so that if I were overbalancing *forwards* I would try to miss the tree and land on the grass). I would know whether it was 'bare' or 'leafy', and thus whether this was winter or summer. Within different cultures 'a tree' may indicate primarily 'shade' or 'water' or 'wood' for various uses. It may be part of 'a forest' (danger) or 'a park' (recreation) or 'an avenue' (high value property). To understand 'a tree' means being able to notice and to respond appropriately to this system of significant distinctions. To sum up, the first step we take when considering objects dialectically is that we identify them within the set of *relationships* which define them (like the point of overlap in the middle of a Venn diagram) rather than trying to define them in isolation, as single entities.

'Objects' here would mean not only trees but such things as 'curricula', 'Martin's attitude to mathematics', 'the head's management style', 'your personality', and 'my consciousness'. In each case we would set about understanding the phenomenon in question by considering: (a) the essential set of relationships which relate the phenomenon to its *necessary* context, and (b) the essential set of relationships between the elements of which the phenomenon consists. Let us consider each of these aspects in turn.

'Contexts' may be either narrow or wide sets of relations. 'My consciousness' has as its *minimum* context: (1) the scene in front of my eyes in this room now, (2) my immediate purpose (to finish writing this section on dialectics), (3) my awareness of my activities over the last hour or so. From this minimal starting point we could expand the set of contextual relations for 'my consciousness' to include, respectively: (1) the house and its neighbourhood where I am writing, (2) the general set of purposes and priorities by which I try to live, (3) my life history since childhood, (4) the language system by means of which all this has meaning. Clearly the outer limits of 'context' are infinite, but this does not mean that we can arbitrarily seize on *any* other phenomena and treat them as 'the context' of the phenomenon we wish to understand. Instead, we must work outwards through what may be thought of as a series of concentric *rings* of surrounding phenomena, where each ring has a necessary relationship with the one 'inside' it. Only in this way can our analysis be 'complete as far as it goes'[3], though it could, of course, always be extended by moving outwards to the next concentric ring.

Consider the following example of such a series of concentric rings, which might be appropriate for an understanding of the party political allegiance of teachers:

a   Individual teachers' current perceptions of their careers;
b   The immediate institutional structure within which they work;
c   The general structure of the system of educational institutions;
d   The relationship of educational institutions to economic and political institutions;
e   Government and opposition party policies towards education.

It is important to note that the sequence (a)–(e) is not predetermined: what constitutes the relevant (and in that sense 'necessary') context for the understanding of a phenomenon needs to be carefully worked out by an analysis which is based on detailed experience as well as on logical relationships between the various phenomena involved. (Also, it is clear that the above sequence relies on a general assumption that political allegiances are mainly related to people's economic interests. A different series would need to be devised if one's *general* assumption was that political judgments are mainly based on, say, moral values, or on religion.) To return to the example, the basic argument is that only by tracing the relationships from (a) to (e) through (b), (c) and (d) could we understand the meaning of statistics concerning which political party was supported by a sample of teachers. Without tracing these concentric relationships our knowledge of such statistics would merely be a linkage between isolated single entities, and would thus *not* constitute a dialectical understanding. (The familiarity of this line of criticism is shown when we sense the doubtful value of opinion polls as to how many people of categories P and Q expressed belief X as opposed to beliefs Y or Z, so that we are not at all surprised when the next poll shows the exact opposite.)

When we approach the 'elements' of a phenomenon dialectically, we again create an analysis which is both based on experience and at the same time logically required. The logical point is as follows: any entity which we can identify is 'complex' in the sense that it can be analyzed into constituent elements, for example, a school into a number of classrooms; a class into, say, a teacher, two parent helpers, plus a number of pupils; a pupil's state of mind into a number of attitudes, goals, memories, emotions; an emotion into . . . and so on! This complexity therefore immediately sets up a contradiction: on the one hand the particular phenomenon is a unity, and only this unity gives form and meaning to each component element; on the other hand this unity can always be broken down into apparently separable elements, each of which can in turn be treated as an independent entity. This is where the purely logical argument ends, however: to decide what particular separable elements comprise any particular phenomenon is always a matter for empirical investigation and interpretive judgment. It is this search for the combination of the overall unity of a phenomenon and the diversity of its elements which characterizes the second fundamental dialectical approach to the process of understanding.

Positivism in general seeks to ignore this, and to concentrate instead on things as simple unities, so that they can be defined and statistically manipulated, and this accords with our practical desire to see the world as a stable and orderly place. But the dialectical approach also accords with our common experience of how complexities can emerge to amaze us just when we thought we had got something neatly pigeon-holed: people suddenly behave 'out of character', a 'poor' class suddenly does an excellent piece of work, a group of 'responsible' adults suddenly goes crazy during a role play exercise on a residential course. We know that simple pigeonholing categories are always provisional and superficial: our awareness of our own complexity (for example, 'I astounded myself: I didn't know I had it in me.') ensures that at some level we know that the unifying labels that we use to categorize experience within the routines of everyday life are merely the beginnings of understanding.

The third step in the argument starts out from the fundamental notion of contradiction which we have just considered. It is because of the fundamental contradiction within each phenomenon between its unity and its diversity that we know it is currently undergoing a process of change. This is perhaps the single most important contribution of dialectical thinking. That the present is different from the past is one of the safest of generalizations, and hence one of the safest of assumptions is that the future will be different from the present. (This holds true whether we are considering the structure of the civil service, a class of learners, or an individual person.) And yet some of the most widespread methods for 'rigorous' analysis (precise definition of discrete entities, identification of linear chains of cause and effect, explanation of integrated systems in terms of the contributory function of each sub-system) create explanations which suggest so strongly how what we have carefully observed *had* to happen, that it neglects consideration of why and how what we carefully observed yesterday will certainly be different tomorrow, i.e., by the time we can get round to doing something about it. In contrast, a dialectical approach urges the principle: any explanation of phenomena which does not explain how and why it has changed, and *will continue to do so*, is a poor explanation.

However: we cannot predict the future. In what sense, then, can the ongoing process of change be analyzed? The dialectical approach suggests that in order to understand a phenomenon we treat it as a set of relations between elements which are different and, in some sense, opposed (i.e., 'contradictory'[4]), and yet at the same time interdependent (i.e., form a unity[5]). It is this instability in the structure of a phenomenon which provides it with a specific and inherent tendency to change. In this way dialectics gives us a principle by means of which we can select, from the infinite number of elements and relations into which any phenomenon *could* be broken down, some as more significant than others: those internal relationships between constituent elements whose instability creates the likelihood of change.

As an example, consider a hypothetical class of students or pupils: I know, in principle, that it is not only a 'unified' class but also a 'disunified' assembly of different individuals. Suppose that I investigate the social structure of the class by establishing the pattern of current friendship choices: I would produce a conventional sociogram which appears to represent a fixed system of interlocking groups. However, I need a way of analyzing the pattern of friendship choices in such a way as to take the change process into account. The dialectical principle suggests that the most significant internal relationships determining a tendency to change are between elements which are both different *and* interdependent. Hence

49

I might conclude that the two groups which are made up of *similar* class members (say: one group of highly enthusiastic individuals and another group of rather hostile, cynical individuals) are *not* significant from this point of view, since the two groups are separated from each other (i.e., not 'interdependent'). These groups, then, are likely to be self-reinforcing, not likely to influence each other, and thus more likely to maintain the current pattern than to change it. I would therefore be much more interested in two other groups, which are both 'unified' (as a group of friends) and also 'disunified', in that each group contains both cynical and enthusiastic individuals. In other words, it is the balance of power within the two 'mixed' groups which is going to be most significant in understanding the social psychology of the class as a whole, since it is there that the two elements — cynicism and enthusiasm — are putting pressure on each other and thus creating a delicately poised situation which is inherently likely to shift one way or the other. In this way, it is the outcome of the tension within those two mixed groups which is the factor most likely to determine the future development of the class as a whole.

This fundamental emphasis on the process of change, gives the dialectical method a specific and helpful perspective on an otherwise very awkward issue which has a crucial significance for the practice of social investigation, namely: how far are individuals determined by their environment? If, using a positivist approach, we attempt to understand a situation as an interlocking system, by observing defined and unified entities and trying to identify lines of cause and effect between them, we create the image of a social system which determines the behaviour of its members (by means of motives, values, role definitions, etc.). But this then suggests that observers of the social system are also determined by it, since they also are members — appointed and paid by institutions, influenced by professional, moral, and class ideologies, worried about their careers, their mortgages, etc. This in turn means that the findings of these observers carry no persuasive authority in their own right (unless of course we already happen to agree with them) since their findings are (like everything else) merely the effects of social causes (i.e., the motives, values, and role definitions affecting the research process). Furthermore, if this description of a static, interlocking social system were accurate, then investigation could not lead to change, since the investigation would itself be part of that interlocking system. Therefore, in order to avoid this absurd self-destructive circle, positivist observers are led to claim that, whereas the people they describe are determined, they themselves, the observers, are able to be independent, by means of their 'scientific method'. They are thus able to create new and independent knowledge which can be 'applied' to the system in order to change it. It is easy to see that this claim is at best highly questionable, and at worst quite incoherent: to adopt the stance of 'the independent observer' in order to interpret others' activities as dependent on forces beyond their control is to deny by your own act the very point that you wish to assert: that people can be understood as determined. And if they *are* determined, how can changes (as a result of 'independent observation') be put into practice? It seems as though other people are both wholly determined by existing forces and yet wholly available to be, as it were, redetermined by 'new' forces.

The dialectical approach avoids these incoherencies by asserting the change process as a fundamental axiom. The argument is as follows. Individuals are the product of their social world, but this social world is structured as a series of contradictions, and is thus in a continuous process of change; its influence upon individuals is thus both conflicting and varying, and can thus never be either unambiguous or final. Consequently, individual consciousness is also structured as a set of contradictions, and individuals thus possess a degree of autonomy as to how they will respond to the conflicting and varying pressures from their social context. In other words they retain a *creative* space for their own interpretation and decision-making. When they act, therefore, they do not simply reproduce their environment; they change it. Hence, although we started by saying that individuals are the product of their social world, we can *also* say that the social world is created by individuals' actions. We can make *both* statements simultaneously because 'action' is not 'behaviour' (the effect of a cause) but 'praxis' (the creative implementation of a purpose). This model of action is applicable both to the activities of someone investigating a situation and also to the activities of those taking part in the situation being investigated: we no longer have that inconsistent dualism which contrasts (without accounting for) the free independence of the observer with the constrained dependence of the observed.

Again, I think this accords with our experience. We are normally wholly sceptical of anyone claiming to speak 'entirely without bias' on any matter in which we have a serious interest; and equally sceptical of anyone claiming to 'explain' to us our own actions as the effects of forces beyond our influence, rather than as the results of our choices between various influences. The dialectical notion of 'praxis' thus cautions us against the temptation of slipping into an 'independent observer' stance when we start to carry out an investigation, and of starting to collect examples of other people's behaviour as patterns of cause and effect.

'Dialectics' puts forward a coherent general theory both of the nature and structure of reality and also the process of analyzing and understanding reality. Even more than 'reflexivity', it is the topic of a substantial theoretical tradition,[6] but this body of theory can be summarized to provide simply a *method* of analysis. Quite simply: dialectics gives us a principled basis for making selections. It thereby helps to contain our potentially vast amounts of data and interpretation within the practical limits (for example, time, resources) of practitioner research. The next section describes 'dialectical critique' as a methodological principle.

Principle Two: Dialectical Critique

Whereas positivist methods suggest that we must observe phenomena exhaustively, and define them precisely, in order to identify specific causes and effects, a dialectical approach suggests we subject observed phenomena to a 'critique'. This entails investigating (1) the overall context of relations which gives them a unity in spite of their apparent separateness, and (2) the structure of internal contradictions — behind their apparent unity — which gives them a tendency to change, in spite of their apparent fixity.

Our first step, then, will be to collect phenomena from the situation we are describing. These may be statements of opinion from interview transcripts or notes, observations of occurrences (for example, in classrooms or staffrooms), or statistics of the comparative frequency of these phenomena (i.e., the *distribution* of attitudes or events). This will give us as a starting point for our analysis a set of phenomena as they have presented themselves to our investigation, in their immediate form, i.e., as entities which appear to be separate, unified, and fixed. Our critique can then focus on any or all of these three apparent characteristics, as elaborated below.

Separateness and the Context of Necessary Relationships

We may start out from a single, separate expression of opinion, or other category of evidence, and explore the general set of ideas and beliefs within which, alone, that opinion or evidence has meaning, and which in that sense forms a 'necessary' context. Thus, for example, a series of collected opinions or test scores relating to school policy on girls' underachievement in science would need to be set within the context of a general set of ideas on the scope and origin of gender roles. In this way opinions on 'girls' underachievement in science' will need to be considered in relation to opinions on 'girls' overachievement in languages' and on 'boys' underachievement in home economics and biology', and thus concerning what might be meant by 'normal achievement'. The latter thus no longer appears to be merely a matter of an individual's performance in relation to his or her individual ability, but clearly points towards a necessary context of motives, social opportunities, and group expectations. We can thus see the sense in which this form of analysis presents 'a critique': each of the relationships noted above opens up a series of questions: what do we expect of different groups of children and why? what makes curricula relevant to different children? how is ability related to motivation? By considering the original opinion in isolation we might well have overlooked such questions and concentrated exclusively on events concerning girls and science. In this way the 'context of necessary relationships' creates the *scope* of the investigation, and shows what range of phenomena must be taken into account for the adequate interpretation of *any* of the data.

Overall Unity but Diversity of Elements

We start out from the series of distinct categories in which we collect our data (a potentially infinite series, since any noun — or combination of nouns — can be a 'category'). Then we analyze these categories in order to find unity concealed behind apparent differentiation, and contradiction concealed within apparent unity. This will give our analysis an initial basis and purpose in making selections, without importing analytical purposes from outside the data, i.e., to see how they match up to some prior theory.

Suppose we are investigating 'disaffection' in a class of adolescent students, and that we have collected data (attitudes, behaviour, etc.) from two groups, the 'disaffected' and the 'compliant', having previously given a working definition to create the distinction. One approach will be to focus on any significant behaviour which is *common* to both groups, or to focus our attention on any individuals who shift from one group to the other, either permanently or intermittently. Alternatively, we will be interested in any attitudes or activities *within* each group which appear to be in contradiction with each other. We will focus on conflicting attitudes, conflicting actions, or attitudes which are at variance with actions. In this way, the dialectical analysis will be a critique of the distinctions between the categories ('disaffected'/'compliant') which were its starting point, by showing their basis in conventions or decisions which can be queried. This will enable the analysis to be a development *beyond* that starting point, a learning process rather than a confirmation.

The Inherent Tendency for Phenomena to Change

Starting from a provisional description of how a number of elements in a situation fit together and thus form a system of cause and effect, we will look for contradictions within and between those elements (as in the previous section). This will enable us to focus on the pattern of opposed forces which make up the history of the situation and give it a specific tendency to change. This will enable our analysis to point from the immediate phenomena of the situation not only to speculations upon their origins but also towards a number of possible futures, and thus towards possible ways of intervening in order to influence which of those futures may be realized. In other words, a dialectical grasp of the process of change enables us to introduce 'effective action' as a criterion for 'valid' understanding.

As an example, let us consider two contrasting ways of understanding the 'disaffection' problem referred to in the previous section. One approach would start by treating 'disaffection' as a unified category referring to a particular characteristic which an individual person may or may not possess. We could then trace the causes of this single phenomenon backwards (to 'lack of parental support' and 'previous failure') and outwards (to 'awareness of poor career opportunities' and 'peer group pressure'). This is plausible enough as a descriptive interpretation, but its format as a static and apparently self-reproducing cause-effect system does not open up any hopeful strategies for intervention. We might therefore even say that as an understanding of disaffection it is 'too easy', since it can lead to a self-justifying excuse for continuing professional ineffectiveness. Admittedly, it might indirectly suggest that one might look for improved methods of classroom control, in order to oppose one force ('disaffection') with another ('authority'), but our analysis already suggests that the problem is so powerfully determined, as the effect of many causes, that one teacher's efforts seem, in principle, unlikely to have much impact.

In contrast, a dialectical approach might run as follows. 'Disaffection' is *not* a unified negative emotional response, on the part of students, to a unified positive educational effort ('developing the capacities of individuals') on the part of teachers. Rather: education is generally structured by (among other features) a contradiction between developing the capacities of all individuals, and legitimating the lack of capacity of some individuals in order to prepare them to accept low status. Similarly disaffection among learners is structured by a contradiction between acceptance of the educational authority which accepts, values, and develops individuals' capacities, and rejection of the educational authority whereby individuals are compared, graded, and rejected.[7] These contradictions will underlie any educational situation I may be investigating (say, for example: a 'Social Skills' class within a 4th-year secondary option scheme). They may also be seen historically as the current expression of a similarly contradictory relationship between nineteenth century educators and (on the one hand) Christianity (a concern to make generally available such universal virtues as perseverance and industriousness) and (on the other hand) capitalism (a concern to control a potentially unruly workforce by promoting precisely those same virtues).

What possible futures does this analysis conjure up? (We can be simple and schematic, because our purpose at this point is merely to gain a sort of chronological perspective on our 4th-year Social Skills class.) One possible future is a robotized production system beyond the reach of 'unruly' workers, who thus need to be educated for a life of creatively absorbing (and hence politically harmless) 'leisure'. A second possibility might be a participatory production system drawing upon the industriousness of all, in which technical know-how is no more important than the skills of collaborative decision-making.

What might these alternatives suggest in terms of intervention strategies? First of all we seem to need an approach which can go beyond the real contradictions between the needs of individual students and the needs of the current economic and political order. (The sense of 'go beyond' here is quite modest: it does not mean *remove* the contradictions; we are not aiming to restructure the social order but to address the problem of disaffection in our 4th-year Social Skills class.) In fact our analysis of possible futures has implicitly begun to suggest two possible strategies for change: *either* move the curriculum towards 'absorbing, creative leisure', and base other curriculum aims around that; *or* move the curriculum towards collaborative decision-making skills, which can clearly be seen to have relevance for situations which are not tied to the current structure of job opportunities. In this way, a dialectical critique constructs a historical perspective, and thereby works towards the exploration of strategies for change.

Unremarkable as the above examples may seem, we might compare them with the strategies which appear to be made available by the previous, non-dialectical analysis. Parental support and peer group pressure are all beyond our influence, so that all we can consider is: how can we manage the presentation of our educational efforts in such a way that they will not be nullified by the 'disaffected response' of the students? But unfortunately this analysis does not in itself suggest any particular aspect of our presentation as being more significant (and thus more worth attempting to change) than any other. In other words, without an analysis of the contradictions involved, we can only take the current situation as it immediately appears and seek improved techniques for manipulating or enforcing our control of it.

The purpose of this brief example is merely to indicate that the analysis of a situation into its constituent contradictions is not a mysterious or a mechanical technique, but a way of ordering one's thoughts. Nor is it lacking in practical relevance: on the contrary, the dialectical approach to analysis always envisages a further dialectic between theory and practice, which will be further elaborated later — see Principle Six.

Principle Three: Collaborative Resource

The problem. The question here is: what is my 'role' as a researcher? What sort of relationships does it require me to adopt with those in the institution who are my hierarchical superiors, with my students, with interested colleagues, and above all with those from whom I am 'collecting data'? In particular, how can I — within these relationships — attempt to be 'impartial'?

Practitioner action-researchers know that they are part of the situation in question, not detached from it; they are not observers, but 'members', as are colleagues, students, caretakers, and any other people who make up the situation. It is collaboration among the membership of a situation (for example, a school, a classroom) which creates it and keeps its processes going, and, it is also through collaboration that the different processes of a research projects are created within the situation. 'Collaboration' here is intended to mean: *everyone's* point of view will be taken as a contribution to resources for understanding; *no-one's* point of view will be taken as the final understanding as to what all the other points of view *really* mean. This is a major contrast with the positivist approach, where the overall assumption is not that investigators are knowledgeable because they are insiders, but that they may be impartial because they are outsiders. We have already seen the forms of incoherence created by the stance of impartiality: it leads investigators to say (usually in quick succession): (a) that steps should be taken to 'ensure' impartiality, (b) that impartiality is in principle unattainable, (c) that particular methods have been adopted because they are 'as impartial as possible', and (d) that owing to 'limited resources' (say £500,000!) the work falls lamentably short of its impartial ideal.

Collaboration is more modest in its claims, and potentially much more coherent in its approach to the question of impartiality. Our inquiry will start by collecting a number of viewpoints (including that of the initiator of the research) and it is this series of viewpoints which gives a preliminary structure and meaning to the situation under investigation. (It *could* be argued that there are as many viewpoints as there are individual members, but — equally — it can be argued that individual viewpoints can be grouped into 'roles', i.e., social positions with more or less recognized combinations of rights and obligations.)

To work collaboratively with these viewpoints does *not* mean that we begin by trying to synthesize them into a consensus, by counting or evaluating them. On the contrary it is the variety of differences between the viewpoints that makes them into a rich resource, and it is by using this resource (the differences between viewpoints) that our analysis can begin to move outwards from its inevitably personal starting point towards ideas which have been *interpersonally* negotiated. If we *begin* by seeking consensus between viewpoints we shall have no counterweight to the subconscious selectivity which makes us tend to notice more readily what agrees with our prior assumptions. Instead, therefore, the first step in our analysis will be to take each viewpoint as a *serious* viewpoint, so that differences between viewpoints constitute serious challenges or questions posed from one to the other. This will be true irrespective of the social status of the member who puts it forward. Pupils' views will thus be allowed seriously to confront teachers', probationers to confront heads of department, and *all* views will confront those of the initiator of the research. To treat all viewpoints as a collaborative resource is thus to suspend the conventional status hierarchy which (outside the research stance) gives some members authority over others, and some members' viewpoints greater credibility than others'. It is thus part of the research process that we shall treat all viewpoints as potentially of equal significance[8] so that our *analysis* of them can be specifically different from our *awareness* of their varying degrees of authority in their (and our) practical context.

The basic argument so far in this section has been that what we collect from other members of the situation is not 'data' (to be fitted into one or other of our anticipated interpretive categories), but a set of resources for creating other interpretive categories, which when we started we had not anticipated. Another way of putting this would be to say that the interpretive categories we start with are to be treated as data alongside the ideas we collect from others. There is a further step, however, which follows from previous comments concerning unity and diversity (see under 'Dialectical Critique'). The viewpoints of members in the form we collect them (through open-ended questionnaires or interview records) will tend to seem more or less unified: that is, after all, implicit in the notion of 'a viewpoint'. But our analysis will not only seek to assemble resources for reinterpretation from the differences (the conflicts, the contradictions) *between* viewpoints, but also from the conflicts and contradictions *within* viewpoints, including of course our own. In this way, the principle of 'Collaborative Resource' indicates a process of simultaneously giving weight to the understandings contributed by all members, and at the same time a process of 'deconstructing' the various contributions so that we can use them as resources for 'reconstructing' new categories and interpretations.

This suggests an important point about 'resources'. Focusing on the *contradictory* elements of a viewpoint enables us to give full recognition to those fleeting glimpses of ideas which we normally dismiss as 'irrelevant' because they don't fit in with the rest of our conceptual framework. What is being suggested here is that the rationally unified expression of a viewpoint is only the verbal tip of a psychic iceberg: the resources we possess for transcending a viewpoint are scattered among a lifetime's accumulation of ideas. They will include our general moral and political concepts, ambiguous images from our dreams, and scenarios from our favourite films and novels, as well as specific professional hypotheses. In seeking to assemble intellectual resources with which to carry out an analysis, we should cast our net as widely as possible (*cf.* the well-known technique of 'brainstorming'), knowing that the appraisal of the usefulness or otherwise of these ideas will come later, as an essential phase of the work.

The following example is taken from a study of my role as tutor on an in-service course on professional self-appraisal for teachers (see chapter nine). At the end of the course I tape-recorded a discussion in which I asked the course members in what ways they thought they had benefitted. Here are extracts from two accounts.

> *Student A*: It's made me braver . . . I'm prepared to say, 'Yes, this is what I think.' I feel as if I've been besieged on all sides by so many ideas . . . (Now) I have the courage to say things that are un-

fashionably so, against the things that are fashionable . . . .

> *Student B*: Now it's had exactly the opposite effect on me . . . It's made me a lot less critical of other people, because I have tended to hold opinions, I think, sometimes, which have been unfounded, and when I really look at them closely, I find that other people's opinions are just as good as mine, if not better.

Firstly, in order to treat these accounts as resources, I have to try to ignore my practical interpretation of A as 'a better student' than B. (Unless I take this step I will not be entering into a 'collaborative' relationship with the accounts, in order to develop my thinking, but *using* them as *evidence* to support my current thinking.)

Secondly, the accounts must be allowed to challenge each other. (In the original conversation it is clear that A and B did indeed perceive their statements as being in opposition to each other.) Thus, in these accounts, the development of assertiveness (Student A) seems to contrast with the development of self-criticism (Student B). The statement 'I'm prepared to say, "This is what I think"' is difficult to reconcile with the statement 'I find other people's opinions are just as good as my own, if not better'. This opposition challenges my belief (important in my original conception of the aims of the course) that the capacity for self-criticism is the most important dimension of assertiveness, of intellectual confidence.

Therefore (thirdly) I am challenged to think again about this belief: it may be a lot more problematic than I had thought. Perhaps there *is* a real opposition involved, especially when one is deeply committed to a set of practical responsibilities (as are both A and B), so perhaps my disappointment at what I take to be the crudity of both statements needs examining. This subjective response (of disappointment) and the set of ideas from which it derives are presumably linked to my own personality, intellectual biography, and professional role, so this challenge, emanating from the two accounts I have collected from other people, can be thought of as the beginning of a move beyond my original subjectivity.

On the other hand (fourthly) my sense that there will be a unity behind the opposition of A and B leads me to look carefully at both accounts, to try to find contradictions *within* them which will blur the simple opposition *between* them. For example, A claims 'I know what I think' and yet feels 'besieged on all sides'. Furthermore, his opposition between what is 'so' and what is 'fashionable' begs the whole question as to how he makes that judgment. So although he says he 'knows' what he thinks, he also presents himself as *reacting* against the external pressure of 'fashion'. Similarly, when B finds his own opinions to be 'unfounded' this sounds like a process of critical examination of grounds for belief, so why does this lead him to be now *less* critical of others than he was before? Perhaps 'being critical' in the latter case means 'being *dismissive* without good reason'; so perhaps the process of 'being critical' needs to be divided into 'asserting the right to be dismissive' and 'requiring good reasons'. Hence the 'opposition' between A and B disappears.

Finally, returning from theoretical possibilities to feasible practicalities, perhaps I need to focus discussion within the course more clearly on what we might mean by 'knowing what we think' and by 'being critical', in order to illuminate more clearly the close relationship between these ideas, and thereby to clarify an important aspect of the aims of the course.

In retrospect, of course, this seems fairly unremarkable, even 'obvious', but this is merely to say that it really might be a feasible and effective thing to do, precisely because it has been there all along, as a concealed possibility which just needed 'unearthing'. The example is intended to illustrate how, by treating other participants as collaborators, i.e., by treating their accounts as resources along with one's own, we can enable such 'unearthing' to take place, and may come up with ideas which are both new (at the time) and usable.

The example also begins to show the nature of the link between the 'collaborative' process of mutual challenge between accounts and 'modest' claims to objectivity. 'Objectivity' here seems to have four senses:

1 The collaborative process acts as a challenge to (a check upon) one's subjectivity (one's personal starting points and assumptions).

2 The process involves examining relationships between the accounts of the various *necessary* members of a situation: the range of accounts which will need to be considered will be given by the *structure* of the situation. (In the example above: a curriculum has to include a teacher and one or more learners.) The selection of which accounts to include is thus never entirely arbitrary, even though it can never be absolutely and finally complete.

3 One outcome of the process is a series of analyses which are based on inherent and necessary relationships, both logical and empirical. (In the example above: between knowledge, criticism, and confidence.) The analyses do not add up to a general law, and they are very clearly both incomplete and speculative; but they are not just opinions, and they *could* be illuminating (in the sense of 'relevant') for a range of situations whose structure is similar to the one from which they are derived.

4 The outcome of the process is a practical proposal. Whether it is based in objective considerations, or is (in contrast) merely a personal, opinionated judgment, will in part at least be seen when it is put into practice and its consequences noted. It is not necessarily the *only* or the 'best' practical strategy, but it has emerged from the analyses (see 3 above) as a theoretically *possible* strategy, and it is now my practical judgment, as an insider and as a practitioner, that it could be a *feasible* strategy. Once again, we end on the theory/practice issue, which will be taken up under Principle Six.

Principle Four: Risk

The problem. As professionals, with established reputations for competence, working under difficult conditions, the research process is going to seem like a *threat* to all the taken-for-granted processes by which we 'cope'. How can we manage this sense of threat? In particular, how can we manage the sense of threat that we (as research initiators) may find ourselves posing to our colleagues, on whose collaborative support we depend?

This principle follows quite directly from the previous one and also from the principles of reflexive and dialectical critique. The principle is: that initiators of research must put themselves 'at risk' through the process of the investigation. This clearly has something in common with the well-known scientific concern that hypotheses should be open to refutation. But practitioner researchers bring more than hypotheses to their research, so that more than hypotheses are at risk. Furthermore, the process is not merely one of exposure to refutation, but of exploring possibilities for transformation.

What may be transformed (and thus in this sense 'at risk') are:

1 Researchers' provisional interpretations of the situation, which become merely 'resources' alongside those of other members;
2 Researchers' decisions as to the questions at issue, and thus concerning what is and what is not relevant;
3 Researchers' anticipations of the sequence of events through which the investigation will pass.

Through involvement in the investigative process, we will therefore not only submit others' accounts to critique, but our own also; we will not only note the contradictions in others' viewpoints which indicate their inherent tendency to change, but will also note these contradictions and possibilities for change in our own viewpoints. We are not 'consultants', advising others how to change, nor 'catalysts', unchanging facilitators of others' development. (We might, however, benefit from others performing both these roles.) In engaging in a process where the purpose is change (innovation at the level of practice and the development of new insights concerning practice) we are part of the situation which is undergoing change. We have no theoretical basis for exempting ourselves from the processes we set in motion, and we do not want to be exempt; on the contrary, we want to change because we want to *learn* as much as possible: insofar as the outcomes of the investigative process seem to be renewed justification for what we were doing (or knew) before, our investigation will represent changes postponed, opportunities not grasped, possibilities not revealed or explored. The only hypotheses we will want to support are those which have newly emerged in the course of our inquiry; those we started out with we will wish to transcend.

The previous three principles taken together give a theoretical basis for this fourth principle, but there is a practical consideration also. An investigation or a developmental project may well be initiated by one person in a situation, but initiators need collaborators for the work to proceed. At the very least they need interviewees, respondents to question-naires, suppliers of documents, etc. Now, initiators may promise that the project will be of benefit to all, but other members may nevertheless be reluctant to become involved, noting that the process will involve them in the expenditure of precious time, worrying that the process will tend to threaten their current practices and assumptions, and fearing that the process will make them (as producers of data) vulnerable to the research initiator (as an interpreter of data). A common sense consideration of the interpersonal politics of the research process suggests that a potentially effective way of allaying such fears and worries is created when initiators can clearly show that the work proposed will subject the initiators them-selves to those same fears and worries. Claims as to the benefits of the pro-cess will then ring more plausibly and may meet with less scepticism. In this way the 'micropolitics' of the research process creates a serious of rigorous requirements, where considerations of ethics (concern for the psychic comfort of our collaborators) mesh with considerations of prudence: after all, we are going to have to work in the situation after the investigative project is over; unlike researchers in the role of outside observers, prac-titioner researchers cannot upset an institutional apple-cart and walk away to present their findings elsewhere.

So, if we propose to observe a colleague's class, let us also propose that the colleague should observe us; if we wish to analyze pupils' work, let us do so within a mutual exchange of materials and interpretations; if accounts are to be broken down into their component contradictions, let us make it clear that our own accounts will be similarly analyzed; and if professional categories and practices are to change as a result of the project, let us ensure that our own categories and practices are among the first to change.

But perhaps it is worth emphasizing that to call this principle 'Risk' is slightly ironic. To say that all participants in an investigation (including the initiator) will place their practices and viewpoints 'at risk' is merely a way of saying that all participants have a capacity for change, for fresh insight.

The following example concerns L, a teacher in an infant school carrying out a study of her work with children on 'The Past', as part of an in-service course. During a visit to a local church, one of her pupils came up to her and, pointing to the lectern, said, 'Can I draw that, please?' L saw that the lectern was carved in the shape of an eagle, and therefore con-cluded that the request was connected, for the child, with earlier work done by the class on 'Birds', which had included 'Observational drawing'.

Her first reaction was that here was 'encouraging' evidence of the child's 'interest' in the work. However, further reflection on the form of this interest suggested a series of possibilities with quite challenging implications. Here was a child who had 'taken over' the meaning of the curriculum devised by L, and was proposing relationships that L had not envisaged. Here was a child who was no longer carrying out tasks set by the teacher, but proposing her own tasks. In other words, L allowed the 'innocent' request to pose a threat to her conceptions of curriculum structure ('Art', 'Birds', 'The Past') and to her conceptions of the role relationships between 'teacher' and 'pupil'. The form of the threat, however, was not the simple, negative: 'What right do we have to *impose* definitions?' — which, in the end, we can answer quite easily. Instead, the challenge was a positive one: if under certain conditions children will treat the exercise of intellectual skills as a pleasurable opportunity, and ask: 'Can I draw that?' — then perhaps a teacher should be able to set up conditions in which pupils will, in the same spirit, ask: 'Can I write about that?' and 'Can I count these?'.

In this way L accepted the *risk* of exposing her sense of professional adequacy to a radically more demanding set of criteria. She went on to examine the rest of her curriculum provision in the light of these criteria, attempting to recreate elsewhere that moment of the eagle lectern. The point of the example is not whether she succeeded, but that her moment of insight became particularly valuable when she allowed it to take the form of *accepting* a *risky* challenge.

Principle Five: Plural Structure

The problem. The research process seeks differences, contradictions, possibilities and questions, as ways of opening up new avenues for action. The initiator of a research process is not an uninvolved observer but an implicated participant, and situations cannot be reduced to a consensus, but must be presented in terms of the multiplicity of viewpoints which make up the situation. So the next question is: how can these features be embodied in a research report?

Research reports conventionally summarize and unify; they are linear, presenting a chronology of events, or a sequence of cause and effect; they are presented in the single voice of the author, who organizes evidence to support his or her conclusions, so that the report will seem authoritative and 'convincing' to readers. This 'unified structure' is an appropriate format for the presentation of positivist modes of inqury. But our dialectical, reflexive, questioning, collaborative form of inquiry will create a 'plural structure', consisting of various accounts and various critiques of those accounts, and ending not with conclusions (intended to be 'convincing') but with questions and possibilities (intended to be 'relevant' in various ways for different readers). We therefore need to consider an appropriate format, i.e., the nature of a 'plural text', which can accommodate a plural structure of inquiry.[9] The following are some general practical suggestions.

In the course of the work, we will have gathered a number of different accounts (from interviews, from diaries, from observed conversations, from documents) and these accounts need to be heard, as independent interpretations, not merely as evidence supporting the author's interpretation. This will be difficult, because the report cannot be too long, but it is possible in principle, since we are not required to describe the situation by means of a summarizing consensus, which has to justify itself by referring to 'all' the evidence, but merely to delineate a structure of oppositions and contradictions. However, although the report will seem to be at one level a collection of fragments, there will have to be a principle by which some matters are included and others excluded. Whereas a unified text is constructed by the links in the author's argument, moving 'logically' from evidence to conclusions, a plural text will need a structural principle which exists separately from the author's argument (since the author's argument will be only one of various voices in the text). One convenient principle which can be used for this purpose is that of the 'necessary range of data' (derived from the notion of the 'context of necessary relationships' — see Principle Two). Briefly, the idea is that the phenomenon one is investigating will have a certain number of elements which must *all* be included if the phenomenon itself is to be comprehensible as such. Thus, for a teaching situation to *be* a teaching situation it must include (at least) a teacher, a learner, educational aims, a teaching interaction, and outcomes. Hence, a study of a teaching situation must contain data relating to all of these, because each can only be interpreted in the context created by all the others. This set of necessary elements thus provides a framework within which the data (no longer merely 'fragments' but parts of a structure) can be presented (see chapter nine for an example in full).

Data and interpretation will be related as follows. The accounts we have collected will include various would-be authoritative claims to describe the situation 'as it is', and one form of analysis we will carry out will be a reflexive critique of those claims (see Principle One). Hence, the text of the report will be more of a collage than a description: it will contain a plurality of accounts and also a commentary on each account. But the principle of reflexivity requires us to go further, of course: in order to ensure that these commentaries are compatible with the role of the author as collaborator and participant (rather than as observer and judge), the commentaries must go on to address their own contradictions, their own reflexive status. Commentaries, then, will contain a high proportion of questions, as opposed to descriptive, interpretive statements.

Like any research report, our text must give readers the resources with which to disagree with it. Hence, just as positivist researchers include 'raw statistics' as well as their own calculations, we will include more data than our commentaries require, to enable readers to focus on other aspects than those which we have selected. There is a difficult judgment here, of course: readers will expect a report to be sufficiently organized to be accessible to a conventional act of reading, as well as sufficiently open to allow for readers' various interpretations.

This concern for readers as further collaborators in the process of the work raises the question: who are our readers? The reason why readers must be thought of as collaborators is that our first circle of readers *must* be the members of the situation from which the report derives. This is helpful, in that it gives us one crucial purpose for our report: to act as a *discussion* document through which the dialectic of theory and practice can move back from the moment of theory (the report) to the moment of practice (what is to be done with the report). (*Cf.* the original meaning of 'dialectics' as 'the art of discussion'.) This again gives us a clear reason for maintaining the emphasis in our commentaries on questions rather than prescriptive statements: our report will suggest to our collaborators a plurality of possible action strategies, and the choice among these possibilities will be a *collaborative* choice, which we (as report writers) have no need or wish to pre-empt, by presenting *one* conclusion or recommendation.

This suggestion, that the primary audience for an action-research report consists of the members of the situation from which it was derived, may trigger off once more the familiar fear (or criticism) that action-research does not lead to the discovery of any truths which are of general significance but only truths which are valid for a particular situation. But the answer to such fears and criticisms is that they are misplaced, relying as they do on positivist notions of validity and significance derived from the natural sciences. Their relevance for methods of understanding human situations is thus dubious from the outset. For example, one does not have to think very hard in order to find work of very general significance which was originally produced for the members of a particular situation: A. A. Milne and Lewis Carroll originally made up their stories in order to entertain individual children, and we now read as 'literature' what were originally political pamphlets, letters, diaries, and personal love poems. Indeed, the very concept of 'art' suggests how familiar we are with the idea that the particular instance can have very general significance. *Hamlet*, *Oliver Twist*, Rembrandt's face, two embracing figures by Rodin, four notes at the beginning of Beethoven's fifth symphony: all of these have been such well known general symbols for so long that we hardly need to feel overwhelmed by the more recent claims of 'science' that general significance can *only* reside in statistical manipulations carried out upon representative samples. In other words, one does not need to address explicitly a universal audience or to utter a statement in the form of a universal law in order for one's words to have a general significance: 'significance' is, in a very important sense, in the mind of the beholder, as an interpretation which *finds* points of contact, of relevance, to which the beholder can relate. The question of significance and validity for a practitioner's action-research report, therefore, is not to be approached via a simple analogy with an experiment in physics or behaviourist psychology, or with a statistical analysis of questionnaire returns. Instead we need to think also of the 'significance' of work in history, documentary, fiction, and (auto)biography, where we have no difficulty at all in accepting that the portrayal of a specific situation can embody ideas of universal 'validity'.

What enables one specific situation to be relevant to many other situations is a similarity of *structure*, so that if our research report has managed to go beyond accidental descriptive details and to grasp the structure of the situation in which we have been involved, then there is every chance that the report will appeal to a wider audience than our immediate colleagues. This audience may consist of anyone with experience of or interest in a situation which is similar in structure to the one which we have analyzed. Hence the importance of the principles of reflexivity, dialectics, collaboration, and risk: in their different ways they embody general and rigorous criteria of relevance, so that the necessarily economical selection of evidence and argument that we make (guided by those principles) may enable our report on *our* situation to achieve relevance for the experiences of others. As *general* principles they help our selective process to avoid the merely accidental, the merely personal opinion, and to grasp structures of experience which will be widely shared.

The open, 'plural', questioning format of our report will make this breadth of relevance more rather than less likely, since it will prevent our presenting a report in the form of a unified, prescriptive viewpoint, which readers may well feel inclined — from their own inevitably *different* viewpoint — to reject as 'just our opinion'. Instead, the plural format of our report will enable it to speak simultaneously to readers with differing viewpoints, and it is in this sense that the report may be able to claim 'objectivity', i.e., relevance and plausibility for readers with widely varying concerns.

Principle Six: Theory, Practice, Transformation

The problem here is very simply posed. What of the crucial relationship between theory and practice, between research and action? How shall we ensure that 'findings' can be 'implemented'?

The positivist conception which still haunts action-research through the continuing influence of Lewin (see chapters two and three) presents us with a crude separation: 'research' strives towards an ideal of disinterested and comprehensive observation of 'the facts', so that 'action' (observed by researchers) is explained as the behavioural effect of specifiable causes. However, we have seen that the stance of the disinterested observer is one which cannot in principle be attained, and the cause-effect explanations of social action always seem to the actors themselves to be a potentially insulting diminution of their experience. Positivism thus creates the theory-practice relationship in the form of an impasse, in which the prescriptive claims of researchers are frequently greeted by practitioners with incredulity, boredom, or mockery, as in the following quip (from the pages of *The Times Educational Supplement*) in reference to a survey commissioned by the NFER:

> Research either tells you something you knew already, or tells you nothing, or tells you something which is obvious nonsense. (Sloman, 1980)

However, by abandoning the positivist conceptions of research and action, we can find a way out of the impasse. The first step is to emphasize that theory and practice are not two distinct entities but two different and yet interdependent and complementary phases of the change process. Thus, first of all, the theorizer-researcher is engaged in a set of *practical* activities: making contacts, arranging meetings, collecting and classifying materials in ways that look as though they are going to be useful, deciding that 'enough is enough', etc. He or she does this as a *person* interacting with other people in a context full of psychological and institutional pressures. Conversely, practical actors carry out their activities in the light of a massive corpus of *theoretical* understanding: their specialist professional knowledge and their common sense conceptions, categories, and rules, concerning what is normal and what makes up the range of foreseeable possibilities. Theory and practice are thus not distinct entities which confront one another across an unbridgeable gulf: each contains elements of the other.

How then shall we characterize a formal process which links them within an investigative project? We can begin by noting that the links between any practical decision and the understandings which inform it can always only be loose and provisional: practical decisions are never entirely lacking in theoretical justification, but these justifications can never show that the action was (absolutely) 'correct', because they can never be complete. The array of potentially relevant considerations available is always so vast and so heterogeneous that no action can simultaneously take it *all* into account: any given action must always ignore or presuppose certain factors in order to respond carefully to others. Thus, although action is always reflective, its reflective basis is always open to question. In taking a particular decision one always excludes certain possibilities, and one's reasons for excluding these possibilities can never be more than 'good enough for the time being'. So, the role of theoretical reflection with respect to practical action is not to introduce new and different concepts 'from outside', nor to present authoritative conclusions based on a claim to have 'gathered all the facts'. Instead, the purpose of reflection is to *question* the reflective basis on which practical actions have been carried out, to offer a reflexive and dialectical critique whose effect will be to recall to mind those possibilities which practice has chosen on this occasion to ignore.

This is the theoretical phase, in which theory *questions* practice. But it is followed by a contrary movement, in which practice questions theory, as follows. Theoretical critiques of practical accounts and events pose questions which recall forgotten possibilities. But these questions and possibilities can never be completely exhaustive, and so they do not have any absolute or final authority. Ultimately they also are produced through personal interactions in practical contexts. For this reason the theoretical critique is itself also open to question: which of these newly recalled possibilities is practically feasible; which of these insights is usable?

At this point, however, it becomes of the utmost significance that we emphasize that this mutual questioning between theory and practice is strictly *unending*. This means that practice cannot simply *reject* theory (as impractical, now) because it must recognize that practical decisions will *always* be open to question. Since the principle outcome of theoretical questioning is the transformation of practice, whatever may seem impractical now may well seem feasible later, when circumstances will have changed. Similarly, theoretical critique cannot simply *confront* practice with an authoritative interpretation of events (as though to say, '*This* is the *real* reality') because it must recognize that theory itself will always be open to question, that the outcome of one phase of *practical* development will be a need and opportunity for further *theoretical* work. In other words, theory, being based in practice, is itself transformed by the transformations of practice. Theory and practice do not, therefore, confront one another in mutual opposition: each is necessary to the other for the continued vitality and development of both. Conversely, it is the separation of one from the other which threatens the stultification of both: theory separated from practice slips into abstract speculation and the ramification of jargon; practice separated from theory slips into self-justificatory reaction or self-perpetuating routine.[10]

It is this final argument, that theory and practice *need* each other and thus comprise mutually indispensable phases of a unified change process, which presents the strongest case for practitioner action-research — as an activity which represents both a powerful (i.e., rigorous and worthwhile) form of practical professionalism *and* a powerful (i.e., rigorous and valid) form of social inquiry. The examples in part two are an attempt to justify this claim.

Notes

1 The academic tradition for the thesis of reflexivity can be drawn up to include: Heidegger (1968), Polyani (1962), Cicourel (1964), Garfinkel (1967), Blum (1974), McHugh *et al*, (1974), Derrida (1978), Lawson (1985). A summary of this academic tradition can be found in Winter (1987), pp. 7–11.
2 See, for example, Augarde (1984) *The Oxford Guide to Word Games*.
3 The term sometimes used in this context is: analyzing 'a totality'.

4 This term reminds us of the link between reality and language, inherent in the world 'dialectic' itself, which was noted at the beginning of this section.

5 This is a restatement of the well-known idea of 'the unity of opposites'.

6 The analysis in this section draws largely on the work of: Israel (1979), Fisk (1979), and Markovic (1984). Other sources for the argument are: Hegel (1969 and 1977), Lenin (1972), and Adorno (1973). The tradition can even be traced back to the ancient Greeks: see the account of Heraclitus by Bertrand Russell, (1946) *The History of Western Philosophy*, p. 62. The academic tradition for dialectics is summarized in Winter (1987), pp. 11–16.

7 See Werthman's (1971) article 'Delinquents in schools' for a clear, elaborate, and highly readable illustration of this point.

8 See Habermas (1972). The argument is summarized in Winter (1981).

9 There is a considerable body of writing on the subject of 'plural texts', e.g., Barthes (1977) and Belsey (1980). The ideas of Bertholt Brecht are also very important in this context; see Brecht (1974). There is a summary of the theoretical argument in Winter (1986) and in Winter (1987), pp. 135–148.

10 See Postscript: Some Notes on 'Ideology' and 'Critique' in this volume.

Figure 2: How reflexive judgments create the illusion of being objective descriptions

PART TWO: EXAMPLES

We never fully know what implementation is or should look like until people in particular situations attempt to spell it out through use.

Michael Fullan (1982),
The Meaning of Educational Change

Chapter 5

Introduction to Part Two: Research and Writing

Part two consists mainly of three 'research reports' to illustrate the six principles of chapter four. There is more to action-research than research reports, of course. Indeed one feature of all three reports is that the format in which they are presented includes an element which is specifically concerned with *practical* developments in the situation where the work originated.[1] But even this simple statement raises two important issues concerning the writing of research reports in the context of small-scale practitioner inquiry: who are they for, and what would be an appropriate format? This chapter will briefly discuss these issues, as an introduction to certain features of the three examples which follow.

The Question of Format

Two suggestions have already been made concerning the appropriate format for action-research reports. Firstly, in chapter two we noted the recommendation by both Kemmis and Elliott that the report should be a 'case study' of the *process* of the work, basically in *narrative* form. Secondly, chapter four, principle five, puts forward the notion of a 'plural text', where the single voice of an author contriving the sequences of a logical argument is partly (at least) replaced by an interplay between the many voices of those who have participated (in different ways) in the work.

Both of these suggestions (narrative case study and plural text) propose a format which differs substantially from the conventional journal article in which research by academic specialists is usually reported. This generally has the following structure:

1 Summary review of the relevant academic 'literature';
2 Methods and techniques used;
3 Findings;
4 Conclusions and implications.

What is (or should be) the relationship between action-research reports written by practitioners and this academic convention? One danger, of course, is that the academic convention can be taken as a *norm* to which practitioner reports should aspire, and in the light of which they will almost inevitably be seen as deficient: review of literature not exhaustive, methods not comprehensive, findings not statistically significant, conclusions of no general relevance. To avoid falling into this trap, it is important to remind ourselves of a number of important points.

Let us begin by remembering that the conventions and norms as to how writing should be structured have been (and are) continually changing. For example, as late as the seventeenth and eighteenth centuries, both philosophical and scientific writings were often presented in verse, or in Latin, or both; and Plato, of course, organized his analytical writing into the form of dramatic dialogues (*cf* 'dialectics'). Similarly, the narrative sequence of the novel has been presented in the form of exchanges of letters between the characters, and in the form of pre-conceptual 'streams of consciousness' from which the reader has to *deduce* the actions taking place. In general, the history of writing shows a continuing process of experimentation, in an attempt to do justice to the always frustrating relationship between the linear sequence of words on a page, the infinite complexities of experience, and the desire to elucidate a wider significance from particular events. The preferred solution to this problem, the form of writing adopted as 'appropriate', depends on the writer's purposes, and these in turn depend on the network of social relationships within which the writing takes place, i.e., the social role *from* which one writes.

In this light, let us look again at the 'academic norm' for research reports — the sequence of: literature review, methodology, findings, conclusions. We can see it as one *possible* format, *one* way of structuring and transforming experience to bring out its significance; and we can also see, I think, that the social role for which this format has been devised as appropriate is that of 'the outsider expert'. The literature review display possession of a corpus of learning, conferring the right to interpret; 'methodology' displays command of complex 'scientific' techniques, (specialized authority as an inaccessible mystery); 'findings' display the authority of knowledge, previously concealed (from everyone, including the participants in the situation investigated) and now revealed; 'conclusions' displays the right to prescribe, based on the forms of authoritative expertise previously demonstrated. This is a format, then, which (like any other format) reflects a type of cultural authority, in this case the authority of the 'scientific expert'.

But one of the general arguments of this book is that, as a basis for the interpretation of the complex social situations which characterize professional work, the 'expert' authority of scientists and academics is both questionable and limited. These questions and limitations need to be carefully noted, in order to 'clear a space', as it were, for our own search for alternative formats for the writing of action-research reports. It is thus worth remembering some of the problems which the conventional academic format serves to conceal. Two brief examples only will be given here, indicating that when social scientists turn their investigative skills upon their own activities, the resulting criticism of social science formats and procedures is fairly severe.

Firstly, Roth (1966), in a paper with the suggestive title 'Hired Hand Research' casts doubt on the quality of the 'findings' which result from the 'methodology' of expensively funded surveys. Roth observes that the directors of large-scale social science investigations have no sound reasons for supposing that the commitment of 'research assistants' to their work situation is different from what sociologists have found to be the case among other low paid employees. On the contrary, Roth had found that, in common with other low paid employees, research assistants devised ways of improving their working conditions by reinterpreting managerial instructions. For example, they queried the value of coding accurately the nth questionnaire form in a large sample, or of carrying out all the observations in a schedule, especially when a) it was Saturday, and b) they 'knew already' what the outcomes would be. So they stayed at home and 'saved time' by ticking the most easily coded responses, and by categorizing interviewee comments that were difficult to classify as 'inaudible'.

Secondly, Becker (1971a) presents the following speculation upon the possible consequences of the policy of editors of psychology journals of only publishing 'positive findings'. If nineteen people investigate a correlation between two variables and come up with a negative result, nineteen research articles will be rejected by academic journals, and no-one else will necessarily be aware that this is the case. The twentieth researcher could then, quite by chance, achieve a positive result which is 'statistically significant at the 0.05 level' (i.e., will only occur by chance once in twenty times). This 'finding' would be published, and would take its place in 'the literature' as a respectable, statistically well-founded result (pp. 20–1). 'Reviews of the literature' could therefore, in theory, be reviews of a systematically generated structure of illusions.

The point behind these examples is simply that practitioners writing reports upon their action-research projects should not be overawed by the portentous format and rhetoric of academic journal articles: they too have their problems! Instead we should accept — and indeed welcome — the point that since our writing emerges from a different set of relationships (collaborative and action-oriented, rather than authoritative and observation-oriented) the format of our writing should also be different.

Although we have as yet no clear-cut set of conventions, some possible starting points have already been indicated. Firstly, in view of the link between the social relationships of the research process and appropriate ways of writing, the narrative format proposed by Kemmis and Elliott can be seen as expressing and recognizing the basis of action-research in the ongoing professional experience of the writer, the *sequence* of practice and reflection. (This is illustrated by the projects summarized in chapter two, and a further example is given in chapter six.) Secondly, the 'plural text' advocated in chapter four, expresses both the collaborative relationships of the action-research process, and the open-endedness of its outcomes. Conversely, certain stylistic features of 'academic' writing could also be seen as *inappropriate* for action-research reports, i.e., those aspects of style, tone, and vocabulary which seem to express the expert role by suggesting a *withdrawal* from personal involvement, and a sustained abstraction from concrete detail.

This, of course, raises the question as to what sort of style and structure can be both personal and detailed and yet at the same time offer general significance. There is an instructive analogy here with the problem of writing as defined by some feminist writers, who ask what format for writing *women* should use in a culture dominated by the conventions for writing created by a system where (on the whole) it is *men* who analyze events in scientific articles, while women make that possible by looking after the necessary domestic affairs. What is instructive for us as practitioners in search of a format for writing analytically out of our professional experience, is to notice some of the innovative formats used by women seeking, very consciously, for ways of writing analytically (politically, historically, philosophically) out of their personal and domestic experience.

One such example is Carolyn Steedman's (1986) book *Landscape for a Good Woman* which blends autobiographical reminiscences with interspersed passages of social history, sociology, and psychoanalysis, to form a sort of theorized biography of her mother. Another suggestive example is Christa Wolf's *Accident* (1989). Wolf's narrator is at home, on the day after the Chernobyl 'accident', doing the housework, gardening, and looking after children, while also watching TV bulletins from Chernobyl and at the same time awaiting news from the hospital about the result of her brother's operation for a brain tumour. Arising from an account of this day in a domestic context, Wolf weaves together, from these varied themes, a series of general reflections — on war, destiny, optimism, bureaucracy, human autonomy, and on the problem of writing.

The similarity between practitioner action-researchers and such feminist writers is the sense of a need to devise new structures of writing, which will link analytically the details of personal experience and the general significance of that experience. In both cases, the problem can be put as follows: we write from a social role where we are supposed not to be fully competent to construct our own analyses, but are supposed instead to await the authoritative analyses of our experience by other, more expert writers.

The Question of Audience

Academic articles on education are primarily addressed to other academics, informing them of a new addition to the corpus of knowledge, and presumably the writers also hope that both teachers and the managers of funding agencies will find their work to be relevant and of interest. Who are action-research reports written for? There are three answers, I think, each of equal importance.

One audience is: colleagues — those with whom one has collaborated in carrying out the work reported, and with whom the practical continuations will need to be negotiated. Action-research reports are always situated both within a specific professional context and within a specific sequence of alternations between theory and practice (see chapter four, principle six). For this reason, each of the examples includes in different ways a 'discussion paper' element, i.e., a form of presentation intended to create the basis for a meeting among colleagues which will be concerned entirely with decisions about changes in professional practice. This element is clearly emphasized in chapter six. In chapter nine a series of asterisked paragraphs concerning practical implications was written into the analysis, and these subsequently needed only to be 'lifted' from the rest of the text to form the basis for the discussion paper presented at the end of the chapter as appendix D. For this audience of collaborating colleagues the 'discussion paper' element is the core of the report, and the rest is, as it were, an optional 'background paper'. The latter would of course be made available to all colleagues, but we might not necessarily expect everyone concerned to have sufficient time or interest to read it before the meeting based on the discussion paper.

The next answer to the question, 'Who do we write for?' is: ourselves. The process of writing involves clarifying and exploring ideas and interpretations. It begins when we start to gather data and to jot down immediate notes on the possible significance of certain incidents. In particular, when our attention is directed towards one area of our practice, little surprising things which would otherwise be noted for a moment and then forgotten are documented, so that they can be recalled. The process of exploration and clarification continues when we first begin to review the whole collection of notes and data, prior to writing. Ideas 'spring to mind' — questions, links, interpretations — and these develop and ramify as we write the report itself.

So, writing up a report is an act of *'learning'*, learning through the act of writing. In this sense, therefore, we write for ourselves: when we read what we have written, we find out what, in the end, we have learned. As such, action-research for professional practitioners can be seen simply as a translation into adult and vocational terms of a theory of the educational process which has long been a familiar platitude in the general education of children and adolescents: the notion of the 'active learner' who learns by 'making' sense of his/her experience.[2] This, of course, is one of the ways in which action-research can be most clearly relied upon to be of professional benefit: the research and the writing up of the research are, in themselves, extremely valuable learning experiences for those who do and write up the research. This effect is frequently commented upon (see for example the summaries presented in chapter two) and certainly I am very conscious of changes in my approach to certain aspects of my professional work as a result of the research presented in chapters six and nine in this volume.

But this emphasis has to be handled with care: the value of action-research to the practitioner who carries it out is eagerly conceded by those who wish then to go on to argue that action-research processes do *not* produce outcomes that are of value to others and of generalizable significance.

For this reason it is important to give equal emphasis to the third audience for action-research reports: interested colleagues, in other institutions or in other areas of the same institution, for whom the underlying structure of the work presented in the report may seem to be similar to situations with which they are familiar and concerned. The report is thus intended to help the process of learning *among* members of a profession. By focusing *accounts* of practice into critical issues relevent to the process of *improving* practice, a practitioner's research report presents situations at the level at which 'useful lessons' can be learned, in the form of *comparisons* between the different experiences of the practitioner who writes and the practitioner who reads.[3]

I hope, therefore, that chapter six will be of *general* interest to anyone who has to mark written work in secondary, tertiary, and higher education; that chapter seven will be of general interest to anyone concerned with the education of children with special educational needs; and that chapter nine will interest not only those who have responsibility for access courses but anyone who has to teach and assess curricula based in the learner's experience. The latter is, of course, a very broad category, and serves once more to make the point that the origin of action-research reports in specific work contexts does not, in principle, limit the scope of their relevance.

Finally, one or two brief comments on how these three reports are intended as illustrations of the points about method made in part one. Chapter six concentrates particularly (and especially in the first section) on the process of *reflexive critique*. Chapter seven (which was written by Susan Burroughs when she was a peripatetic special needs teacher in primary schools) concentrates particularly on the process of analyzing a collection of accounts into *contradictions* — using the technique of 'dilemma analysis' which was the original formulation of 'dialectical critique'. Chapter nine is a more elaborate piece which attempts to illustrate comprehensively the overall approach. For this reason, to make the process as explicit as possible, chapter eight is included, as a description of the way in which the methods presented in chapter four were actually utilized in order to make the practical decisions required by the process of 'writing'.

Notes

1   I am aware that (unfortunately) my overall emphasis on the details of the process of analytical reflection (in order to counteract positivist ways of thinking about the relationship between knowledge and evidence) may appear to reduce the emphasis on the process of practical institutional change. This is not my intention. My argument at this point would be that — in the face of powerful managerial hierarchies — only very well founded procedures for critical reflection and collaboration will be able to create the space and the opportunities for institutional change to be initiated by practitioners.
2   One is tempted to question why it is that, whereas we know so well that children 'learn by doing', the education of teachers still offers such comedies as the hour-and-a-half *lecture* on, for example, resource-based learning.
3   At the moment, problems of publication and distribution intervene in this interchange, but we may look forward to improvements brought about by — on the one hand — local meetings for networks of interested practitioners and — on the other hand — advances in information technology such as 'desktop-publishing' and computer link-ups, which will enable practitioners to 'access' and 'print off' each others' work directly between the institutions where they work.

Chapter 6

'Objective' Judgments? — The Problem of Marking Written Work

Acknowledgments

I should like to express my appreciation of the contribution to this work of the following staff and students at the Anglia Higher Education College: Ron Best, Irene Clarke, Joe Haves, Ralph Henderson, Judith Houghton, Tom Hughes, Marilyn Nickson, Pauline Sweetingham, Helen Thorne. I am grateful to them for allowing their words and ideas to be included. All saw an earlier draft of the chapter and the various comments made have been incorporated.

Introduction

No-one ever told me how to do 'marking'. It seemed to be one of the many things one was expected to 'pick up'. This study is thus a belated attempt to examine critically (and thus — belatedly also — to improve) the methods I have more or less spontaneously devised for writing comments on students' work.

A number of factors led me to this topic. Firstly, it seemed to be an example of how my role as a teacher involved the use of institutional authority, which a previous piece of work had suggested as a theme that I was more concerned about than I cared to admit (see Winter, 1986). Secondly, I had become interested in Donald Graves' ideas on teachers' responses to children's writing, ideas which pose a radical challenge to the conception of 'marking' as the passing of authoritative judgments (see Graves, 1983). Thirdly, my work on reflexivity formulated both the problem and a method of approach, by suggesting that the sort of judgments involved in 'marking' create the illusion of referring directly to external realities (i.e., in the students' work), while actually relying largely on subjective values and concerns. Altogether, then, a growing sense of unease began to creep over me every time I found myself wielding a pencil over students' scripts.

So I began to collect data. I mainly collected copies of students' assignments and written comments upon them by myself and colleagues, but I also asked one group of twenty students to fill in a questionnaire concerning their feelings about the comments on their work, six of which were completed. All the 'students' referred to were experienced teachers undertaking award-bearing in-service courses. Their written assignments were either critical essays on educational research, reviews of research articles, or short analyses of their own teaching. The sort of assessment criteria involved were, therefore:

personal insight;
clear style and organization;
effective use of reading;
understanding of the personal relevance of theoretical ideas.

(The sort of criteria which — in various different forms — probably underlie the evaluation of learners' written work in many different contexts, from lower secondary school to degree courses.)

As so often happens when you turn your attention in a particular direction, you begin to notice things happening. In this case there were four key incidents, spaced over eighteen months or so, so that I had time to reflect on one incident (and in some cases to alter my practice) before the next one occurred. The main part of this report is organized around these incidents, which — because they seemed revealing and worrying at the time — I documented as thoroughly as I could. Other data (for example, changes in my own practice, quotations from the student questionnaires) are introduced in relation to the four incidents. The first two incidents in particular provoked a sense of urgency about the study, by suggesting some of the difficulties for students created by the issues surrounding the supposed objectivity of one's judgments as a marker. The incidents are presented here in chronological order, so that the report has the overall structure of a narrative (of which the final phase is the writing of this report), and ends with a proposed staff discussion paper.

Incident 1: The Case of Steve and Margaret

Steve and Margaret had each written an essay in which they presented their professional situation in terms of a series of 'role conflicts'. The two essays provoked very different reponses, from me and from a colleague, which are the subject of the following discussion. Substantial extracts from the essays are therefore included, and readers might like to note their own reactions. It should be borne in mind, however, that the extracts have been chosen to illustrate the basis of my *negative* response to Steve's work and my *positive* response to Margaret's. It is the *questionable* features of these reactions which will be analyzed. Here are some extracts from Steve's essay.

> All the world's a stage,
> And all the men and women merely players:
> They have their exits and their entrances;
> And one man in his time plays many parts...

This oft used citation has frequently been used to introduce the discussion of role, but it is inadequate to circumscribe the multiplicity of functions of the modern pedagogue....

[X] In the early days of state education, the teacher was an instructor and a guardian of certain moral principles laid down by those in authority. Indeed as recently as 1947 when George Tomlinson, the Education Secretary at the time, raised the school leaving age to 15... the emphasis was on 'instruction and care'. Gradually the teacher has become much more than a conveyor of knowledge. He has become a parent-substitute concerned with children's welfare....

[Y] My hypothesis, therefore, was that the divergence of the roles of a contemporary teacher... (has) led to a situation where his class-room performance is severely impeded, and role strain is inescapable....

Robert Merton, the American sociologist, in his theory of conflict in the role set, suggested that 'what is an educational essential for the one, may be judged an educational frill or as downright subversion by the other'....

[Z] When asked to consider the roles of others most respondents were incapable of objectivity and sanctimoniously sought justification of their own positions. Perhaps the most apocalyptic disclosure of all was the egocentricity of students whose self-absorption recognised only those roles which directly affected their needs (such as the provision of interesting lessons) and appeared oblivious to the needs and demands of other role members....

The 'incident' began when I gave Steve a 'B' for his essay, rather than the 'A' he expected. In my written comments, I criticized, among other things, his logic at point X above; I also suggested that he had not really checked his 'hypothesis' (Y) but had written 'polemically' to justify it, and that therefore he himself was doing what he criticized in others (Z). Steve asked that his essay be marked by another tutor, and indicated that he was not clear on what basis I had given other students' work an 'A'. For example: Margaret's, of which extracts are given below.

I decided to concentrate on the sets of expectations of the tutor's role partners and role set, and in order to explore how they see the tutor's role I asked them to cooperate in completing a questionnaire. At first I asked two questions only:

[P] 1) What are your expectations of a tutor? (What do you expect him/her to do?)
2) What are your perceptions of a tutor? (What does he/she actually do, from your point of view?....)

[Q] At first glance it may seem that there is a large degree of consensus of opinion regarding the tutor's role, but when looked at closely several areas of potential conflict come to light: a) All groups stated that they expected tutors to relate theory and practice, and to have regular ward contact for teaching. One senior tutor expected tutors to 'uphold standards of care'. However, the perceptions of the tutors in particular show that they feel the demands of classroom teaching, administration, and meetings leave little time for any regular commitment to the wards. If this is so, then how can they 'uphold standards of care' or 'relate theory to practice'?....

[R] Hargreaves says that 'within a single role... a hierarchy of obligations... dictates which expectation is to be accorded priority'. This sounds quite straightforward until one asks who decides on the order of the hierarchy, and what criteria are used when deciding on those priorities....

In my comments I complimented Margaret on her neat distinction between expectations and perceptions (P), on her analysis of the contradictions within her data (Q), and her critical point on the limitations of Hargreaves' observation (R).

A colleague — 'C' — marked the two essays, and we tape-recorded a discussion about our differing responses. C suggested that he would be inclined to reverse the grades. For him, Margaret's work was 'descriptive' rather than 'analytical', because it did not 'explore the wider implications' of her detailed observations. In contrast, Steve's work was an impressive display of 'perceptive analysis' and 'high quality discussion'.

Commentary

My discussion with C clarified aspects of the 'reflexive' problem of marking. Behind our use of categories such as 'analytical' and 'descriptive' and 'A' and 'B' grades lie our own different priorities concerning academic work. C attaches great importance to demonstration of having mastered a body of reading, and the elaboration of evidence in relation to that reading, whereas my particular interest is in a careful use of empirical evidence. Consequently, what C sees as a 'lack' of elaboration, I see as an 'impressive' modesty in making claims. My general interest in research-based work leads me to value 'description' stripped of prior value judgments, but C, more frequently concerned with the 'scholarly' criteria for essay work, sees 'mere description' as fundamentally limited. Thus, in apparently making statements about the work of Steve and Margaret, C and I are also justifying our own professional lives.

From the Student Questionnaire

Question: What criteria do you think were used in writing comments on your work?
Student 1: ...The commentator's own view of knowledge...
Student 2: ... The luxury of personal intrusion and comment of the marker's own views...
Question: Are you fairly clear as to 'how well' you did?
Student 2: ...Not totally convinced. One marker seemed to perceive more weakness in the work than the other...
Student 3: ... There did seem to be a measure of inconsistency in the comments of the two markers. For example, P's point (i) compared with R's point (4). Also, P seemed more prepared to agree with (my point of view) than did R...

The justificatory dimension of marking also took another form. I explained to C that, as the *teacher* of the unit, I was using as a criterion: does the student's work show that they have learned from the course?

> RW: I'm saying: everyone on the course should develop; that what one is giving marks for is not how much they knew before they started, but how much they have moved on from wherever it was they started....There is nothing in what Margaret wrote to suggest she knew anything about (role theory) beforehand, and therefore what she does is starting from a zero starting point: one couldn't have expected any more. Therefore: an 'A'. Given Steve's starting point, which was a long way down the road, one could have expected him to develop more.

> C: You see, that now raises the question for me: how would you see an *external* marker, not familiar with the course, just being presented with these two essays, but having to moderate the marking (which is a very important part of our system)? I've always found it difficult to mark an essay where I haven't been involved in the course, and yet I get

them all the time! So all I have to go on is the title. (As an external examiner) I've just marked a whole set of (X College) scripts: I only have the internal markers' comments . . . . Very often I'm working in the dark, so I have to adopt a certain set of standard criteria. I would still maintain, though, that it would be difficult to suggest that a person has got something from a course if they do not give evidence of at least a limited range of reading related to it. Because, surely, when we talk to them . . . we are only raising issues, but we are also recommending broader reading.

RW: In this particular unit we didn't. We specifically said to them, 'Don't bother to read up about role theory; just carry out the task.' So I'm worried that Margaret was paying me a compliment. She was complimenting me *as a teacher*, by doing *exactly* what she was supposed to do, nothing more and nothing less.

Commentary

C, as *external* to the teaching, manages his responsibilities by invoking 'standard criteria' (and particularly 'evidence of reading') which relate less to the course than to C's management of his role as an external marker. In contrast, I am seeking specific feedback on *my* activity as a teacher. Thus I am inclined to compliment Margaret (with an 'A') as a reward for her compliment to me. And yet my 'compliment' is deeply ambiguous. I seem to be quite pleased that she has done nothing less but 'nothing *more*' than the task set, and that she had a 'zero' starting point. ('Margaret' subsequently pointed out that she did *not* have a 'zero' starting point: she *did* have prior knowledge of role theory but decided that the instructions for the assignment suggested that it was not relevant.) Thus, my search for evidence that I have been effective as a teacher denies the relevance of what Margaret could bring *to* the work, apart from compliance with my instructions. In noticing the reflexivity of my response (its roots in my concerns rather than in objective features of Margaret's essay or her knowledge) I am — regretfully — made to recognize an authoritarianism within my practice which previously remained hidden from me — but not, of course, from Steve!

I described to C my response to Steve's work in the following terms:

RW: I felt rather irritated by Steve's essay . . . . I felt he was saying to me, by the way he wrote, 'I challenge you to exercise any superiority over me.' So I rose to the challenge . . . things like: 'There is a contradiction in this paragraph'. (See X in the extract from Steve's essay, above.) He wishes to argue that the teacher's role has *become* broader, that it *used to be* narrower. But what he wrote doesn't actually suggest that, because if you are responsible not only for 'instruction' but for 'care' as well, he's actually saying that teachers *always* had that broader role.

Commentary

The 'rigorousness' of my criticism here is thus activated mainly by an emotional response. Not surprisingly, C rejected the necessity for my criticism, saying:

> I interpreted that as, 'And gradually the teacher as *instructor* has become more than a conveyor of knowledge'. That was my interpretation.

The general point here is that the form of attention we bring to an act of reading is a *choice* (on the part of the reader), that readers *invoke* criteria as part of their *response* to what is written. C and I might perhaps agree that Steve '*could* have phrased his point more neatly', but that is not to say that there is a logical flaw *in* Steve's text. I blow my whistle, but C doesn't. One is not supposed to argue with the referee but that is merely a matter of keeping order: controversy over decisions is universal and usually undecidable.

One can attempt to make explicit this interpretive function, by adopting a 'diagnostic' approach to marking, but this brings its own problems:

> C: I was fully aware (that Margaret and Steve had) different starting points. Yet my feeling was really to give *credit* for the fact that Steve started a long way down the road....
>
> RW: Yes, that's one point. Or you could say: where someone is creates different standards by which they are to be judged.... It's like a Piagetian model of 'stages'. You judge learners by standards that they generate for themselves.... This is the issue, for me, in how we mark.... Is it possible to mark *not* the final standard reached in the work, but how far they have developed... how much they have learned by doing it?
>
> C: There's a slight worry I have there, though, as to what you take your starting base from. How do you identify where it is they've started from? Are you saying it shows through in their writing? Is it possible to do that in any sort of accurate way?

Commentary

If there is a contradiction between assessing a *product* (a piece of written work) and assessing a *process* (what was learned by doing it) then it is not very convincing to suggest that the process can be assessed simply by assessing the product. (This is clearly exemplified in my assessment of Margaret's prior knowledge.) Producing and marking written work takes place within a complex interaction influenced by an enormous range of factors. Markers bring their own concerns, and learners bring theirs. Steve, for example, said that he had been told to undertake the course in order to gain a qualification appropriate for a position he already held. So it would be quite reasonable for Steve to write an essay with the express purpose of displaying a prior competence: to show that he had learned from the process would have been to concede that he needed a learning experience, whereas from his perfectly justifiable point of view he may well have felt that what he needed was a qualification which would document his *previous* learning. In other words, the meaning of the process of producing written work (whether an essay *or* a comment on an essay) is a highly variable personal matter. How then could it possibly be reduced to 'how much' has been learned, on a scale from A to E?

This is the general point about reflexivity. For practical purposes, grading from A to E can be made to take place, but only by ignoring the inevitable reflexivity of the judgments on which it is based. For practical purposes these judgments have the apparent form of statements about what is 'in' the piece of writing. But when we have made explicit the reflexivity on which they depend (their inevitably personal significance) a number of alternatives spring to mind, as ways of conceiving of the *relationship* between writers' and markers' concerns. Marking as an assessment of the writer's competence, is one extreme. Marking as a confrontation within a power relationship is another. Marking as rewarding compliance is the other face of the same extreme. In between might lie, for example: marking as diagnosis and the prescription of remedies; marking as the facilitation of development; marking as one move within a collaboration.

Postscript to Incident 1

My considerable sympathy with Steve's irritation was increased recently, when I received a letter from the editor of an academic journal, rejecting an article which I and a colleague had submitted. The referee had commented:

> It purports to be a discussion starter, why not, therefore make the issues more clear cut?

(But as far as we were concerned the issues were as 'clear cut' as necessary.

What is meant by 'clear cut' is a reflexive judgment, relating to the intellectual style (and perhaps even also the personality) of various readers and writers — in this case those of the journal referee and ourselves.)

> A promising piece of work cast rather in the form of an outline which needs fleshing out.

(But this 'need' is not *in* our article, but a reflexive reference by the 'marker' to a *different* sort of article that he or she 'would have' written. The ideal amount of 'flesh' is notoriously a matter of taste.)

> How do tutors ensure that the biographies are stiffened with relevant theoretical perspectives?

(The phrasing ('stiffened') suggests that, for this writer, manhood is at stake where theoretical perspectives are concerned, a dramatic illustration of how academic judgments are deeply rooted in biographies!) (As is, of course, my interpretation of this comment . . .)

My own sense of irritation (at receiving reflexive statements presented to me as though they were objective judgments) makes it hard for me not to add that the article was accepted, unchanged, immediately afterwards by another journal.

Incident 2: The Case of Joan

In an effort to be 'helpful', when I mark a piece of work, I put numbers in the margin against particular passages and write a comment on a separate sheet. In an effort to be 'open-minded', I usually begin reading without a precise sense of what I am looking for, but wait until 'something strikes me'. The problems of this procedure became apparent in the following incident. In response to her first piece of written work, Joan received a page of detailed comments. The first *eight* were all negative. For example:

> 'Somehow I don't seem to be able to understand this sentence . . . '.

> 'Yes. I think you are afraid of saying, "This is my concern and this is how I can see this method contributing to my study." But this has to be said, and supported.'

> 'This seems a little vague.'

> 'Careful: you sound very sure of this: how do you know?'

Altogether, out of eighteen comments, four were positive. For example:

> 'Yes, I like this argument.'

> 'From here, the next half-page is good — clear and precise.'

> 'This seems more in keeping with Kelly's approach. It is well

described and clearly linked to your theme. Your best paragraph
(I think) so far.'

After I had written the detailed comments, I added, squashed up at the top
of the page:

'You have worked hard at this, and there are lots of good ideas. I
have been *very* "nit-picking". Can we talk about it after you have
read it through?'

Instead, Joan wrote me a letter. She referred to difficult personal circumstances and also to her worry that she had found the set readings very
difficult. She concluded that she would not be able to reach the 'required
standard', since (among the other factors mentioned) my comments made
her feel that she could not understand what it was that I could not understand, and that she was unclear as to what was unclear to me. In the end,
Joan decided to leave the course.

I gave Joan's work and my comments to a colleague, 'P'. P's marksheet
began with the comment:

There needs to be a description of what the Parental Involvement
in Reading scheme is all about, in order that we can appreciate
what is to be analyzed.

Altogether P listed six suggestions (for example, 'All of this would have been
better placed at the beginning, where it provides the context for your
discussion.') and five questions (for example, 'What are "personal
constructs" and why are they used?'). She concluded that we were both
being 'fairly gentle' and 'reasonably constructive' but suggested that my
comments may have included 'one too many "I don't understand's"'.
Another colleague, 'N', agreed with P's implication that 'I don't
understand' is unhelpful, and suggested, 'I reckon you need to talk her
through it and maybe do some positive "stroking".'

Commentary

Surely, N is right. But more interesting is the fact that my final comment,
squashed into the space at the top of the page where it was intended as the
first thing Joan would read, already expresses an awareness of what N
suggests as a remedy: 'You have worked hard and there are lot of good
ideas . . . . Can we talk about it?'. So my marksheet contains within itself
both the 'remedy' as well as the problem. In this way it presents an implicit
acknowledgment of the contradictions within the marking process. It is
negative — but acknowledges the need to be positive: without 'encouragement', criticism may well be counterproductive. It presents the students
with judgments in a written form (and thus apparently fixed, judicial,

authoritative, unalterable, the 'final' word). And yet it acknowledges that to be of value to the student these judgments need to be negotiated within the teacher-learner relationship ('Can we talk about this?').

Within these contradictions, the ambiguity of 'I don't understand' does indeed seem to be particularly revealing. On one level it seems that the marker is admitting an inadequacy and suggesting that the student will have an opportunity to 'explain'. And yet, as both P and N noted, the comment also seem particularly *oppressive*, a verdict against which — in its Kafkaesque elusiveness — there can be no appeal. Neither can there be a remedy, since the comment refers to what is beyond the control of the student, even though it is supposedly a reference to a feature of her work. This is an illustration of the peculiar *power* and the limitations of the *written* word. When the teacher says, 'I don't understand', the learner can explain her thoughts (especially if reassured by a tone of voice), but when the marker *writes*, 'I don't understand', the recipient of the marksheet receives a form of condemnation which renders her helpless.

P seemed to sense similar contradictions when — immediately after noting the problem of 'I don't understand' — she continued:

> On the other hand, my own questions may provoke even more anxiety on the part of the writer. What was important in assessing this piece of work is not to be destructive . . . .

A marker's 'question' would seem to invite a continuation from the student, but if what is taking place is 'assessment', then a reply to the 'question' may not really be relevant: what appears to be a question is a disguised form of a judgment. Thus P expresses an awareness that her marking, like mine, is awkwardly caught between a process of constructive developmental dialogue and a process of authoritative assessment.

Perhaps the issue, then, is one of *confusion* between different functions which are in contradiction with each other, and which the conventional procedure of 'marking' runs together. Perhaps it is this which generates 'anxiety' (both in the student and in the marker). If so, it cannot easily be removed. Joan's work did not *need* to be 'assessed'. It was an interim piece, not a final assignment that had to reach a set standard in order to 'pass'. P and I could, in principle, have responded with *advice* pure and simple, and avoided explicit evaluation. There are examples of this process in Graves' (1983) work, where teachers pose questions which lead the learner onwards, without any implication that the teacher knows what the learner *ought* to be writing (see pp. 107 ff, and p. 127). But this is with primary age children, where the purely *educational* purpose (of developing all according to their abilities) is not yet explicitly tangled up with the other purpose which determines what goes on in schools and colleges: grading learners in ways which outside institutions can use in order to allocate social roles. Older learners know that they are implicated in this 'social grading' process – though they may be highly critical of the injustice of its outcomes:

they know that it is significant whether their work is 'good enough' (to pass, to get a distinction, to get a reference which will support a bid for promotion), and thus they *want* to be assessed. So this contradiction is part of the structure of education systems, and thus part of the awareness which learners and markers bring to their interaction.

But although both learners and markers are 'aware' of the contradiction, it is learners who are at risk from it, whereas markers — being in the position of power — can perhaps afford to treat it in a fairly routine way. Marking, after all, *is* a routine. Looking back over my marking of Joan's work, I notice that I 'delivered' my comments in the order in which they *happened* to occur, as responses to the text, without considering the balance or sequence of positive and negative impact, until the very end, when I squashed up my positive overall comment in such a way that it must have clearly signalled to the student that it was an afterthought.

Perhaps by carefully analyzing the single routine process of 'marking' into its different contradictory elements we may be able to manage more effectively the various elements and the relationship between them. My immediate reflections in the incident with Joan suggested one practical method of separating out the contradictory elements. It is embarrassing in its simplicity. I decided to begin my notes on individual passages half-way down the space available on the marksheet, leaving plenty of space to add, at the beginning, an overall comment of carefully phrased evaluation, with the emphasis on encouragement. That at least increased my sense of control over the process. Instead of simply delivering an almost accidental sequence of detailed responses, I had a procedure which enabled me explicitly to take responsibility for managing their overall impact.

Incident 3: The Case of Sheila

The incident with Sheila raises another aspect of the marking process which takes the form of contradictory elements needing to be separated out. The immediate issue is quite stark: who is the audience for one's marking? Consider the following extracts from my marksheet for Sheila's end-of-year assignment — a critical review of two research articles:

Question 1: This is a most satisfactory critique....

Question 4: This is quite an adequate general appraisal, but it is disappointing that so little reference is made to ideas from the course, as was explicitly required.

General: Question 1 ensures a pass. Questions 2 and 4 are flawed as answers to set questions, but nevertheless indicate an adequate grasp of the research process and its issues.

Commentary

The phrasing here indicates that this was written to my fellow markers — including the external examiners. Its critical vocabulary ('most satisfactory', 'adequate', 'flawed') seems intended to demonstrate a 'judicious' application of standards, i.e., a demonstration of the academic competence of the *marker*. However, there is already an irony here, because it later became clear that what I had perceived as a 'flaw' in the answer was at least partly due to an ambiguity in *my* wording of the question, which the student and the marker had thus interpreted differently.

From the Student Questionnaire

Question: What criteria do you think were used in writing the comments on your work?
Student 4: Arbitrary categories legitimated by the achievement of 'consensus' among markers. Who assesses these criteria? . . . . To what extent are markers' marks a form of display *(of knowledge, status, etc.)?*

The comments I had written about Sheila's work suggest, then, that they were intended for other examiners. However, Sheila herself received a copy — as routine 'feed-back' on her work — and she was somewhat taken aback by what she perceived as its 'harshness', which was, of course, never intended as such. In retrospect it seems surprising that this confusion of the two audiences should have taken place. How could the difference between the two audiences not be treated as a crucial matter? It seemed almost as though — on one level — the difference was not felt to be significant. With this issue in mind I looked closely at a complete set of marksheets relating to the equivalent assignments of the previous year's students.

The group consisted of seventeen students, and since each script was marked by two tutors there were thirty-four marksheets. Of the thirty-four, six seemed to be addressed to a fellow examiner (for example, they referred to 'the student') and twenty-eight to the writer of the assignment (containing such comments as, 'You have not shown that . . . .'). This seems to confirm that we had not clarified for ourselves to whom the comments on the marksheets were *supposed* to be addressed.

This ambiguity may explain another feature of the set of marksheets, which relates back to the case of Joan. Of the twenty-eight marksheets addressed to students, not a single one began with an overall encouragement. Instead, all of them began with a comment on a particular passage. Of these opening comments:

> Sixteen pointed out a deficiency (for example, 'What are the grounds for claiming the inadequacy of the sample?')

Eight were complimentary (for example, 'I very much agree with
all of this')
Four were (perhaps) 'neutral' (for example, 'Having drawn our
attention to this, what comment would you make?').

In other words, the majority of the marksheets addressed to students
seemed largely to ignore what we otherwise knew to be an important issue:
the need for encouragement ('positive stroking'), the danger that negative
criticism can be destructive. If we had been *talking* to the students, instead
of *writing*, we would certainly have *started* with a general encouragement.

Commentary

It seems that there is a curious ambiguity as to the audience for markers'
comments. From the data described above, it seems almost as though the
audience *does not matter*. Sheila received comments which were written
for an examiner. Of the marksheets analyzed, some were written for fellow
examiners and others for students, but students received both marksheets
anyway. Furthermore, marksheets apparently addressed to students did
not seem to have been structured to take account of students' emotional
needs. And yet we are otherwise perfectly aware of students' needs, and
know perfectly well that the audience for a statement plays a crucial role in
determining its meaning and its appropriate form. Comments addressed to
examiners are intended as judgments of academic quality, and thus displays
of academic competence, whereas comments for students are intended to
be helpful suggestions. The difference could not be clearer. So where does
this apparent vagueness as to the audience for markers' comments come
from?

Marking, as was noted previously, involves *both* functions and *both*
audiences. Students therefore receive suggestions *and* questions as implicit
forms of judgment, and judgments as implicit forms of advice. Examiners
also note the academic standards implicit in their colleagues' choice of
advice and questions. But this familiar combination — familiar as the
practical routine of 'marking' — covers two (at least) distinct functions,
and Sheila's response suggests that it might be helpful to separate them.
Consider, finally, the following plea from one of the student questionnaire
forms:

> *I think each marker should have put a general comment at the
> end, in addition to judging stylistic competence, and some guides
> as to how to remedy the weaknesses in the work. Positive
> constructive advice on how to reduce errors is not the same as
> indicating the error.*

Incident 4: The Case of Vera

The previous three incidents suggested in different ways the need to clarify, within the marking process, the relationship between judgment and advice. Problems, for students at least, seemed to have been created by the tacit fusion of the two. So when, a few months later, I received a piece of work from Vera and felt worried by the fact that parts of it seemed to me to be 'unclear', I did *not* (this time) write her a list of detailed criticisms and suggestions. Instead, after discussing the problem with a colleague, I arranged a tutorial. This, of course, signalled that I thought there was a problem about her work, and she indicated subsequently that she had indeed felt very worried before the tutorial. However, this would seem to be inevitable: submitting work on a course that can be passed or failed is to 'submit' oneself to academic authority. My problem as an adjudicator of standards was: how 'serious' were Vera's lapses from 'clarity'? If they were 'not serious' I wished to avoid unnecessary undermining of her self-confidence.

Within the face-to-face situation it was possible for us to begin to take control of the tensions involved, through some general discussion in the first few minutes. I then gave Vera her work, on which I had merely placed a tick against passages which seemed to me to be 'clear' and a question-mark against passages which I thought 'unclear'. I asked her to explain and to suggest modifications of the passages I had questioned. This she was able to do quite easily. At that point we were also able to discuss — without apparent tension — what might be the nature of the 'problem', which *she* defined as 'not making assumptions explicit'. She then went on to suggest that an important contributory factor might be the fact that, as the Head of a very small school, she was used to communicating (both orally and in writing) within a small closed community, where — indeed — shared assumptions could be taken for granted. In this way, Vera's 'problem' could be seen, not in terms of an intellectual inadequacy ('lack of clarity') but in terms of being out of practice in the techniques of a certain form of communication: writing for readers who are (theoretically) unfamiliar with — and potentially hostile to — the argument one wishes to develop. Clearly I could not have expected Vera to have practised these techniques before writing her assignment, since neither she nor I (until that moment) could have described the nature of what it was she needed to practise.

In the end, then, there was no real 'marking' (apart from ticks and question-marks intended as merely cues for our discussion). The outcome of the interaction (writing — reading — tutorial) was a specific piece of advice for Vera and a valuable clarification of both her and my understanding of what 'clarity' might mean. I also felt that I had at last taken a practical, as well as a theoretical step forward in my grasp of the contradictions of 'marking'.

MARKING WRITTEN WORK —
A STAFF DISCUSSION DOCUMENT

Arising out of a recent investigation of the process of 'marking', I think some of our current procedures would be worth reconsidering. (Copies of the full report are available on request.)

Here is a typical official marksheet format of the type currently in use:

TITLE OF COURSE:	NAME OF STUDENT:
INTAKE YEAR:	
ASSIGNMENT TITLE:	
NAMES OF MARKERS:	GRADE:

1 ....

2 ....

AGREED GRADE: ....

COMMENTS:

DATE .... (PLEASE RETURN TO COURSE TUTOR)

This format expresses the general institutional purpose of marking — the creation of apparently objective data on the quality of a student's work. Detailed comments are used to amplify a general assessment. This information is filed and used to provide documentary justification for future decisions. This is the process which the institution *requires* markers to carry out, and which students are prepared to accept — with varying degrees of compliance. But what this format conceals is the complexity of the marking process. Behind the conventional routine of 'marking' lie a number of disparate and potentially conflicting processes. My investigation suggests that a number of students find the tacit fusion of these different processes into one routine either confusing, or frustrating, or emotionally difficult to handle. Perhaps, by separating out these elements, it might be possible to agree on procedures which are more flexible, and more explicitly justifiable to students than those implicitly encouraged by the current marksheet format. Would it be possible to introduce one or more of the following suggestions?

1 Separate Different Audiences

Markers might be encouraged to write separate sets of comments addressed a) to students and b) to fellow examiners or other academic authorities. (Students perhaps should have *access* to both.) This might enable comments to be more precise and clearer as to their purpose, which would be helpful both to students and to markers.

2 Include Written Comments and Tutorial Discussion as Separate but Equally Important Aspects of Marking

Some responses to students' work may be so unambiguous and unproblematic that they can be written on students' work without fear of controversy or dissatisfaction. Other responses may be very much matters of choice and interpretation, and these might be best handled through face-to-face discussion.

Perhaps, therefore, markers should *not* be under an obligation to *write* at length in response to a student's work, but rather under an obligation to *discuss* a student's work. If so, would it be possible to allocate time for this within general curriculum arrangements? (This process — of using student written work as a basis for discussion – might well borrow from some of the procedures described by Donald Graves as a 'Writing Conference' — see Graves (1983).)

3 Separate Different Types of Written Comments Addressed to Students

For example:

> General comments expressing appreciation and encouragement;
> General comments indicating the quality of the work;
> Specific comments indicating error, omission, or inadequacy;
> Specific comments of appreciation;
> Specific comments giving advice for future work
> > — on content
> > — on presentation;
> Questions intended to stimulate further thought (*without* intended criticism);
> Questions intended to draw attention to problems in the student's work.

We would then need to decide what combination of these (and in what order) might constitute an *effective* response, in the sense of generating in the student a positive attitude towards further work. This leads to:

4 Separate Comments to Justify a Judgment From Comments To Promote Learning

This is partly equivalent to 1 above, concerning different audiences, but not entirely so. Students, as well as colleagues or external examiners, will expect academic judgments. The important thing is that students — unlike fellow examiners — may reasonably demand that judgments are followed by detailed practical advice. But perhaps detailed practical advice might arise better from individual discussion, within which students can participate in deciding the direction of their development.

This is perhaps the key to developing more effective and appropriate procedures. The current marksheet format tends to focus our attention on marking as a summing up of what the student has so far achieved. But what we all know needs equal emphasis — and does not seem to receive explicit encouragement in our prescribed procedures — is that marking is also an interpersonal moment in the development of the student's thinking.

Chapter 7

Dilemmas in the Role of the Support Teacher

Susan Burroughs

Editorial Note

This chapter is an abridgment of a longer study written by Susan Burroughs (see Burroughs, 1984) when she was working as a peripatetic teacher of primary school children with special educational needs. The following extracts concentrate on her use of the method of 'dilemma analysis' (see Winter, 1982), which was the original sketch of the principle of 'dialectical critique' presented in chapter four.

The method of dilemma analysis involves, basically, analyzing verbal data (for example, interview transcripts) in terms of contradictions. The method rests on a set of general assumptions:

> 'that social organizations... are constellations of (actual or potential) conflict of interest... that motives are mixed, purposes are contradictory, ... relationships are ambiguous, and that the formulation of practical action is unendingly beset by *dilemmas*....Hence a statement of opinion in an interview is taken to be a marginal option which conceals a larger awareness of the potential appeal and validity of different and even opposed points of view. (Winter, 1982, p. 168)

The detailed procedures are described as follows:

> The technique... involves (a) formulating the dilemmas at roughly the same level of abstraction at which they are originally presented in the interview scripts, (b) choosing as a starting point the most elaborated formulation of any given dilemma from among the various statements in the scripts, (c) formulating each dilemma so that it balances non-controversially between the potentially opposed points of view, and (d) building up the perspectives for each role by *adding* together the various dilemmas thus formulated. (*Ibid*, p. 169)

Susan Burroughs' report uses the method in two ways. Firstly, she produces a set of practical discussion documents — which illustrates chapter four, principle six, the link between theoretical analysis and practical development work. Secondly, she intersperses the analysis of contradictions with illustrative quotations from interview transcripts, which results in a form of plural 'collage' text, and enables the writer of the report to give space to the voices of those who collaborated with her in the research — the pupils, the classroom teachers, and the members of her special needs support team.

Written in 1983, the report occasionally uses the term 'remedial' teacher, 'remedial' education etc. In this abridgment the more modern terms 'support' teacher and 'special needs' education have been substituted. One other editorial change has been made. The original report uses the distinction (from the 'dilemma analysis' article) between contradictions referring to background *ambiguities*, those referring to the complexity of professional *judgments*, and those referring to *problems* in the situation which undermine the basis for rational action. Subsequent experience has suggested that these distinctions are difficult to operate with any degree of confidence, and so in this abridgment each section of the analysis is presented as a single series of 'dilemmas' (contrasts, tensions).

The extracts from the report include: sections from the introduction; the complete set of discussion documents based on interviews with pupils, members of the support team, and the class teachers with whom they worked; the expanded version of the pupils' perspective document in full (including illustrative quotations); brief extracts from the expanded analysis of the perspectives of the support team and the class teachers; extracts from the conclusion.

Introduction

My original problem was easily identified as a sense of growing unease about the way in which I felt constrained to operate in my current role as a peripatetic support teacher. Defining this unease into an operational set of objectives for investigation was a more rigorous and demanding task. Two strategies were evolved for refining my definition of the problem. One took the form of extended group discussions with other teachers outside my usual contact area, a teachers' centre warden, and an HE lecturer experienced in social and educational research. Parallel with these discussions, I engaged in a detailed subjective analysis of how I perceived my present role — including a description and evaluation of patterns of conflict/accord between the sets of expectations of all those involved. This is an essential preparatory stage for using interviews as a research tool, where the researcher is also the interviewer investigating attitudes in her own professional environment. This allows the unavoidable presence of bias to be made explicit and examined as an element, both in the collection of data and their analysis . . . .

I then conducted a series of interviews, over a period of approximately a term and a half, including those children already identified as having learning difficulties, the Heads and class teachers of these children, and members of the peripatetic team to which I belong. These interviews were tape-recorded in full and expanded by occasional notes by the interviewer. The interviews were then transcribed, partly by me and partly by secretarial help . . . .

(The method adopted for the analysis of the interview material was 'dilemma analysis' — see Winter, 1982.) The results of the dilemma analysis are presented in two forms here. The 'skeleton' versions, which it is intended might also serve as a discussion document for in-service use, appear on pages 98, 103, and 106 below. These versions of the dilemma analysis might be used separately or collectively as instruments for raising the issues involved in providing for special educational needs in terms of the participants' current experiences and perceptions, and as an essential preparation for developmental planning.

In this report I have followed these 'discussion document' versions with an amplified presentation, where the dilemmas are interspersed with extracts from the interview transcripts. Extracts from these expanded versions are on pages 98–9, 103–5, and 106–8 below. It soon becomes obvious to the reader that these extracts rarely exemplify any one aspect of a dilemma, or even pertain to only one area of concern. As such they show the difficulty of analysis of any kind where complexity is inherent and must not be lost through over-simplification. The extracts are included, therefore, not as merely illustrating the particular point, but also as 'giving a flavour' of the whole field and providing examples of the tone and language of the interviews. As 'bald' print on the page, they may allow for many differing interpretations by the reader, but the analysis has to be based on the total input of data, i.e., the recording, the transcript, the shared experience of the interview, the shared knowledge of the area being focused upon, and the interviewer's examination of self-bias. These elements combine to enable the researcher to assess the dilemmas as underlying expressions of meaning . . . .

Section One — The Pupils' Perspective

An analysis of the dilemmas in the attitudes of pupils receiving support with literacy skills, based on transcripts of interviews with groups and individual children, aged between seven and eleven years.

1 *The provision of extra help with literacy skills*
On the one hand pupils are aware of their own inadequacies, and peer reactions often confirm these; on the other hand the receipt of extra help, meant to alleviate the difficulty, may itself reinforce the labelling process.

2 *The difficulties that their classroom needs pose for the teacher*
On the one hand pupils are aware that they need a lot of the teacher's time to help them; on the other hand they also feel that the rest of the class should have a 'fair' proportion of the teacher's time.

3 *Parental attitudes*
On the one hand the children know that their parents want them to

progress at a normal rate, and that their school experience should make this possible; on the other hand the children feel their parents do not want them singled out for extra help.

4 *The link between the levels of difficulty of tasks and likely progress*
On the one hand pupils have an awareness that the literacy support programme is designed to help them; on the other hand they are undecided as to whether being presented with 'hard' work or 'easy' work is the best route towards progress.

5 *Successful learning styles*
On the one hand pupils feel that if they are interested they can learn easily on their own; on the other hand, with some tasks that they find difficult, they need speedy access to help.

6 *A successful learning environment*
On the one hand they find it easier to concentrate if the atmosphere is quiet; on the other hand they appreciate that some kinds of work are necessarily noise producing.

7 *The link between volume/frequency of reading and reading progress*
They have an awareness that 'good' readers read a lot; BUT they get frustrated when they can't read and are pressured to do so.

8 *The selection of reading material*
They like to read 'easy' books/comics with pictures; BUT they want to be seen by their peers to be reading 'harder' books.

NOTE: **This analysis is now expanded to include extracts from the interview transcripts.**

1 *The provision of extra help with literacy skills*

> On the one hand pupils are aware of their own inadequacies, and peer reactions often confirm these;

You used to bunk off, didn't you, T? Because you didn't think much of the school. They used to keep on at him because he was slow. They used to take the Micky out of him.
T: They don't now 'cos they know I can hit 'em. 'Cos some third years used to take the Micky out of us. But now we are fourth years we can get 'em back.

> On the other hand the receipt of extra help, meant to alleviate the difficulty, may itself reinforce the labelling process.

They reckon to know everything, because they don't go in groups, do they?

Once last year they said, 'You go to baby work.' They think they're more brainy.

It doesn't matter about people calling you names. You've just got to learn and read.

He says things like that because they think you can't do the work they do. He's thicker than us. He goes, 'So I've improved miles more than you.' He keeps showing off.

2 *The difficulties that their classroom needs pose for the teacher*

> On the one hand pupils are aware that they need a lot of the teacher's time to help them;

It's good coming here because the teachers don't have time to help you read.

I think it's better like this, 'cos teachers — when they've got a load of people in the classroom — they can't tell you what you want. So it's better having groups, so you can hear one read at a time.

> On the other hand they also feel that the rest of the class should have a 'fair' proportion of the teacher's time.

Then the teachers don't have so many people in there. So it helps them. 'Cos they've got to have about twenty-nine people to read, so we only get one time to read a week.

The teacher is busy with the children, so it helps coming here.

3 *Parental attitudes*

> On the one hand the children know that their parents want them to progress at a normal rate, and that their school experience should make this possible;

Only my Mum: she goes, 'Oh, you're not trying at your reading.' She says, 'Bring your book home.' I read it. If I get a word wrong — I don't know — she never helps me.

I told Mum. She said, it's good, because it helps me read and it helps me write.

> On the other hand the children feel their parents do not want them singled out for extra help.

She didn't want me to have help; she wanted me to read on my own.

My Mum doesn't know about me coming here.

4 *The link between the levels of difficulty of tasks and likely progress*

> On the one hand pupils have an awareness that the
> literacy support programme is designed to help them;

We come to learn to read and write — try — learn.
You can help us to read, and that. Help us spell, and that.
It makes us learn in here.
We come 'cos we need help with the reading, and that.
It helps you read and write, and we play games.

> On the other hand they are undecided as to whether
> being presented with 'hard' work or 'easy' work is the
> best route towards progress.

You get away with the work in the classroom when you're in here.
Last week I missed the spelling test. It's easier work here.
The words we do here are easy: I wish they were a bit harder.
It's harder work here, but I can do it.

5 *Successful learning styles*

> On the one hand pupils feel that if they are interested
> they can learn easily on their own;

I like books in the box in the library (Cliff Moon). I can read them.
They're easy to read.
You learn well if you're left to work it out.
If you're in the mood for reading or writing, I can do it quickly.
If you like it, it's not so hard.
It sticks in your mind, 'cos you enjoyed it.
It's easier if it's a good story. You get tired if it's boring.

> On the other hand, with tasks that they find difficult,
> they need speedy access to help.

Ask your Mum or Dad. Ask your teacher.
Go up to teacher to ask, or wait a minute.
I'm doing some splitting up words with my Dad. That helps: two
syllables, like my spellings.
I try and spell it out, and read it to my Mum when I'm going
swimming.
I had to write out my hardest word: 'Card board hydrates'. I
sounded it out.

6 *A successful learning environment*

> On the one hand they find it easier to concentrate if the
> atmosphere is quiet;

I prefer to read to myself, in my mind. I can follow it better like that.

Just don't listen to other people. If they try to disturb you, ignore them.

(I like it) when the classroom is all quiet and not noisy. If it's all noisy you can't concentrate on the reading. It's all right if you're all reading together in your head.

> On the other hand they appreciate that some kinds of work are necessarily noise producing.

We play games 'cos they learn you reading your letters and words. You have to read the sentences.

That helps, 'cos teacher can read as well, and we can read out loud.

Going to reading groups and read to the teacher when it's all peace and quiet. Both got the same book, and read to each other.

That helps when you're not shy, 'cos you can ask about things.

7 *The link between volume/frequency of reading and reading progress*

> They have an awareness that 'good' readers read a lot;

I get the feeling sometimes that I can do much better. Like, some of the fourth years: they've got big books they can read lots of chapters out of. I feel a bit left out, a bit jealous.

I like Topsy and Tim. They're quite hard sometimes. My sister reads them to me. It's got harder words, longer words.

I read a lot now. I didn't read much.

I prefer one big story. I can find the ones I can read now.

I think I'm getting on better than last year. I can read more harder words.

I take a book home each day to read at home, and I quite enjoy it.

> BUT they get frustrated when they can't read and are pressured to do so.

If you're reading a book to her or doing the spellings, I get so up-tight with her that I don't want to do them. I keep on trying; she keeps on going on at me.

When I can't get a word I get in such a mood I throw the book about.

My Mum keeps saying to me: 'If you don't start reading in the fourth year, you'll have to go to a special school.'

If I don't get a word and keep on trying it and give up, she starts shouting at me.

Mum says, 'It's because you can't read very well that you come here.'

8 *The selection of reading material*

They like to read 'easy' books/comics with pictures;

I like the easy books. I look inside at the pictures, 'cos they've got easy words in them.
I like comics — that's all. I think they're easy, with the pictures. *Bangers and Mash* is good to read 'cos it's quite easy. I like funny books.
I read the first page, and that. I choose ones I can read.

BUT they want to be seen by their peers to be reading 'harder' books.

I want to get on higher books, 'cos when you get on lower books, people make fun of you.
I've read just about all the fact books in our classroom.
We ain't no good in class at reading, are we? 'Cos we're on lower books.

Section Two — The Support Team Perspective

An analysis of dilemmas in the attitudes of members of a peripatetic support team, based on transcripts of tape-recorded interviews.

1 *The allocation of peripatetic team time*
On the one hand, time blocking could lead to a deeper sense of involvement in school curriculum development; on the other hand, the long gap between blocks could pose difficulties for sustaining the programme, and would not accommodate new entrants.

Time blocking could enable a support plan to be tried and evaluated by both team member and class teacher, leading to its confident continuation in the gaps between blocks, BUT any rapport and counselling effects between team member and pupil would be lost in the long break between contacts.

2 *The role of the peripatetic teacher in the school*
On the one hand, where there is a lack of mutual involvement in the pupils' support programme, misunderstandings about the role of the peripatetic support teacher are common; on the other hand, contact time with the staff, away from the children, is difficult to organize, and is dependent on the teacher's priorities.

On the one hand a specialist teacher has the interest and motivation to keep abreast of developments in her field, and can be a useful resource; on the other hand their specialism may limit their career prospects, and lead them to lose relevance in the wider school context.

On the one hand a peripatetic relief teacher could free the class teacher to work with those children with special needs, while she took the remainder of the class; on the other hand some teachers may resent the disruption to the major part of their class, and/or lack the interest or expertise to use the time with special needs children to the best effect.

3 Record keeping
On the one hand there is a need for constant, up-to-date, *informal* exchange of information, between class teacher and team member, on pupil progress; on the other hand a formal, *written* record is permanent, and can monitor both the plan and recorded progress.

Written records may be overlooked by the class teacher, whereas oral communication is at least received, whether or not action results, BUT written records can provide any enquiring agency with information about the pupil's educational history and present level.

Effective record keeping, relying on observation as a major element, requires completion close to the event, BUT time taken in record completion may be taken away from contact time with the pupil.

4 The best environment for learning
On the one hand, carry-over relevance of a supportive activity is most easily achieved if worked on in the classroom, observed by all; on the other hand, some distractible children may need an environment of quiet and freedom from conflicting activities to successfully carry out parts of their programme.

On the one hand, some needs (for example, language development) are best met by working with compatible groups of pupils from different classes; on the other hand, depending on the characteristics of the school, this may be a disruptive arrangement for pupil and/or teacher.

Flexibility of working situation means you can meet the pupils' and teachers' needs more sensitively, BUT the use of bulky resources (for example, computer) can render constant moving of working situation less effective in terms of learning, because of effort and time expended on relocation.

5 Mutual cooperation between class teacher and team member
If a planned approach to meet a pupil's special needs is to succeed, cooperation is essential, BUT this implies a common philosophy on effective strategies, which may be difficult to establish, or only achievable over time.

6 Parental involvement
On the one hand, many parents think teaching reading is a very specialized thing, and the involvement of a peripatetic support teacher confirms this;

on the other hand, providing parents with the opportunity to make a positive contribution can relieve anxiety in both parent and pupil.

A pupil's having problems outside school is often associated with reading failure in school, and teachers feel they must try to compensate for this, BUT involving the family in a pupil's progress, far from imposing an additional burden, can prove effective counselling, by allowing an opportunity for discussion the problem and ways of tackling it.

NOTE: In the original report the analysis is expanded at this point to include extracts from transcripts of the interviews with the support team members. Unfortunately there is space here for only one illustrative example.

4 *The best environment for learning*

> On the one hand, carry-over relevance of a supportive activity is most easily achieved if worked on in the classroom, observed by all.

I think you have got to look at several areas. You've got to look at the school's organization, the child you're working with, and the practicalities . . . . I have just moved to an area in a school, rather than have a little room. I've moved to an area which we have made, and actually the children don't seem to be as distracted as I had thought they would have been. I think it all depends, with special needs children: a lot of them are visually distracted very readily. As long as you've got them facing somewhere blank or something reasonably blank, there isn't a lot of movement. It's not so much sound as visual things that interrupt . . . .

If you are a long way from the classrooms, it adds to the stigma, if you like. You are tucked away, you're hidden, they can't see what you are doing, and the rot sets in. If you are close to the classrooms, they see you talking to the teachers, they see the kind of things the children are doing: if they are enjoying it, if they see them working with tapes and the computer. You're seen and you are part of the school.

> On the other hand, some distractible children may need an environment of quiet and freedom from conflicting activities to successfully carry out parts of their programme.

If you are recording, you need quiet for that. So a little spare room somewhere tucked away is handy. An ideal situation would require one of these, an area for your hardware, but it would also include an involvement in what the teacher is doing, and what the child is interested in . . . .

Although I'm in the corridor, it's a nice enclosed area, next to the book area, so I can use both, and although it gets cold, I have got places to hang things, which I can leave up permanently (reference charts, or pictures I can use), so I feel that's quite nice. Although it's a corridor — people coming and going — we don't really notice it; we've got used to it . . . .

You see, I can't say, 'Go and find it; go and look at it; go and do it', because it has got all the apparatus (maths apparatus, library books) all in there, and people are coming and going all the time. I had a cupboard, which I lost; so all my things were just on the floor. You never seem to get organized.

Section Three: The Class Teachers' Perspective

An analysis of dilemmas in the attitudes of class teachers, based on transcripts of interviews.

1 *Curriculum content*
On the one hand, in a centre-of-interest, topic approach to learning, skill-getting is contained within that curriculum framework; on the other hand, some children do not readily generalize their learning to other situations, and need a planned progression, including an element of overlearning.

On the one hand, using written resources and keeping their own records are integral parts of the topic-centred curriculum; on the other hand, this approach (if not modified) is inaccessible to the children experiencing difficulty with literacy skills, and highlights their inadequacy.

2 *Responsibility for meeting children's special educational needs*
On the one hand, the presence of a visiting specialist may lead the class teacher to believe she can relinquish responsibility for her pupils' special needs; on the other hand, brief and infrequent contact between the child and the specialist means only a support role can be provided, and responsibility for meeting children's needs must remain with the class teacher and the school.

3 *The allocation of time within the school*
On the one hand the child with special needs demands a disproportionate amount of the class teacher's time, and the teacher feels a duty to allocate accordingly; on the other hand, the support teacher, being available only infrequently, may not be able to contribute greatly to easing this demand, where an immediacy of response is vital.

A concentration of support in the early years may bring most children to a level of independent learning quite quickly, BUT the teacher cannot abandon a programme that is proving successful, until the independent level is reached — whenever that is.

4 *The allocation of time between schools*
On the one hand, some children's needs might be best met by an intensive teaching programme of short duration; on the other hand, for some individuals, a short-span, regular support programme may lead to most effective progress.

Allocation of time should be according to the number of schools covered, because the need to relate to a school's curriculum and its members of staff is the same in each, BUT administratively it seems logical to allocate team contact-time to schools according to the numbers of children with special needs in each, where it is viewed as an allotment of direct teaching time, and not as an advisory role to the school staff.

5 *The best location for support teaching*
On the one hand a support teacher working within the classroom aids a class teacher's awareness of the ways of meeting special needs which she can continue to support; on the other hand, where the school is large and the allocation of support hours meagre, the contact time in any one class may be so reduced as to be ineffective, unless some grouping from several classes takes place.

On the one hand a support teacher working within the classroom aids the child in the transfer of learning across the curriculum; on the other hand, some learning activities may be most effective in a quiet, distraction-free environment.

6 *Counselling the child on his/her self-concept as an achiever*
On the one hand there is a need for honesty between teacher and child in identifying learning difficulties; on the other hand there is a need to instil confidence in the learner, to facilitate progress.

7 *Resources for learning*
On the one hand a team member may be welcomed because of access to, and familiarity with, extra resources; on the other hand the most valuable (and expensive) resources the school has are its own teaching staff.

8 *Grouping according to needs*
On the one hand some children's needs are best met by working within their own age group and interest level, and this may be simpler to organize; on the other hand some pupils may have common problems across the age/class bands, and economies of support teaching time and effort may be made by grouping according to need.

On the one hand, the times when a support teacher is available will demand timetabling considerations for those classes and individuals involved; on the other hand, where this support is valued, meeting this challenge can be an innovative curriculum development for all the class.

9 *The effects of labelling*
Where individuals or groups are extracted for help, this labels them as different, and (even where the rest of the class are supportive) affects their self-image, BUT they already sense that their difficulties have made them different, and may see 'help' positively, as a means of becoming more like their peers.

Where a class activity is taking place simultaneously, modifying it for some children may make them conspicuous, BUT if no modification takes place, then their difficulties may become more apparent, and (equally) lead to adverse labelling effects.

10 *Record keeping*
On the one hand, accurate teaching records are valuable to all persons concerned with the child during his/her school life; on the other hand, record keeping should not encroach too greatly into non-teaching time, nor be so copious as to deter quick and easy access.

There is a need to communicate continuously on the work being done, to avoid confusion for the child, BUT informal, oral communication can immediately and effectively meet this need, but may prove transitory.

Most teachers have a good idea, in their minds, of the stage each child is at, and what he/she needs to go on to next, BUT absence of a definitive hierarchy of learning in reading and literacy make attempts to formalize this into written records very fraught.

11 *Teacher training to meet children's special learning needs*
On the one hand, it is felt that there is insufficient input in initial teacher training to enable a new teacher to plan adequately to meet special learning needs; on the other hand, school-based in-service work — after experience of teaching children with learning difficulties — may be more effective in terms of a teacher's professional development.

12 *Reported parental attitudes to support teaching*
On the one hand, many parents still see it as a stigma, if their child has to receive help from a support teacher; on the other hand, some parents are well aware of their child's difficulties, and have a positive attitude towards any efforts to help their child.

On the one hand there is a need/duty to keep parents informed of the school's efforts to help the child who is experiencing learning difficulties; on the other hand, the parents' attitude may be counter-productive, unless efforts are made to involve them positively in their child's progress.

NOTE: At this point in the original report the analysis is expanded to include extracts from the transcripts of interviews with the class teachers. Unfortunately there is space to include here only one example as an illustration.

10 *Record keeping*

> On the one hand accurate teaching records are valuable
> to all persons concerned with the child during his school
> life.

So I think you have to devise a record keeping system which is very easy to use, very easy to read; and I think the most important aspect of record keeping is what the teacher knows about that child in her mind. So I think the talk, the way things start over a cup of coffee, is in a way far more valuable for record keeping than anything you can write down ...

One of the ways I work in my class, is that they have a little blue book, and every day now I insist they take their reading book home, with the blue book, and their parents sign to show they have read every day, and they comment if necessary (if they think the book isn't interesting enough, or it's too difficult or too easy); and we have built up quite a conversation with one of the parents about the stories. Also, the children are encouraged to see their progress. I do find that a very beneficial way of keeping a record. At the end of the year, with your written notes, I can amalgamate anything onto the actual record....

I quite like the idea of a book, plus any verbal explanations that are required — particularly as one might forget. But if it is written down, what you have actually done, and any follow-up work.....I write down what I've done: often I do forget what I've done, especially if you are only coming in once a week. A lot can happen.

> On the other hand, record keeping should not encroach
> too greatly into non-teaching time, nor be so copious as
> to deter quick and easy access.

I think record keeping is very important, but I do think it can become a god, and then teachers spend most of their non-teaching time filling in record sheets and writing copious notes. When you think of the normal busy day a teacher has, how many times do they pick up the child's record sheet and really thoroughly read it?

I think there is a danger of having too much paperwork around, because often, if it's only a few children in your class, I think it's probably up to you (as up to me) to look and see what they have been doing, and to ask them....

I think it would be one more thing to put in a record card, and it would be one more thing that wouldn't be read by the next teacher anyway.

Some Conclusions

NOTE: **The concluding section of the original report includes a detailed discussion of the relevant literature. The extracts below are the passages which refer to the data from the interview transcripts.**

Individualization is the central theme of strategies to meet children's special needs. Multi-professional cooperation may be seen as operating at either the planning or the operational level, or both. Where the implementation involves the extraction of children, it may be pertinent to ask how missing out on those amounts of class activities might affect the progress of average children. Certainly, my study shows a general feeling that record keeping should exist; but in what form, for what purpose, and for whose use, seems very unclear. Where two or more professionals are involved in direct teaching, there is the need to plan, coordinate, and constantly exchange information about progress. Yet my study reveals staff's suspicion of too formal record keeping, which they feel is seldom maintained, read, or noted thoroughly, amongst the day-to-day pressures of classroom life; so they tend to rely on informal verbal interaction for communication . . . .

Change involving people's specialisms and areas of responsibility is always problematic. Yet comments in my study show a readiness to change at all levels, providing people feel that their experience — gained under previous set-ups — is not devalued in order to demonstrate the need for change. In the case of the support team, they feel professional enhancement is the key to their becoming effective instruments in supporting and furthering the benefits of organizational change . . . .

There was unanimity in my study about the need for much extended in-service work . . . echoed also by my validation discussions with similar persons to those within my study . . . .

The role of the support service should be reassessed. The present practice of abstracting children only after failure is a negative approach. (Document prepared by members of the Essex Institute — now Anglia HEC — In-service course 'Children With Special Educational Needs', 1984)

I feel my study supports this view, where that aspect of the service's role is all that is observed or attributed to them. Changing the school's perception of the role of the support teacher is just as crucial as changing the structure under which it operates . . . .

(Can a support teacher act in the role of consultant?) My dilemma analysis illuminates the difficulties between team members wanting to develop this role, their own feelings about their ability to do this, and the perceptions of the children and class teachers about the possibility or need for this as part of the support teacher's role.

A Personal Response to the Issues Raised

A certain amount of helplessness and lack of direction emerges from my study, by all concerned, but there seems to be a willingness to change and a genuine concern expressed. A complete reappraisal at LEA level is indicated, in my view, to rationalize the provision for children with special educational needs:

(a) A general raising of levels of awareness of special needs, for all school staff.
(b) A consultant team of *classroom* teachers, to support development of whole-school strategies for children with special needs.
(c) A special needs coordinator on every staff (or shared between two small schools, at most), without responsibility for a class, and with frequent time-tabled meetings of all coordinators with any other local representatives of special educational provision.
(d) Special needs input on *all* in-service provision.
(e) Review of capitation and staff remuneration, as between special schools, units, and mainstream.
(f) A training and career structure for teachers especially concerned with special needs, to attract and retain staff capable of supporting the changed concepts of ways of meeting pupils' special educational needs.

Chapter 8

From Principles to Practice:
A Description of the Process of Writing
a Research Report

Introduction

Chapter four gives a set of guiding principles, but it is clear from the examples in chapters six and seven that in practice these principles can (and will have to be) interpreted in many different ways, depending on the varied characteristics of different research projects. Chapter nine gives a further (more extended) example — a research report evaluating a specific course — of an attempt to work in accordance with these guiding principles. However, many of the activities involved in organizing and drafting the report are not immediately obvious from the text of the report itself — the sequence of procedures, the worries, the decisions as to what to include and what to exclude and on what basis, etc. And the principles themselves have been intentionally given in a very general form, so they also do not necessarily convey the sort of practical decision-making processes which they will entail when one is sitting at one's desk confronted by a pile of paper. This chapter is therefore included as a 'bridge', describing directly the process by which the report presented in chapter nine was written in the light of the theoretical rationale provided by the six principles in chapter four. Some of the points it contains could perhaps be deduced by carefully comparing the two chapters, but that seems rather a burdensome task to impose, and so I hope that the following account will be helpful in indicating some of the main procedures and issues involved.

It is worth noting, however, that the 'six principles' relate to the *whole* research process, not just to the writing of a report. It is merely a feature (and perhaps a limitation) of this particular project that I collected the data over a long period and then sat down to compile an evaluation, as a preparation for the next phase of work. It would have been more in keeping with the spirit of action-research if the work described comprised more clearly several cycles of movement between action and analysis. Indeed, action-research would ideally hope to generate a culture of innovative professional practices, rather than an accumulating corpus of research reports, but it is part of the argument of this book that where it *does* generate research reports, these can stand comparison with those of conventional social science, in terms of their intellectual rigour and generalizable relevance. It is as part of this argument, therefore, that the example in chapter nine is presented.

The following explanation of the process considers in turn the various decisions involved in (1) the choice of data, (2) the choice of format, (3) the implications (for the writing) of the audience(s) envisaged, and (4) the criteria by which interpretations of the data were made.

The course which is the topic of the report was an in-service course for teachers, where the 'students' were engaged in compiling a collection of descriptive analyses of what they had learned from their professional experiences. Since I was new to this type of course, I wished to evaluate it carefully in order to consider appropriate teaching methods, and so I collected quite extensive data from the outset. I also asked a colleague on secondment from another institution to sit in on sessions as an outside evaluator. Further details of the course are given in the introduction to the report itself, at the beginning of chapter nine.

Which Data?

Having decided to evaluate the course, I had accumulated a mass of data in a rather hamster-like fashion during the two years during which the course had been running. There were transcripts from tape-recorded teaching sessions, interviews, and discussions, comments from the external evaluator, students' work, written comments on students' work, and examiners' reports, as well as all the official course documentation. Reading it all through, as a preliminary step, led to a sense of oppression: it was all, in a sense, 'relevant', but there was clearly far too much for it all to be included, so on what basis could I decide what to include and what to leave out, without introducing an obviously subjective bias from the very outset, by (say) using a criterion of what 'seemed interesting'?

I resolved this issue by using the principle of 'the context of necessary relationships' (see chapter four, pp. 47–8) as follows. I started from the idea that the phenomenon I was trying to analyze is 'a course of study', and that 'a course of study' *must necessarily* include (at least): (1) students' background experience, (2) course aims, (3) course activities, (4) the teaching methods by which those activities are organized, and (5) course outcomes, since each is only intelligible in the context of all the others. So: I needed to include a selection of data referring to each of these elements.

This line of thought helped me to make two decisions. First, I realized I would need to include a section on students' previous education and experience, even though the data was very minimal (see chapter nine, section 3). Second, I was able to decide to leave out a vast amount of data referring to one student who had seemed throughout to be experiencing difficulties and thus seemed to be an interesting 'case', since although this material was indeed very interesting, it was not — unlike the rest of the material — *essential* to an understanding of the course. (Clearly, if the focus of the report had been on, say, the phenomenon of 'assessment' rather than 'course evaluation', then the material relating to this student *would* have been essential.) I also concluded that, if 'course outcomes' are a central element, then it was essential that I should discuss these with the examiners, rather than relying on their official report sheets, in the same way that I had discussed the pedagogical process of the course with the students: this seemed important in terms of the symmetry and balance of the data. Thus, although I had originally felt oppressed by the amount of data I already possessed (when it confronted me as an undifferentiated mass) I now felt sufficiently clear about the range and types of data I required to decide to set up *another* discussion, and to make *another* transcript! (see chapter nine, pp. 150-2)

Which Format ?

The above solution to the problem of 'which data?' was also helpful in tackling the problem of the format for the report. The problem here took the form of a dilemma. On the one hand, how could I present a 'plural' text which would be a collection of different, 'collaborative' voices from the research, rather than the single, prescriptive voice of the researcher marshalling evidence to justify a conclusion? (See chapter four, principle five.) And yet, on the other hand, the text cannot be merely a random collection; it must have some form of unifying thread, if it is to be coherent and readable at all. But if the unifying thread is not to be an argument leading to a conclusion, what could it be? The practical problem about a text which presents a unified argument is that the unity of the writing needs to be worked out in advance, so that it often seems very difficult to start writing at all: every paragraph is burdened with the meaning of the totality, and yet when you first put pen to paper, you don't know what that totality is going to amount to. So it was a relief, at first, to feel freed from the burden of a unified argument. But the usual alternative — telling a personal story, using the chronological sequence of one's own experiences as the structure — didn't seem adequate. After all, I hoped that the report on this particular course would raise general issues, would present an ordered agenda of proposals for consideration by the colleagues I had worked with, and a structure of ideas that would be relevant to numerous readers in other contexts. For these purposes, a sort of elaborated diary format seemed too timid, too private — whereas the unified argument format seemed too authoritarian, too prescriptive. (Note that in chapter six the narrative format *did* seem appropriate, since the investigation had focused on a sequence of separate incidents.)

In view of the considerations above, I decided to use as a connecting thread the series of elements listed above, in the previous section, as the necessary components of the phenomenon being analyzed: student background, aims, activities, teaching methods, outcomes. This had the merit of also being a form of logical analysis of the topic, and thus provided an objectively justifiable structure — unlike a simply autobiographical sequence. At the same time it suggests a sort of generalized temporal sequence, which is only to be expected, since the phenomena which we are likely to want to research (for example, courses, teaching strategies, management processes) will necessarily have a temporal dimension. Since writing a research report is also an activity with a temporal dimension, the series of elements provided an obvious and convenient starting point for my presentation (the students' previous experience). It also seemed to promise that there would be a suitable point on which to end the report (the course outcomes), and it gave a rationale for moving from one heading to the next (the sequence of the necessary elements) without the need for a connected argument based on particular interpretations and conclusions.

But a format is more than the structure of a sequence of headings. How would I present the data; and how would data be linked to interpretation, in the absence of an overall argument which would organize data as evidence to justify a conclusion? Here also, the guiding principles of chapter four provided practical answers.

First: in order that there should be other voices in the report besides my own, I needed to include *substantial* extracts from transcripts, documents, reports, etc. i.e., extracts which would be substantial enough to stand on their own, to make a point in their own way. Data therefore would normally take the form of a quarter-page extract, rather than a two-line quotation to *illustrate* a point. My own interpretations would then simply be placed after each extract under a sub-heading 'Commentary'. If more than one interpretative argument arose from a given data extract, they would be labelled 'Commentary, A, B, C, etc.' These lengthy data extracts would also allow the general atmosphere of the course to emerge independently of my own interpretations, and thus enable readers to formulate their own commentaries and alternative agendas of concern.

Second: a basic criterion for interpretations was that they should lead to proposals of practical possibilities, and it seemed important to keep these separate from both data and commentaries, so that these sections could be used in themselves with colleagues as a working document on which to base decisions about future developments of the course. After wondering about giving each of these sections a subheading 'Practical suggestions', I anticipated that this would become very tedious, and interrupt the flow of the text as a whole, and therefore decided to use simply an asterisk and indentation. It would then be a simple matter to identify and collect these passages into a discussion paper which could form the basis for a meeting about practical changes to the course. (This is presented as appendix D to chapter 9.)

In this way, then, I thought I had a format which had enough underlying coherence and forward movement to be readable in a conventional manner, while following the suggestion — from principle five — that the report should be a sort of collage, a 'plural structure' which would be sufficiently open and loose as to enable the interplay of voices from the research process, and to facilitate varied responses by readers in the light of their differing professional and personal relevancies.

Which Audience?

It was clear from the outset that I was writing for various audiences: (1) those with whom I had worked on the course — students, colleagues, and the external evaluator, (2) colleagues with whom I would be working in making changes to the course, and (3) a wider audience of educators who might be able to relate my account of this course to their own experiences of similar courses, and indeed to 'courses of study' in general. These three audiences are, I would suggest, those which would almost always be envisaged in this type of writing. However, for this piece I also had two other audiences in mind: (4) academic social scientists, whom I wished to convince of the rigour and richness of this method of work, and (5) teachers on in-service courses, for whom I wished this report to be a usable model for their own work. Finally, of course, one can (and ought) to say that for any significant, authentic writing one's *first* audience is oneself, but that takes us somewhat aside from the direction of the present argument.

The immediate practical question concerned the first three of my audiences: how would the report have to be presented, such that these three audiences simultaneously could feel that their differing purposes and concerns were taken into account? Put in these terms, that seems a difficult question, but in fact I felt the existence of these complex audience constraints to be a helpful discipline, rather than a hindrance or an inhibition, because it meant that I was not in the worrying position of being apparently able to write 'how I liked', and thus of having to *decide* what I liked. On the contrary, I obviously had clear reasons for writing in one way rather than another; it just needed to be worked out: the differing demands of the three audiences overlapped in the centre, I could assume, to provide me with precise and rigorous guidance, as follows.

First, the report could not be too long: each audience would have limited time available, and there are practical limits to the length of a chapter in a book or an article in a journal. So I had a simple reason for selecting only a small proportion of all my data.

Second, the 'practical decisions' sections must easily be separable from the rest, and yet not interrupt the text as a whole, so that the report could function both as a working document and as an analytical account. Hence the asterisks and indentations mentioned in the previous section.

Third, the report must make sense to 'outsiders'. This meant, for example, that I would need to phrase some of the commentaries to bring out the wider implications of the points being made concerning this particular course. It also meant that an explanatory introduction would be required, providing enough context and rationale for readers with experience of different types of educational establishments to approach the report with a sense of its potential relevance for their concerns. And finally it meant that I would need a concluding section, which would bring together the various general issues which would have emerged at different points in the commentaries.

But the audience factor that played the most important part in shaping the writing was my sense that I was addressing colleagues and students with whom I would need to be on amicable terms *after* they had read the report. Indeed, they would need to grant permission for its publication. This consideration is often presented as a regrettable matter which can imperil 'the truth': insider researchers, it is feared, are not 'free' to say what they 'really' feel (for fear of hurting people's feelings) and are thus not able to tell 'the whole truth'. But 'the whole truth' here is what might be presented by an inquisitive and reckless gossip, which may be fun to overhear, but has no warrant of reliability, and is a poor model for a research stance! In contrast, as I sifted through my materials, it seemed to me that the requirement of discretion created another constructive and rigorous form of intellectual discipline, helping me to discard lines of thought which were merely my own prior value judgments, political and moral concerns, personal responses to individuals, etc — all of which I was continually tempted to elaborate directly into categories for *organizing* the data, without allowing them to be *transformed* by the data. I always started by regretting that such and such a point would have to be left out because it would be 'tactless', but in the end always discovered that what I had taken to be tactlessness concealed other, purely analytical weaknesses, and thus ended up feeling relief rather than regret at its disappearance.

This requirement — that I was going to have to maintain a professional relationship with at least two of my audiences — led to several practical decisions. It meant that I sometimes changed the gender of a speaker or writer, in order to try to make their anonymity impenetrable even by other members of the same small group. It meant that I avoided transcript extracts which appeared to reduce the plausibility of the speaker because of the very different rules and expectations concerning coherence which govern spoken rather than written language forms. This in turn made me decide to 'tidy' occasional details of grammar and syntax in transcripted statements, and also to *punctuate* them very fully and carefully, so that they could stand in a written text with more of the authority of voices offering interpretations, and less of the raw quaintness of 'evidence' for what the author wishes to present. Finally, it meant that, as has been mentioned before, I decided to arrange further discussions with one group of colleagues (the examiners) whose interpretations of the course were only represented in the data by their formal reports: I suspected that they would otherwise (rightly) feel that their perspective was not properly documented, and that any interpretations I might make of their reports in the absence of such discussions would be inadequate. In this case, once again, my awareness of the anticipated audience for the work seemed to create an entirely helpful pressure towards greater adequacy and objectivity.

Which Interpretation?

It was as a set of criteria for the interpretation of data that the guiding principles were most directly relevant, and it was in this respect that it was most helpful to feel that I had grounds other than my own interests and value commitments for selecting among the various lines of thought which occurred to me as I pondered over the data I had collected.

My first preparatory step had been to assemble all the data in chronological order in a large loose-leaf binder, and to number each document, so that I had a fairly efficient retrieval system. I then read quickly through it all, jotting only the briefest notes as I went. This was in order to lodge somewhere in my mind an overall awareness of the material, so that as soon as I started to carry out the detailed interpretive analysis there was a good chance that connections would 'spring to mind' between different parts of the data.

It was at this point I decided that the basic structure of the report should be the context of necessary relationships which made up the phenomenon I was studying. This meant that I would use as section headings the series of course elements (i.e., students' prior experience, course aims, activities, teaching methods, outcomes) constituting the course of study, where each element depended on all the others for an adequate interpretation of its meaning. This was a further reminder of the importance of an overall awareness of the body of data, and so I read once more through all the material, this time carefully making notes under three headings: 'contradictions', 'making reflexivity explicit', and 'themes and thoughts' — the latter a residual category for ideas which seemed not to fit either of the other two. Each note took the form of a brief phrase and the number of the data document to which it referred, so that I could easily cross reference. (Towards the end, a note often involved merely adding the number of another data document to an existing phrase. Examples of some of these notes are given in an appendix, at the end of this chapter.) Quite early in the process, I rediscovered that I had my own personal and practical agenda for the work — the search for teaching methods appropriate for courses based on students' experience — and so I added this heading to my note-making process. It is also important to mention that many of the commentaries in the text of the report did not figure in these early notes, but were developed in response to particular data during the writing of the report itself.

The preparatory work completed, I then began compiling the report, by writing an explanatory introduction (aimed at my third, 'wider' audience) and went on to assemble the first section of data, the students' prior experience, and sat back to consider my first paragraphs of 'Commentary' and 'Practical suggestions'. It was at this point that I realized how useful the preparatory stage (of overall familiarization with the data) had been: I had no difficulty in formulating an interpretation (of even the very minimal data I had on the students' prior experiences) which linked this element in with other elements of the data, i.e., teaching methods (see chapter nine, p. 127). In other words the preparatory work had succeeded in creating for me that 'necessary context' of meanings which would provide, throughout the report, one of the basic frameworks for interpreting data. Indeed, I was surprised to find that I did *not* need to go back repeatedly to my preparatory notes and work directly from them, since I was not constructing a unified, linear, summarizing argument requiring all the evidence to be marshalled towards a conclusion: instead, the general awareness generated by the preparatory note-making seemed to be sufficient to create the links necessary for the looser structure of the 'plural text'.

Throughout the rest of the interpretive work of writing commentaries and practical suggestions, the six principles of chapter four provided guidance in various ways.

First, all commentaries had to be presented in terms of *either* the principle of dialectical critique *or* the principle of reflexive critique. Lots of other ideas swarmed in, clamouring that they were 'interesting', and indeed they were: curious misunderstandings, curious blunders (my own and others'), particular incidents which beautifully illustrated general patterns, perfect examples of important educational, sociological, psychological, and political themes, surprising phenomena of all sorts. But all were excluded if I could not formulate them in such a way that they conformed to one of these two interpretive principles. With some ideas I struggled until I finally found such a formulation; with others I struggled in vain, and ended by leaving them out. Some readers may experience a sense of outrage here. 'But,' you exclaim, 'surely, this means your report is *incomplete!*' However, those of you who know the anguish of confronting a mountain of data, plagued by the endless fertility with which possible and 'interesting' interpretations spring to one's mind, will know the sense of relief with which I wielded my scythe, feeling confident as I did so that the excluded ideas had 'failed' a rigorous, theoretically based test of their objectivity and significance, and that therefore, although they had initially *seemed* interesting and important to *me*, I could now no longer be sure that they necessarily were so for anyone else: they might have only seemed 'interesting' because (for example) they were familiar, or confirmed my prejudices.

Second, all commentaries had to lead to the formulation of possibilities for action (see chapter four, principle six). Again, I usually found that, sometimes after a struggle, this could be done. If not, I had grounds for believing that the interpretive idea was in some important sense lacking in significance, so — out it went! (There were a very few exceptions to this rule, where further data extracts on the same issue intervene between a commentary and its associated practical suggestions (see for example chapter nine, pp. 140–2).)

Third, I had to work hard at avoiding commentaries which placed me, as the researcher, in the superior role of one whose analysis of other people's words shows that I understand what is going on, but they don't. (See chapter four, principle three: 'Collaborative Resource'.) In other words, I had to analyze the documents from the research in such a way that the commentaries upon them represented a process of *learning* from the data, rather than 'sitting in judgment' upon it. In practical terms, this meant analyzing the relationship between — on the one hand — the contradictions and apparent unreflexiveness in particular pieces of data and — on the other hand — the further levels of contradiction and apparent lack of reflexivity in my own response to that data. (See chapter four, principle four: 'Risk'.) For an example of this, consider chapter nine, pp. 147–50. My first inclination was to leave the argument at the point where I had indicated disagreement among the examiners, thereby vaguely implying some sort of inadequacy ('inconsistency' perhaps, or 'lack of proper grounds') in their judgmental process. But this treats *their* work as subject to *my* judgmental analysis, leaving me 'in the clear'. So the next step was to argue that I had to assume, on principle, that their disagreement represents a form of response to the situation with which I must collaborate (rather than dismiss as faulty), from which I can therefore learn something of value, and on which my own interpretation can build. Consequently, their disagreement may represent, for example, a problem in the guidelines they were using, which I had provided, and which thus need further critical analysis. The commentary thus swings round to place me, the researcher, also 'at risk', and the overall analysis at this point is, I think, all the better for it, in purely intellectual terms, as well as in terms of the interpersonal considerations outlined in the previous section on the relationship between the report and its audiences.

A particularly interesting problem arose when I came to use the external evaluator's material. Having kindly provided an official evaluative report, at my request, she obviously needed to be mentioned by name, in order that her contribution should be appropriately recognized.

My dilemma was as follows. If I were to treat her report as a final, objective evaluation, it would undermine the whole idea of my own evaluation as an action-research project by a practitioner-researcher, by implying that there was, ready-to-hand, a 'correct' interpretation of the situation, provided by an outside observer: her report, therefore, has to take its place in the overall research report as one voice among many, and thus subject to dialectical and reflexive critique. On the other hand, to name a colleague and then subject her interpretations to a critique could seem on my part to be professionally churlish and even defensive.

After some thought about all this, I decided that it would be acceptable to analyze extracts from the evaluator's *official* report, which after all had been carefully composed for use in a public arena, but that I would also have to include the report itself more or less in its entirety as an appendix, as a tribute to its status as an overall commentary. But I did *not* feel that I could quote the evaluator's 'private' comments (her written comments on students' work, extracts from tape-recorded discussions, etc.) without obtaining her permission in advance and also sending her a copy of the whole report, so that she would be able to see the whole context in which her remarks and my commentaries upon them would be placed. This shows very clearly the significance of procedures for ensuring anonymity: where collaborators are *not* anonymous, they really need to become co-authors. This would indeed have been an interesting step to take, but in the end I decided it would be an unnecessary complication in this instance. Firstly, she was by this time once more working in her own institution on the other side of the world; secondly, I found that all the points which emerged from the external evaluator's private comments were also covered in the analyses of the other materials.

Clearly this decision (not to quote the evaluator's comments) would have been much more difficult if I had been writing a conventional report, which makes claims for its interpretations on the grounds that they are supported by 'exhaustive evidence'. In this report, the methods for the *use* of evidence are extremely rigorous, but the crucial matter is no longer the *amount* of evidence collected or cited.

Conclusion: Delegation, Rigour, Objectivity, Ethics

This explanation may have given the impression that the method of writing illustrated in the next chapter is laborious and time-consuming, so I would like to emphasize that for me it was neither. The process of compiling the report seemed (in comparison with other pieces of writing I have done) both more straightforward (because its structure did not depend on working out beforehand the details of one's own interpretations and arguments) and also (perhaps for the same reason) more explorative and thus more enjoyable.

There was a sense of freedom about the process which I could try to explain by suggesting that this 'plural structure' represents an act of 'delegation'. Rather than being burdened by the thought that the whole report had to present *my* argument, *my* choice of evidence, *my* conclusions, etc, I felt I was delegating part of this responsibility to the 'voices' (within the data and within the text of the report) of those with whom I had worked. These seemed less like 'objects of investigation', who had produced data that I was under an obligation to analyze 'convincingly', but more like co-authors of a text of which I had the job of editing, and like colleagues with whom I was entering into discussion. A further part of the responsibility for the writing was being delegated, in a sense, to *readers*. Rather than offering a finished product — a ready baked cake whose colour, taste, and consistency would all represent *my* professional judgments — I felt as though I was offering something more like a set of resources — a mix- and-serve pack, where a recipient still has to make important decisions, may add a favourite ingredient, may add less sugar than recommended, and may know very well it will need baking for ten minutes longer in his or her particular oven. In this way, the plural text, as a 'semi-delegated text', expresses action-research's spirit of open-ended possibilities for continuation and development.

I also felt that the use of the guiding principles enabled me to make those awkward decisions involved in presenting a research report (which data? which interpretation? where to start, how to handle one's own bias, etc, etc.) with greater confidence and clarity. They generated rigorous criteria for rejecting my first thoughts and cudgelling my brains to disentangle new arguments I was only dimly aware of, and they ensured that new thoughts did not spin off into fanciful speculation but retained a focus on professional practice. Furthermore, the rigour of the process did not depend on mastery of nor deference to any corpus of prior literature concerning the matters I was investigating, but was a matter of my own response to the data to hand. Objectivity, likewise, did not depend on exhaustive amounts of data nor on time-consuming jigsaws with cross-references, but firstly on careful analytical treatment of each piece of data, and secondly on careful political and ethical concern for the continuation of professional relationships.

But the proof of the writing is in the reading, and so the work presented in chapter nine must now stand or fall on its own merits or otherwise, not just as an example of a 'plural text', but as 'an evaluation' and as 'a research report'.

Appendix

Examples of Preparatory Notes

NB. The following phrases are taken verbatim from the preparatory notes, where each one was followed by the number of the data document(s) to which it refers. The page numbers below refer to chapter nine, i.e., to one of the places in the report where the note is utilized.

Contradictions

* MEd (external standard) v. self-appraisal (internal standard) (p. 127)
* Diagnosing need v. assessing level of work (p. 138)
* Standard from within individuals v. standard by comparison with others (p. 127–8)
* Pedagogy: tutor dominated v. collaborative learning (p. 134–5)
* Students: well-motivated v. sense of lack (p. 126).

Reflexivity not Explicit

* 'Extend', 'develop', 'critically', 'deeper understanding': Meaning??? (p. 129)
* An 'interesting' example — 'Being interesting' as a THREAT (p. 135)
* The problem of my distinction between 'confidence' and 'understanding' (p. 140–2).
* The difference between giving and receiving criticism: a problem of authority and also of defining a tutorial role?? (p. 142–3).

Chapter 9

The Learner's Experience and the Teacher's Authority: Evaluating an Access Course

Acknowledgments

I should like to express my appreciation of the contribution to this work of the following colleagues and students at the Anglia Higher Education College, Brentwood. I am grateful to them for allowing their words and ideas to be included, directly or indirectly in the report. Vaughan Collier, David Crowe, Helen Thorne, Pamela Weston, Mary Campbell, Irene Clarke, Paul Eiken, Ian Ellis, Alex Gibson, Frankie Heywood, Ron Best, Jan Cheesmer, Ron Cooper, Steve Decker, Tom Hughes, Tim Hull, Yvonne Larsson, Teri Moore, Peter Wilson.

Note:

Possible practical developments, for discussion and action, are marked * and indented.

1. Introduction

This course evaluation report concerns the access course for the part-time MEd in Educational Research and Evaluation, at the Anglia Higher Education College. The MEd access course was designed to enable students to gain academic credit for learning which had taken place as a result of their professional and general life experience. Students on the course must carry out a series of tasks requiring them to reflect on their educational and work experiences, and thereby to demonstrate a level of understanding equivalent to a BEd Honours degree or In-service Diploma in Education, one or other of which is normally (for applicants other than those from the access course) a necessary entry requirement for the MEd course. In the context of vocational education the course illustrates 'the accreditation of

124

experiential learning', and in the context of education in general it illustrates an 'individualized curriculum'. In both contexts it offers contrasts with the tradition of 'a prescribed course', and thus raises important issues concerned with (1) the role of the teacher, (2) the nature and source of academic standards, and thus (3) the process of assessment.

There was also a more practical starting point. At the time of writing, the MEd access course had had two complete intakes. In the first year there were four students, and in the second year, six. The evaluation report covers both years. It is a new type of course, both for me as a tutor and for the Higher Education College where I work, so that a detailed evaluation seemed to be necessary in order to accelerate the development of an adequate understanding of the processes involved, and thus to be able to implement practical changes with some degree of confidence.

2. A Necessary Range of Data

An educational course may be minimally defined as consisting of (1) students' prior experiences, (2) a set of educational intentions, (3) a series of activities, (4) methods for organizing these activities, and (5) a set of formal and informal outcomes. An evaluation of a course of study therefore needs to be based on data from — at least — each of these dimensions. This is the basis for selecting the range of data presented below, which are arranged as a series of sections concerning:

Students' prior experience (section 3);
Course aims and objectives (section 4);
The series of coursework tasks (section 5);
Notes on or transcripts from course sessions (section 6);
A report on the course made by an outside observer (section 7);
Retrospective evaluations by both intakes of students, by means of
questionnaire returns and tape-recorded discussions (section 8);
Assessment comments made by staff acting as examiners for the
students' final coursework portfolio (section 9).

One of the preliminary steps in the compilation of the evaluation report was to read through all of the data collected and to make a note of 'significant' issues, i.e., those where the existence of contradictions, paradoxes, dilemmas, or tensions suggested a potential for or likelihood of change or development. The 'commentaries' are thus not only derived from specific, isolated data, but also from a general awareness of the range of data and issues which are to be presented as an evaluation of the course. For example, the commentary on aims involves consideration of assessment processes, the commentary on coursework tasks relates back to the question of aims, and the presentation of students' background experience relates to the issues of teaching method, and so on.

3. The Students

First Intake

— Headteacher, large urban junior school, sixteen years experience (Teaching Certificate, Open University Arts degree).
— Headteacher, small rural primary school, twelve years experience (Teaching Certificate, Open University Arts degree).
— Head of Sixth Form, comprehensive school, nine years experience (BA (Hons), Theology, PGCE).
— Scale 2 teacher, primary school, ten years experience (Teaching Certificate, Open University Arts degree).

Second Intake

— Head of Art, comprehensive school, twelve years experience (Teaching Certificate, Open University Foundation course — Arts).
— Head of CDT and TVEI, boarding comprehensive school, sixteen years experience (Teaching Certificate).
— Headteacher, large urban infant school, nineteen years experience (Teaching Certificate).
— Lecturer in Outdoor Pursuits, further education college, sixteen years experience (Teaching Certificate).
— Lecturer in Social Work, college of higher education, eleven years experience (BA (Hons) Fine Art, Certificate in Social Work).
— Schools–Industry Liaison Officer/Advisory Teacher, thirteen years experience (Teaching Certificate, Open University Foundation Course — Science).

Commentary

(A) The wealth of experience and previous study possessed by this group of students contrasts strongly with their status as students who *lack* a necessary qualification and therefore *need* an 'access course'. One is tempted to ask (on the one hand) whether the access course is really necessary, and (on the other hand) whether the students see themselves as possessing a 'wealth' or a deficit. As regards the latter question, one student specifically said, during discussion, 'We know we are not as well qualified as other students', but another said, 'We are a highly-motivated group . . .'.

*Perhaps not all students need the complete procedure of the whole access course. Instead, particular sections might be

required, depending on prior qualifications and experience, and
on negotiations during application.

(B) The *diversity* of experience and previous study possessed by the students
suggests strongly that a process of collaborative learning, of learning from
each other rather than from the tutor, would be both possible and desirable
as a fundamental process of the course. But although this diversity could be
an important resource for learning, it could also be a distraction, leading
merely to fascination with each others' anecdotes. In this way, diversity
could easily lead merely to fragmentation. So the question is: what sort of
skills and curriculum materials would be required to enable students to see
links between their own situations and the manifold experiences of their
colleagues, and thus to take advantage of diversity as an opportunity for
learning? Or does this question itself reflect my 'teacherly' preoccupation
with *telling people things*, my need or desire to 'teach skills'? Is there *really*
a problem of a diverse group learning from each other?

> *A set of guidelines could be written suggesting how students
> could organize learning sessions largely for themselves, based on
> the exchange of diverse professional and academic experience.

4. Intentions, Aims, and Objectives

The title of the course is 'MEd Preparation and Professional Self-appraisal'.
All students whose work reaches the required standard are given a place on
the MEd course, and numbers entering the access course are restricted so
that there need be no competition among the students on the access course,
even though the overall demand for places on the MEd exceeds the number
of places available. This arrangement embodies an intention that the
course experience should be collaborative, mutually supportive, and positive, thereby reducing the danger of experiencing failure (through competit-
iveness within the group) to a minimum. Students who complete the tasks
but whose work does not reach the required standard, *or* who choose not to
proceed to the MEd, are given a 'Certificate of Attendance for a Course of
Professional Self-appraisal'. These arrangements are an attempt to ensure
that the course should be *intrinsically* valuable (a process of self-appraisal)
as well as *extrinsically* valuable (a means of gaining access to a course which
carries career prestige).

Commentary

(A) The course title and these basic arrangements immediately suggest a
contradiction within the course between externally prescribed criteria

(MEd requirements) and internally derived criteria (self-appraisal). This contradiction is the source of the uncertainty and worry concerning 'standards' which was one of the main themes to emerge from discussions with students (see sections 6 and 8 below).

> *One might attempt to reduce the ambiguity and anxiety created by this contradiction by either (i) more precise definition of external standards (specific objectives and assessment criteria distributed to students), or (ii) more precise definition of internal standards (negotiation of individualized 'learning contracts').

(B) In general terms, this tension between internal and external standards characterizes all educational processes where an element of *selection* is involved, since educational processes are supposed to be both worthwhile in themselves and at the same time to measure the student in relation to an external norm — whether the norm is derived from a group average or from a prescribed level of competence. In this sense the issues concerning the access course are not untypical of those relating to other formally institutionalized courses of study.

The specific aims of the course, derived from the BEd Honours course, are set out below in their practical form as a set of criteria used by examiners to assess the portfolio of coursework submitted by the students at the end of the course.

The Portfolio should:
1 Demonstrate a high level of understanding of the teaching process, by relating practical experiences to theoretical issues.
2 Demonstrate a capacity for critical evaluation of ideas and arguments concerning education.
3 Demonstrate a practical awareness of how a research project might contribute to the understanding of an educational issue, by discussing the strengths and limitations of the methods selected.
4 Demonstrate an awareness of educational issues concerning institutions of a type other than that in which the teacher–student works.
5 Demonstrate a critical and informed awareness of current thinking in one aspect of education.
6 Demonstrate standards of written presentation characterized by clarity of expression, logical consistency, and the structuring of material within a clear organizational framework.

Commentary

Like any set of objectives which is not expressed in strictly behavioural terms, this list requires examiners to make judgments that seem as though they might be objective, but which actually must be highly personal and reflexive. For example, examiners will have to decide what they will interpret as being 'a demonstration', 'an awareness', and 'a capacity', and they will have to judge what they will consider to be *sufficiently* 'critical', 'informed', 'clear', 'logical', etc. Even criterion (1), which tries to give an objective definition of what is to be considered a 'high' level of understanding, still leaves examiners with questions as to what are to be considered 'theoretical' as opposed to 'practical' issues, and what manner of relating them will be expected or acceptable. The point is illustrated in a particularly interesting way by criterion (6), since although it looks quite precise, it could actually refer to writing at any level from a primary school project to a PhD thesis. There is thus a contradiction between the fact that the list of criteria seems to have been precise enough to be usable in practice and the obviously questionable nature of the judgments that the criteria require. The contradiction arises because the inevitably reflexive basis of evaluative judgments is being ignored.

*It will be important to discuss with examiners the actual process by which they use the list of criteria to make the assessments. (See section 9, below)

*Are there ways in which the grounds for these judgments could be made more open to scrutiny? Would it be worthwhile asking all examiners to make explicit their grounds for their assessment of one portfolio, and making this document — the portfolio and the various examiners' judgments — available to students before submitting their own work? (See section 9)

5. Coursework Tasks

Students were asked to complete the following series of tasks. The tasks were devised as a translation of the aims of the BEd Honours course from what might be called an 'academic' mode into an 'autobiographical' mode. Each task corresponds to one or more of the BEd aims. (See appendix A.) Meetings were held at monthly intervals to share the experience of carrying out each task and to consider preliminary ideas for the next.

Task A
Write an autobiography of your full-time education, describing the details of your experience as a learner, and your experience of teachers and their teaching procedures . . . .Focus on your exper-

ience of education (at different ages): consider your own experiences in relation to your assumptions about the attitudes and
motives of those you currently teach.

Task B
List all in-service courses in education attended.
Take one course of which you have a vivid memory and describe
what you learned from it . . . .Contrast this with another course
where either your learning process was very different or where
you learned very little, and account for the difference.
Describe a learning experience which took place *outside* a formal
educational setting — what you learned, how you learned, and
how you knew that you had learned something.

Task C
Read a recently published book which researches an area of your
own professional specialization and write a critical review of it,
explaining the basis of your criticisms.

Task D
Select an aspect of the educational process which is directly relevant to your current professional work and describe the problems
and issues which you feel concerned about. What sort of investigation can you envisage which would throw light on one (or some)
of these problems and issues, and what difficulties would you
expect to encounter if you attempted to implement such an investigation?

Commentary

There seems to be a tension between this strongly prescribed sequence of
tasks and the individualized, 'experience-led' curriculum philosophy.
However, this may be an inevitable consequence of the fact that this is an
access course with a single destination (the MEd course). On the other
hand, the sequence of tasks is *not* based on an analysis of the demands
actually made by the MEd course, by the competencies which will be
required, but on the supposed outcomes of the BEd course. In this way the
course takes for granted the hierarchy of levels of courses (Cert Ed – BEd –
MEd) which is enshrined in the administrative rule: MEd applicants must
already possess a BEd. And yet the provision of the access course is itself a
response to a *doubt* about the necessity of this rule.

*The sequence of tasks which comprise the access course might be
more securely founded if it were derived from an analysis of the
competencies actually demanded by the process of the MEd
course. This suggests two interesting lines of investigation: (a) to

discuss with third year MEd students the nature of the skills, knowledge and personal qualities which they felt the course had demanded of them; (b) to discuss with former access course students currently on the MEd course how far they felt that the access course had been a relevant preparation.

6. Course Sessions

Note: The following extracts are from the session concerned with Task C (the book review). The first set of extracts are from the beginning of the session, which I discussed with one of the students some weeks after the course was over, and her 'success' was established. The interspersed commentary is largely derived from the points which emerged in that discussion. I chose to discuss the transcript with this particular student because she was the only one (out of the four in the first group) who in the evaluation questionnaire at the end of the course said that she found aspects of the sessions 'a little confusing at times'.

> RW: What I'd like to start with is to ask you what you thought you learned from doing this task. I know that's a difficult question, but it's a way of getting into a discussion, so that from what you say you might get ideas as to how to change (your written work).

Commentary

It is not clear whether I am asking them to say what they had learned from the content of the book or from the process of trying to write a review. For me this was not an important distinction, but for the students it *was*, since they were concerned as to what would and what would not be an acceptable response. Flexibility and openness (in the tutor) is intended to *encourage* student response, but it can easily create uncertainty (in the student), which then inhibits response by creating anxiety.

> A: I think you have to read it so much more carefully. I read it in an entirely different way to the way I usually read a book. You know, I usually just read it for enjoyment or to find something out; but this time you had to *really* read it and then think about the point, and try to analyze what it means . . . .
>
> RW: So for you the learning process was being forced to read more sort of analytically?
>
> A: Yes.
>
> B: I agree . . . .I must confess that most of what I've read —

> largely professionally — I've looked for what I've wanted in a book, and having found what I've wanted, to suit my purpose, I've ignored the rest, whether it conflicted with my point of view or with what I was taking from the book.
>
> *RW*: And what did you do which was different from that?
>
> *B*: I was very conscious of having to sort out *my* views on the points the book was covering, and seeing whether I accepted what the book was saying: did it line up with my views or not? And if it did not, why? Why did I take an opposing or slightly different view to what the book was saying?
>
> *RW*: So it made you ask why?
>
> *B*: It made me question *myself* as much as what I was reading.

Commentary

I am trying to base my teaching process on a model derived from counselling, in which I attempt to 'probe' responses in order to stimulate further thought. It is interesting that at the time this session took place I had no doubt that 'further thought' was needed, but as I *now* re-read them, the various statements seem 'already' to be full of valuable insight, so the purpose of my 'probing' seems less clear. So: what is the relationship between 'discussion' as a teaching technique and the facilitation of 'self-clarification' as a counselling technique? One crucial difference between counselling and teaching concerns how far the objectives of the interaction are determined by learners for themselves and how far they are imposed. This has already been noted as an ambiguity in the course aims and tasks: perhaps this same ambiguity reappears as an uncertainty in my role in these discussions.

> *C*: I think that what happened for me was that I read the book and fairly quickly afterwards wrote out my rough draft, that I was just going to polish up for the final presentation, and left it for a while before I actually did that...and I think that delay gave me the opportunity. It wasn't really a conscious process, to be honest, but things settled in my mind, and that gave the different emphasis, and perhaps the clarity.
>
> *RW*: Suppose I had asked you to write a short essay on pastoral care, are you saying you couldn't have done that 'cold'?
>
> *C*: Well, yes, perhaps I could have done, but ....
>
> *RW*: But would it not have been as complex as what you have written here? (. . .)

Commentary

It was at this point that the student with whom I was discussing the transcript said she felt 'in the dark', and suddenly I can see why: I am carrying out a series of dialogues with each student in turn about the details of a piece of work which the others in the group do not know about in any detail.

> *It is clear that the process must be amended so that students can tell each other about what they have done. Otherwise the tutor may remain the focus of the interaction. (See next commentary)

RW: OK, can I just ask you the question, D: what do you think you have learned from writing about that book?

D: Well, it clarified my thinking. My first reaction was fairly amorphous . . . and then I found myself getting increasingly irritated, and then I thought, 'Now, come on, you can't base anything on irritation; it might just be you.' So that disciplined me into saying, 'Well, is there any actual basis for this irritation?'

A: Would you have finished reading it if you hadn't had to?

D: Not really, no, because it irritated me so much.

RW: So you said it clarified your thoughts?

D: Yes it did, it clarified my thoughts a lot. I chose this book because it's an area that interests me, the teacher role and what exactly *is* a teacher trying to do, and it has clarified my thoughts.

RW: But 'clarifying' is quite an easy word to say, and it's very nasty when people say, 'Can you give me an example?'.

D: 'Can you clarify what you mean by "clarify"?' (*Laughter*)

Commentary

The student with whom I was discussing the transcript ('D' in this extract) explained that, for her, 'clarification' was not so much an intellectual problem as a social dilemma created by the presence two crucially different audiences: the tutor, who had already read her work, and her fellow students who hadn't. She therefore could not decide 'how much detail' would be appropriate: enough detail to make the account comprehensible for her colleagues risked being redundant and repetitious for the tutor; but pursuing issues for the tutor (taking for granted what she knew the tutor already knew) risked being incomprehensible to her colleagues. D's problem here neatly illustrates the contradiction between an experience-based curriculum and tutor domination of the interaction.

*In the second year of the course, time was devoted to allowing students in turn to describe their work to the others. This was not felt, however, to be an adequate solution (too mechanical, difficult to concentrate, etc.), and so another suggestion was made: all students should bring along copies of a single page summary of their work for their colleagues to read over at the beginning of the sessions, as well as a full account for the tutor to mark and for inclusion in the portfolio. In this way there would exist the necessary pattern of resources for a collaborative learning process.

Note: The following extract is taken from near the end of the session, where the discussion has become a general conversation about 'educational issues' arising out of the students' work.

> RW: I see. I just wanted to throw some light on B's notion of relevance, because there are different forms of relevance. Intrinsic and extrinsic is one distinction one could make. Because everyone wants to *claim* relevance. I remember hearing about someone being interviewed about their education and its relevance to their work, and they said they had a classics degree and BP had employed them because BP thought that people with classics degrees were good at selling oil.
>
> C: Yes, employers are more complex and subtle in the qualities they are looking for, not just five 'O' levels but the ability to get on with people . . . .
>
> B: The trouble with relevance is that you have to ask: relevant to *whom*, and it's not only relevant to the child but relevant to society.
>
> RW: Sorry. As soon as I hear 'society' I hear it with a capital 'S', and I wonder, 'Who is "Society"?' It suggests a consensus . . . .

Commentary

My interventions here represent attempts to 'challenge' expressions of certainty, authority, and consensus, to make available 'alternatives', and to pursue a train of thought at an abstract level in order to see the conceptual links between anecdotes. However, this is my very personal interpretation of the function of these sessions, and I am not sure how far the purpose of this style of conversation and of my role in it was clear to the students. Thus, since the process and its purposes had not been made explicit nor negotiated with the students — it risks being another form of tutor domination, especially since the tutor himself is *not* challenged in this way.

*If this is a mode of thinking that the course is intended to foster, then students should be given opportunity and specific encouragement to practise it, i.e., to challenge as well as to be challenged.

Similar questions arise from my notes and transcripts from other sessions. For example, in the following extract from the discussion as to what types of learning experiences would be appropriate for Task A, the notion of what is 'interesting' arises as another example of the problem of concealed reflexivity:

> *RW*: You just give the most interesting examples you can think of . . .I mean you could contrast a badly run course with a well run course, but that wouldn't be so interesting as two courses that were both well run in different ways, and you learned from them in different ways.

Commentary

(A) 'Interesting' is used as an evaluative judgment, yet its meaning is ultimately quite private. For a teacher to give students the instruction, 'Be interesting!' is thus highly threatening, since it is — almost by definition — impossible to specify in advance what will count as 'interesting'. The attempt to do so in the above example clearly raises as many questions as it answers: it is arguable that the one sort of contrast is really only 'more interesting' than the other according to my own private agenda, and yet is is presented here as a generalizable prescription. The almost wholly reflexive meaning of the word provides a strong contrast with my suggestion that it can operate as a criterion. What I ought to have said, then, is that this is a reflexive judgment, which students *must* make for themselves. Indeed, in an individualized course such as this, the fundamental reflexivity of evaluative judgments arises explicitly as a key problem (for example, internal versus external 'standards', in section 4).

> *To fall back on 'interesting' suggests that important underlying criteria and objectives have not been specified. The 'General Introductory Notes' issued to the second intake of students (see appendix B) may be seen as an attempt to explain and to specify what is likely to be seen as 'interesting' in the context of the course.

(B) Another set of questions arises from the importance of personal experiences as 'curriculum content' and the dilemma this creates for the tutor: what form of pedagogical comment is appropriate, for example, when a student writes about what he learned from the death of his father? At this point the course seems to resemble the sort of 'writing conference' described by Graves (1983) and thus to require tutorial responses which are supportive and facilitative but *not* evaluative. But how could that be reconciled with the existence of an external assessment standard? When personal experience becomes curriculum content, 'teaching' can seem like an invasion of privacy. Consider the following example, from a course session concerned with students' educational autobiographies:

> RW: Yes, I wonder what you think the link might have been between your work in art and social work. Did writing that up suggest any link between the two? I mean, in your exper- ience, what seemed to move you from one to the other?
>
> G: Well, I got interested in art therapy . . . .I don't know why I went into social work.
>
> RW: It's interesting that you don't say, 'I don't know why I went into art', because that's the one you went into and then gave up. But you are in a sense still in — well, *are* you still in social work? Have you gone back to education, now that you are teaching social work?
>
> G: I don't feel I'm a social worker any more. I feel I'm a teacher.
>
> RW: So you've been an artist and a social worker and now a teacher: three different identities! . . .(Long pause, finally broken by another student)

Commentary

This pressure by the tutor for public self-analysis now, on re-reading, seems embarrassingly oppressive. Why did it seem appropriate at the time? Because 'self-awareness' is an apparently innocent course aim? But progress towards self-awareness may require an educational process which has certain qualities (for example, acceptance of non-explicit understanding, respect for privacy, for problematic emotion) which offer quite a strong contrast with the process of intellectual challenge and debate which is char- acteristic of other, less personal curricula. In this case I seem to be treating someone's sense of identity as a curriculum resource, as a potentially illum- inating set of *ideas*, which suggests a problem in the relationship between my role and function as a tutor and a curriculum based in students' person- al experience.

7. Outside Observer's Perspective

A visiting colleague, Dr Yvonne Larsson, sat in on most of the course sessions and read the students' work. Dr Larsson's final report is included as appendix C; the following extracts from the report take up themes which

were part of our continuously developing discussion during the running of
the course.

The skills component was obviously a very important part of the
course, and the need for students to develop an analytical
approach and 'critical edge' to their appraisal was clearly
outlined.

Commentary

'An analytical approach' and 'critical edge' are further examples of reflexive expressions which are widely used in making apparently authoritative
judgments. There is no doubt that they are 'needed', but there are limits to
how clearly they can be outlined. (See the commentary on 'interesting' in
the previous section.) What is the nature, then, of the 'skills' referred to?

By the conclusion of the five evening sessions and the completion
of each student's portfolio, the expectation is that each student
should be able essentially to replace common sense with systematic thinking, replace anecdotal knowledge with generalizable
knowledge, and replace generalized knowledge with detailed
knowledge.

Commentary

This is a helpful clarification, which was partially incorporated into the
'General Introductory Notes' the following year (see appendix B). The
suggestion that one form of thinking might 'replace' another is to ignore the
problem of reflexivity, but it is a strong indication that despite the difficulty
of making these qualitative judgments, the criteria are real and important.
Unfortunately, having provided the lists of criteria in the 'General
Introductory Notes', I did not feel that they had much impact on the
students' work in the second year of intake. It seemed that the notes were
filed and forgotten. Perhaps, then, there is a contradiction between
prescribing a form of analytical thinking and the necessarily personal form
it must take for each individual.

*The Introductory Notes' may thus be much more difficult for
students to use than I had assumed, and practical activities based
on using them may be necessary if the notes are to be of benefit.

Additional activities could be inbuilt, based on the individual
needs of the students enrolled.

Commentary

There is a tension between individual needs and prescribed course require-ments. This can be resolved by emphasizing 'constructive diagnosis' as a course objective, but then a further tension arises between diagnosis (of individual need) and assessment (in terms of final pass or fail). Dr Larsson and I had frequent discussion concerning the wide range of students' needs, both actual and potential, for example:

1   Knowledge — concerning either self-awareness or educational issues and research findings;
2   Skills — intellectual (critical analysis), practical (information retrieval), or interpersonal (collaborative discussion);
3   Emotional qualities — confidence, toleration of uncertainty, etc.

The list raises the question: what is the relationship between these various needs and the priorities among them; and thus: what is the function of the course? Is it 'assessment of suitability' or 'diagnosis' or 'diagnosis plus remediation'? The latter seems to be implicit in the quotation from the observer's report. However, given the complexity of the list of needs indicated, it is likely that many of them could *not* be remedied within the limitations of an access course, and if one made a diagnosis of need explicit but then failed to provide adequate 'additional activities' for the need to be remedied, one might expose students' vulnerabilities and then subject them to an experience of highly personalized failure.

> *Perhaps, then, the real issue within the course is not so much how to meet individual needs, but how to make the objectives of the course both more explicit and more clearly justifiable, and this — once more — suggests the necessity of analyzing the competen-cies required by the MEd course itself. It would then be possible to discuss with students which competencies they thought they *already* possessed (for which they would need help in providing documentation), and which other competencies they thought they would need to acquire (and what experiences would enable them to do so — including other available in-service courses). Perhaps, therefore, this suggests the need for a *general* Inset/career counselling service, which might begin to address the currently uneasy relationship between need and provision, as il-lustrated in the MEd access course. This in turn might require a rethink of current applications procedures.

8. Students' Evaluations

After the end of the course, the first group of students filled in an evaluation proforma (see figure 3). Given the tiny numbers involved, the results of this 'questionnaire' are the merest indications, but are nonetheless interesting. Firstly, the high overall ratio of 'very important' to 'not all that important' in the students' scoring (21:6) suggests that, in spite of its shortcomings, the course managed to create a generally positive experience for the students. Secondly, the only factors ticked as 'not all that important' by more than one student were 'the particular form and sequence of the tasks' and 'the suggestions of the tutor', which gives further support to previous arguments that the course is perhaps as yet conceived too prescriptively. Thirdly, one of the students noted that 'listening to others' had been an important factor in her learning, although it did not seem to be listed — a significant omission, it now begins to seem.

Figure 3: MEd Access Course: Evaluation Form

1   In what ways do you think you benefited from the course?
2   Would you say that you had increased more in confidence or in understanding?
3   Each of the following factors could have been more or less important in your view of what benefit you derived from the course. Please tick either column A ('very important') or column B ('not all that important') and — if you wish — add your own comments . . . .

		A	B
a	Being made to think about experiences		
b	Being made to write about experiences		
c	Being made to talk about experiences		
d	The particular form and sequence of the tasks		
e	Meeting as a group to exchange professional experiences		
f	The formal discussion of the tasks		
g	The suggestions of the tutor		
h	The critical challenge of the tutor		
i	The support and encouragement of the tutor		

(The following year, when 'listening to others' was included in a list of factors for discussion, it was indeed mentioned frequently as being of importance.)

The final session of the course ended — in both years — with a general evaluative discussion, which was tape-recorded and transcribed. From these discussions, two main themes emerged as particularly significant, the first of which, the relationship between 'confidence' and 'understanding', is also anticipated in certain of the responses to the questionnaire:

Confidence and Understanding

The following comments were made in response to question 2 (above): 'Would you say that you had increased more in confidence or in understanding'?

> *Student B*: More in understanding my professional development, the antecedents to my present   job and views on education. Greater confidence in my perspective on education. I accept it as one of many perspectives, but I believe it.
> *Student D*: Yes, both. More professionally confident.
> *Student A*: Both — to some extent, but also more thoughtful.

Commentary

The students' replies undermine the distinction implied in the question in a number of ways. Perhaps to be 'more thoughtful' (student A) involves a combination of confidence and understanding; perhaps a 'professional' confidence (student D) must entail a degree of self-conscious understanding of one's role; and perhaps to understand the *basis* ('antecedents') of one's opinions (student B) is an integral part of an increased confidence in those opinions. Since these lines of thought seem immediately plausible, and even 'obvious', it becomes interesting to consider why I posed the original question in a form that seemed to presuppose so dubious a distinction. What assumptions underlie the distinction, and why did the assumptions seem so 'natural' as to pass unnoticed? In other words, what were the ideological pressures which led me to treat my reflexive interpretation as an objective distinction?

One important set of ideas which may be relevant here concerns the way in which we think of intellectual qualities as relatively fixed characteristics, leading to various 'meritocratic' hierarchies ('levels of ability', 'levels of qualification') which are a particular concern of educational institutions and of educators — like myself. In contrast, we tend to think of emotional qualities, such as 'confidence', as variable responses to particular circumstances. Thus, we regularly say, for example, 'That was a nasty experience: it undermined my confidence', but not, 'That was a nasty problem: it undermined my understanding.' Instead, we say simply, 'That problem was difficult: it was *beyond* my understanding.' Clearly, once we focus on the issue, we can easily think of contrary examples: emotions as fixed into patterns which form 'personality', and understanding as a faculty which 'develops'. But the point, here, is simply that although the connection between emotional states and intellectual performances is well known (especially to us as educators), we live within an ideology which tends continually to separate them (to such an extent that 'artificial intelligence' is treated as a problem of 'processing information').

In the light of this argument, it is interesting to note that the official criteria for assessing the MEd access course make no mention of any affective qualities (see section 4, above) although they do figure quite substantially in the examiners' responses to the students' work (see section 9).

This line of argument was corroborated by comments made by students during the evaluative discussions at the end of the course. For example:

> *Student C*: As the others were talking I was thinking about how (the course) had affected me in terms of convictions, and how to hold them in public, in the staffroom arena. There's always an interesting mix in staffrooms, and there are some quarters of staff opinion who would hold out quite vehemently against the practicality of educational theory and evaluation, and moves based on that; and I think it's helped me insofar as it's given me the opportunity to step back from the crisis management of, 'Gosh . . . this one's got to be in by yesterday' to actually consider the working situation that *I'm* in, and in distancing oneself from that, and — I hope — looking at it a little more objectively, and on the basis of wider reading, which this (course) has stimulated. It has given me greater conviction . . . .
>
> *RW*: Greater confidence?
>
> *C*: Yes . . . I think there are times in school when you have to stand up . . . and state very firmly your beliefs, and I think that I've gained in that respect from the course. It's certainly underlined some things for me which I've held for a long time.

Commentary

I was originally very downcast at the statement that the course had given this student (whose work I had very much admired) greater conviction concerning previously held ideas, rather than 'new' ideas. But this disappointment now seems to be due at least in part to my excessively 'rationalist' view of understanding, as a series of propositions which one acquires, rather than as part of an overall state of mind (and feeling). The complexity of the link is nicely presented in the following comment by another student, the following year, during a similar retrospective discussion:

Student F: I think I've become more self-confident in how I approach things. I haven't been so dogmatic. I've tended to look more *round* the problem, instead of straight through the middle looking for the answer straight away.

*This distinction, then, is one that I may need to abandon, in my approach to students' work, i.e., in evaluating it and in my guiding comments beforehand: 'new ideas' are *not* going to be the main outcome for all the students, and this does not necessarily represent any degree of 'failure' on their (or my) part.

The problem of internal and external standards

This is the second of the two main themes which I noted in the students' comments on the course. There is a contradiction between the prescriptive elements of the course (the external standard of the BEd, the predetermined sequence of tasks) and the individualized curriculum based on student experiences and areas of interest. This creates a dilemma for the tutor concerning what forms of intervention are appropriate, and a dilemma for students as to what is 'required'.

One student, writing (on her questionnaire form) that 'the support and encouragement of the tutor' was 'very important', went on to add: 'Too important. I should have been more self-reliant'. In noting that an *excess* of 'support and encouragement' can be an educational disadvantage, she was pointing to a paradox at the heart of this course, as well as other educational processes. The students' immediate problem of 'the required standard' is illustrated by the following:

B: I had to struggle, as I think most of us did, with the situation of producing something and not having a mark at the end of it. I knew we weren't going to get marks, but obviously that's why we pressed for some kind of feedback. I can see your difficulties: the course is not set up to give yes/no feedback, 'this is right and this is wrong'.

C: From my point of view...we were aiming to produce a...standard to enable us to get a place on the (MEd) course, and therefore there *is* a level we are aiming at...and sometimes it's difficult, looking at your comments, to necessarily see whether — I suppose it's a matter of insecurity (isn't it?) that you need some confirmation along the way. However, having said that: with my 'A' level students for the first couple of terms I don't give them any grading at all, so I mean it's been quite a useful exercise looking from the other side of it.

Commentary

Student B's use of the vocabulary of 'having a mark', 'yes/no', 'right/wrong' links his own experience with that of the children he teaches, and this is made quite explicit by C. The paradox that teachers should themselves feel anxiety in a situation which they readily create for their pupils suggests the possibility of a general communication gap between teachers and learners: perhaps the 'insecurity' of learners is such that a need for 'confirmation' is more or less permanent. (Just at the time of this discussion I presented a paper to a group of my fellow staff-members, and felt deeply wounded by criticisms from amicable colleagues who presumably felt that they were offering to me the same sort of 'constructive challenge' as I felt I was offering to my students.)

> *As a result of this discussion, I attempted, the following year, to address the question of 'the required standard' by issuing guide-lines at the beginning of the course (see appendix B) which were intended to clarify the nature of the dilemma which faced us (tutor and students alike), and I also distributed an extract from a piece of student written work to illustrate 'a good standard'. But this did *not* resolve the problem, as is indicated by the following extracts from the evaluative discussion with the second group of students:

G: That piece of work you gave us: to me it was more harm than good.

F: In the early tasks I was hanging on to every phrase you (RW) used, because I was very uncertain as to what you wanted. You said things like, 'Don't be simplistic' and then you said, 'Did I say that?'

RW: Did anyone else feel that that first example was distracting?

H: Yes, I did.

J: It was useful to have read it, but not to keep taking it away and keep burning my fingers on it and looking back on it.

H: I enjoy talking in the group. And I didn't think there was enough (talk), and I felt at times that your presence was in-hibiting. I don't think you did this deliberately, but we did treat you as the expert, and phrases like 'hanging on your every word' are . . . .

Commentary

The contradiction between the prescribed standard and the individualized curriculum is dramatically summed up by the suggestion that the illustrative example could be *dangerous* ('harmful', 'burning my fingers'), and that the tutor's presence could be counterproductive.

In future, therefore, I will: (a) provide detailed guidelines for a collaborative learning process based on discussion of the tasks, (b) ask students to provide a summary of their work for each other's use during the discussion, and (c) *absent* myself from at least half of the discussion. This will have the further advantage that it might enable two parallel groups to run more or less simultaneously, which would double the ratio of students to staff, and thus make a very 'expensive' course much more 'economical'.

However, there was a strongly urged oppositional voice here, arguing that the tutor's presence *is* crucial: all students agreed that the tutor's written comments were of central importance, and one of them went on to say:

I think that the written comments make sense in the context of a relationship with you, of listening to you. I think that people are very uncertain as to whether they are good enough, and that's the reason why the tutor should be there, and that's why we hang on your every word, because we don't feel we are the genuine — not quite like some of the other people who come onto the MEd.

Commentary

There are two points here: (a) written comments, in order to be fully effective, need to be embedded in a substantial face-to-face relationship with a tutor, and (b) access course students have *low* self esteem, since they are categorized in terms of a deficit. Is there a link here? For example, if point (b) is accepted, then point (a) might seem to be very important.

*Rather than two opposed categories, 'dependent' and 'independent' students, it might be helpful to think in terms of a developmental objective for the course ('the increase of intellectual self-confidence'). So perhaps the tutor should be continuously present in, say, the first session, but should then *gradually* withdraw as the course progresses.

9. Assessment: Examiners' Comments on Students' Coursework

Examiners were sent (together with the student coursework) a copy of the task descriptions (see section 5) and also a copy of the following guidelines (part of which was discussed in section 4). All examiners were experienced in marking BEd Honours dissertations and some also taught on the MEd course; none were involved in teaching the access course. Each coursework portfolio was assessed by two examiners, and was judged by both examiners to have reached the necessary standard, although some were judged to be 'bare' passes by *one* (but never by both) of the examiners.

MARKING THE MEd ACCESS COURSE PORTFOLIOS

Guidelines for Examiners

General

The portfolios were created in accordance with the Task Descriptions set out on the attached sheet. In assessing the Portfolios the main question is: 'Does the portfolio demonstrate that the student possess at least an equivalent understanding of issues relating to education and educational research, and a similar intellectual ability as an In-service Honours BEd student whose dissertation is awarded a *minimum* pass (i.e., 3rd class Honours)?'
  In other words, the assessment is on a Pass/Fail basis....

Assessment Criteria

The following assessment criteria should be used. They were constructed by synthesizing the In-service BEd 'General Aims' and the assessment criteria for the Honours dissertation. They are thus designed to be compatible with the criteria used in assessing the Honours dissertation, and examiners may also be guided by their *impression* as to whether a portfolio demonstrates an 'equivalent quality' to an acceptable Honours dissertation.
The portfolio should:
1 Demonstrate a high level of understanding of the teaching process, by relating practical experiences to theoretical issues;
2 Demonstrate a capacity for critical evaluation of ideas and arguments concerning education;
3 Demonstrate a practical awareness of how a research project might contribute to the understanding of an educational issue, by discussing the strengths and limitations of the methods selected;
4 Demonstrate an awareness of educational issues concerning institutions of a type other than that in which the teacher-student works;
5 Demonstrate a critical and informed awareness of current thinking in one aspect of education;
6 Demonstrate standards of written presentation characterized by clarity of expression, logical consistency, and the structuring of material within a clear organizational framework.

Commentary

Students who read this report prior to publication were critical of the fact that they had not seen these assessment criteria before submitting their portfolios. This is further evidence of their worry that an external standard is being invoked, but that they don't know what it is. However, the commentaries in this section suggest that publishing the criteria (which now does take place) will not entirely remove this problem, which is inherent in the assessment process.

Although the procedure for establishing equivalence between access course portfolios and BEd dissertations is based on quite careful and detailed work at the level of objectives, the reference to an 'impression' of 'equivalent quality', and the implicit query created by the quotation marks, seem to invite examiners to make use of this detailed work in rather a general way. This may perhaps be a recognition that although the notion of 'equivalent quality' may have to be invoked administratively (as an explanation for passing and failing) *as though* it could be an objective description, its meaning is necessarily reflexive, and can thus of course never be independent of examiners' interpretations of their 'impressions'.

However, during a discussion of the criteria, examiners were concerned to reject the term 'impressionistic' in describing the process, and preferred 'integrated' or 'holistic' instead, which is another way of suggesting, perhaps, that the distinction in which 'general impressions' are contrasted with 'analysis based on specific criteria' is too simple. The following example of an examiner's report — given in full — illustrates the tension and the close links between general qualities and precise criteria, and shows the way in which general qualities *and* specific qualities are both invoked in order to make and justify a judgment.

Examiner's Report

1 There are a number of strengths to this study that contribute to the 'pass' grade awarded. The candidate writes extremely well and has produced a most articulate and readable portfolio. Each section is well organized and maintains a clear focus on the set task. The final section is extremely well discussed and contributes most to the 'pass' grade.

2 There are differences between this study and that of a BEd Hons dissertation. Reference to the literature is almost non-existent here, and the text selected for the critique is dated. There is also minimal awareness shown of the current major debates about schooling and the curriculum. The investigation discussed in Task D contains many pertinent comments but very little discussion or reference to the limits of such an approach or the style of research on which it is based.

3 The candidate demonstrates a capacity for critical evaluation, although much of the portfolio is descriptive. However, her clarity of expression, logical consistency, and structuring of material are of a very high standard.

Commentary

Paragraphs 1 and 3 justify the positive judgment ('pass') by reference to *general* intellectual competencies, but paragraph 2 contains references to *specific* deficiencies of information and awareness. It seems then as though 'equivalence' between the portfolio of coursework and the BEd dissertation is established by means of a notion of 'general intelligence' or 'general intellectual competence', and thus in another case where the examiner went on to praise *all* aspects of the work (including the level of specific knowledge and awareness), it seems significant that the examiner wrote, at the end of the first paragraph:

> In particular, the organization, presentation, and style of written argument are extremely good: it is no exaggeration to say that I thoroughly enjoyed reading (the work).

However, previous arguments have suggested the limitations of purely intellectual categories, and the relevance of affective qualities. The resulting complex mix of criteria (*not* referred to in the guidelines, but invoked nevertheless) is neatly presented in the following opening paragraph by another examiner:

> This is a clear pass. It is a collection of insightful and honest accounts which show someone 'making sense' of their experiences. I was particularly impressed by the autobiographical accounts.

Commentary

'Insightful', 'honest', and 'making sense of experiences' are all expressions which can refer either to intellectual understandings or to emotional self-awareness, and thus serve to indicate clearly the close links between intellectual and affective qualities. It is interesting that the other examiner of this same student's work made no references whatsoever to affective qualities, since the report was based entirely on the listed criteria:

Examiner's Report

Criterion 1: There was more practice than theory but some im-

portant links were made, and implicit understanding under-pinned much of the work.
Criterion 2: There is evidence of critical analysis.
. . . .
Criterion 5: This was a bit disappointing — there was some dis-cussion, but little in any depth.
Criterion 6: Certainly a strength. This work was well put together and clearly expressed.

Commentary

Both examiners passed this student's work, but one appeared to use purely intellectual categories, and the other used criteria which merged intellec-tual and affective qualities. One possible line of argument, then, is that the distinction 'intellectual/affective' is spurious, that underlying the intellect-ual criteria listed on the examiners' guidelines there is a set of implicit af-fective criteria which are deeply relevant to the course aims. This makes sense: the course is a preparation for a vocational, professional role, and it is obvious that any attempt at assessment for vocational suitability must include moral, emotional, ('personal') qualities alongside qualities of the intellect.

> *The 'General Introductory Notes' drawn up for the second year of the course (see appendix B) already contain suggestions which implicitly include affective qualities (first paragraph, headed 'Aims'). Perhaps more attention needs to be directed towards this aspect of the course, especially in preparation for the tasks and in written comments on the coursework. And this might usefully also be made more explicit for examiners.

A related set of issues arises from the following report (another examiner, another student):

> I found this study a difficult one to evaluate and assess according to the criteria.
> She shows a very pleasant and sensitive approach to her tasks, and writes in a style which may be more appropriate to a reflective novel, rather than an academic paper, in both Tasks A and B. This was pleasant to read, and certainly raises appropriate issues, but I feel she may need some help in appraisal of styles of presen-tation . . . . Tasks C and D were presented in a more critical and 'informed' manner.
> I could not with all honesty say that the criteria were fulfilled in a manner that I usually expect, but I feel that this individual style should be encouraged and channelled in a beneficial way.

Commentary

This examiner finds difficulty in using the list of criteria provided, and implies that different criteria may be needed to appraise the autobiographical tasks (A and B) as opposed to the more academic tasks (C and D). This draws attention once more to the potential conflict between assessments based on general qualities as opposed to specific qualities in the writing. The examiner also notes a tension between the *intellectual* criteria presented in the guidelines, and other qualities (sensitivity, individual style) which are felt to be of value (worth encouraging) and yet do not seem to be recognized as such in the criteria provided. In awarding a 'pass', therefore, this examiner has clearly had to carry out quite an elaborate act of interpretation with respect to the listed criteria.

> *It might be useful to provide criteria for the individual tasks *as well* as general criteria.

The following is from the other examiner's report on the same student:

> Criterion 1: Very well expressed accounts and analyses, mostly discussing practical issues. Closer connections could have been made to theoretical underpinning, but this is probably due to the rather practical bias of her in-service experiences.
> The taught parts of the MEd course together with the required reading should help redress the balance.
> Criterion 2: A critical capability ably demonstrated.
> Criterion 3: Some very sound ideas centred around a realistic research proposal, but rather uncritical of implications of chosen methods. This again is probably due to lack of experience...
> Criterion 6: Very high in all aspects of this criterion. A most readable profile.

Commentary

(A) It is interesting that this examiner found no difficulty in using the listed criteria to find that the student's work could be judged as adequate. This marked difference between the two reports is a reminder how far academic judgments may remain highly personal, even where the same set of criteria are apparently being used, and thus how fragile is the basis of shared interpretation on which the use of those criteria depends. What is common to both reports, however, is that in different ways they take advantage of the ambiguity, the questionableness of the criteria in order to pass students whose work displays qualities that the criteria do not seem explicitly to take into account. In other words, the examiners took full advantage of the interpretive freedom created by the reflexive basis of the listed criteria, even though the list of criteria *seems* to be an attempt to reduce precisely such interpretive freedom in the pursuit of 'objectivity'.

(B) The examiner's comments in relation to criteria 2 and 6, contrasted with those relating to criteria 1 and 3, suggest that a distinction is being made between general intellectual capacities (which the student possesses) and particular experiences (which the student lacks but which can easily be remedied). This is a familiar distinction, but it is implicitly contradicted by the underlying rationale of the access course itself, which rests on the claim that theoretical understanding can be derived from reflection upon practical experience. Perhaps this contradiction derives from an interesting ambiguity in the notion of 'theory' itself: theory may be taken either as a body of knowledge derived from books, or as a series of generalizations and connections derived from experience. So this examiner is saying that it is the *former* (book-based learning) which the student may lack, and that this does *not* reflect adversely on her ability to theorize her experience, in the latter sense.

> *This distinction may be worth clarifying both for students and in future versions of the guidelines to examiners.

Some of these issues were discussed, by most of the staff who had taken part in the assessment process, at a meeting from which the following extracts are taken:

> *M*: Do you not find that whereas in a dissertation the student can effectively *mask* their personality behind the quotations and the rest of it, the portfolio is very revealing of their personality?
>
> *RW*: ...Are you saying that that makes them a *good* basis for making academic judgments?
>
> *M*: What's the track record of these students? I don't believe in these predictions. I think these portfolios are as good a way as any other ...
>
> *RW*: As good as a BEd dissertation?
>
> *M*: Well, probably slightly better, but that's just a guess, especially as there is a lot of tutorial help in a dissertation. It does seem that you are getting a judgment about *the person*.
>
> *N*: I'd like to enter a murmur of dissent here. I felt myself trying to resist the power of the personalities coming through, because I still have in my mind some sort of distinction between personality and academic potential and achievement. I'm looking for something a bit more rigorous, a bit more objective, so I think I did put more weight on the book review and the research proposal than on the autobiographical bits, although I found the autobio-

graphical bits more interesting . . . . But I'm not happy with the idea of equivalence to the BEd dissertation, as it is here: 'Up to BEd Honours standard, or NOT up to BEd Honours standard'. I think that's a misconception. When we assess the BEd Honours dissertation we are assessing a level of attainment: when I assess a portfolio, I am assessing a student's potential ability to complete an MEd. I'm not asking myself the question, 'Are they as "good"?'

Commentary

There is a tension between personal qualities as inseparable from (and even as a dimension of) intellect, and personal qualities as a plausible rhetoric which can disguise (and even masquerade as) intellect. Later in the discussion, this led to the suggestion that the function of itemized criteria is to act as a *check* upon a 'holistic' appraisal, so that even though itemized criteria may appear to be *directly* related to the final judgment, their use in the process of making the judgment is always *indirect*, with some form of overall appraisal always intervening at some stage in the assessment:

N: But about this holistic approach: do you cross reference as you do it, or do you do it retrospectively, at the end?

Q: I had them (the detailed criteria) in front of me as I read the work.

N: So you were engaged in this dialectic between the whole thing and the individual criteria —

M: Didn't you find that very difficult?

Q: I read each task and then I looked at the criteria.

N: But did you also say: 'Taking the thing as a whole it also feels right?'

Q: Yes, that was my ultimate judgment . . . .

M: . . . That does seem to me to be the most demanding way of doing it.

N: But isn't it the only way? Don't we make all our judgments in that way?

Commentary

The detailed criteria refer to and are based upon a notion of equivalence between the access course portfolios and the BEd dissertation, but examiners were more concerned to make judgments in the light of their interpretation of students' potential ability to undertake the MEd course, to which the list of criteria does not refer. There is thus a dramatic contrast between the formal detail of the assessment procedure and the practical awareness of the *purpose* of the assessment which guided examiners in making their judgments.

> *Students who read this report prior to publication said that they wanted the criteria for establishing equivalence between the BEd dissertation and the portfolio to be made more explicit (as was suggested earlier). However, this discussion suggests that 'making criteria explicit' is easier said than done. The staff involved thought it would be more helpful to rework the assessment procedure on the basis of analyzing the competencies required by the MEd course:

> If we analyze the needs of the MEd we may well come to the conclusion that the BEd Honours...doesn't meet the criteria as well as the MEd access course. In fact, I'll bet that's the case. Which comes back to what you said earlier about driving a coach and horses through what are considered to be appropriate entry qualifications.

Commentary

This is fundamental: the contradiction inherent in a course which is intended to validate individual experiential learning, and yet which is organized around tasks and criteria derived from an *academic* requirement, rather than from competencies which are required because in the end they will be used. Now that this contradiction has been made explicit, it may create pressures for a change in the conception of the course, which in the end may be difficult to resist. We are well aware of the institutional power behind the system of 'appropriate qualifications', but 'a coach and horses' is a force to be reckoned with too . . . .

General Commentary

Clearly, any evaluation must be a small selection from a vast array of potentially relevant data and a vast array of potentially relevant comment upon the data collected. I have tried to guide my selections by (a) including data from the range of different sources and aspects which seem essential to the course process, and (b) focusing the commentary on those aspects which seem to offer opportunities for practical change. These potential amendments of practice, which have been indicated throughout the report in various places, will need detailed consideration by those who may be responsible for their implementation, and these have been collected into a discussion paper — see appendix D. What follows here is a summary of the key issues which have emerged from the commentaries at a number of different points in the data. Listed together, they may serve to map out a general area for reflection, not only on this particular course, but concerning courses such as this, which are tied to an academic standard, but which are based upon the appreciation of individualized experience.

1 What is the relationship between a teaching process based on collaborative discussion (in order to maximize learning from individual experience) and the counselling process of facilitating self-clarification? What is the role of the teacher within collaborative learning?

2 On what basis is a teacher in a position to offer a 'challenge' to students' presentations of what they have learned from their own experience? What form of 'expertise' could a teacher draw upon in order to do so?

3 How can statements of educational objectives and assessment criteria give greater recognition to the close association between intellectual and emotional qualities, processes, and skills?

4 How can greater clarity be given to the function and usage of *general* evaluative concepts (such as 'critical', 'analytical', 'interesting', 'insightful') which are necessarily matters of individual interpretation but which are (inevitably?) treated as professionally shared objective meanings?

5 How can the relationship between holistic appraisal and specific listed criteria in the operation of an assessment process be made more explicit and more public?

6 How can the inevitable tension be reduced between externally prescribed standards and internal standards derived from the detailed qualities of students' individual work?

7 Is the function of the course of study diagnostic, remedial, developmental, or evaluative? Or what combination or sequence of these?

8 Can course tasks and objectives be tied more directly to competencies which *will* be required at the *end* of the course, rather than to equivalence with a set of competencies derived indirectly and notionally from another course of study?

At this level, the evaluation of the MEd access course provokes a consideration of the general relationship between the academic procedures of educational institutions (from infant schools to universities), the educational achievements of individual experience, and the competent performance of social roles, which *both* are supposed to promote.

Appendix A

The Aims Statement of the In-service BEd

1 To extend the teacher's understanding of teaching;
2 To develop the teacher's ability to evaluate critically the areas of study in (1) above;
3 To extend teachers' awareness of educational research as a means for informing their own teaching experience and practice;
4 To allow teachers to share their professional experience with teachers from different institutions and sectors;
5 To allow teachers to develop a deeper understanding of one or two areas of study related to their own perceived professional development;
6 To provide teachers with opportunities to undertake investigations into aspects of education appropriate to their professional interests.

Appendix B

MEd Access Course — General Introductory Notes

Aims

...The link between the MEd and the MEd Access Course is the idea of 'research' as learning-from-experience. In order to *learn* from experience...the following are felt to be important:

a Willingness to consider alternative explanations and to avoid (temporarily) choice between them;
b Willingness to explore 'new' ideas or fresh combinations of ideas;
c Willingness to accept, make explicit, and explore one's own uncertainties.

All of these imply a considerable degree of self-confidence (of a particular type); and an increase in self-confidence has been found to be a (perhaps *the*) major outcome of the course.

Assessment

It is expected that the qualities listed above will *develop* during the course, and thus the question of whether the *early* tasks are 'up to' a standard should not arise directly. BUT: the writing you do will be highly individualized, and yet you will feel that someone, somewhere, has an external yardstick against which you will be measured. There is indeed an inescapable tension here: don't expect NOT to feel worried about it! Even after noting the following points:

> The course tutor's role . . .is thought of as encouraging and challenging you to explore your ideas 'further', no matter 'where' they are at present.
> It is *expected* that everyone on the Access course will be offered a place on the MEd.
> If there is any doubt about this, arising out of your work, you will be contacted individually . . .and any problems and worries will be made quite explicit. So, if this does not occur, you should not interpret 'critical suggestions' as a disguised threat that your work isn't 'good enough' . . . .

Discussion

There are a number of types of question which will guide the discussion process, and these are another way of indicating the aims of the course. For example:

Can you generalize from that anecdote?

Can you give a specific example of that generalization?

Can you suggest various possible explanations of that?

What evidence might you need in order to choose between those explanations?

What did you find surprising, contradictory, etc. in that experience?

What do those different experiences, ideas, etc., have in common?

What important discrepancies, contrasts, etc. do you see between those various experiences, ideas, etc?

Appendix C

MEd Access Course — Final Report

Yvonne Larsson

1   The aims were clearly established in terms of preparation of the students for entry into the MEd programme and the development of professional self-appraisal, a most important concept in terms of teacher awareness of his/her classroom ability, and particularly for educational research.

2   The tasks set were designed to extend the teacher's deeper understanding and more detailed knowledge of specific areas of enquiry relevant to the professional development of those participating.

3   The small group situation was crucial to the achievement of the aims. The student needed plenty of guidance, structure, and reassurance in the tutorial sessions.

4   . . .The tutor's role was vital in establishing the standards required. It is considered that if the student feels inadequate to the tasks, the comments should be structured appropriately. It would also be worthwhile having individual sessions with the students at times to explore aspects in depth.

5   The skills component was obviously a very important part of the course, and the need for students to develop an analytical approach and a 'critical edge' to their appraisal was clearly outlined. Although skills are essential, content is also part of the training process . . . .

By the conclusion of the five evening sessions, and the completion of each student's portfolio, the expectation is that each student should be able essentially to replace common sense with systematic thinking, replace anecdotal knowledge with generalizable knowledge, and replace generalized knowledge with detailed knowledge. . . .The course is invaluable preparation for students without BEd Honours. It certainly opens up the opportunity for students without (the BEd Honours) to develop the necessary skills (including thinking processes) to embark on worthwhile research. The Access course . . .should be continued in its present form, but additional activities could be inbuilt, based on the individual needs of the students enrolled. There are safeguards also for students who do not reach the required standard in the time allocated, for example, advice to enrol on Diploma courses.

Appendix D

MEd Access Course — Discussion Paper on Future Developments

(This paper is based on a detailed evaluation report)

Formulating More Precise Course Aims

Would it be preferable to reformulate the course based on an analysis of the competencies required by the MEd? How should the latter task be carried out? Is there any other way of making the aims explicit?

Are the following acceptable as overall course aims?

The development of intellectual self-confidence.
The ability to make theoretical interpretations of one's own professional experience.

Are there any other aims (at this level) which would be worth specifying, in advance of an analysis of the MEd requirements?

What role (if any) does book-based theory have in the course aims for the Access course?

Do All Students Need the Whole Course?

Should the first stage of the course, perhaps, involve the negotiation of an individual learning contract with each student, in relation to a statement of objectives (derived perhaps from an analysis of the MEd)?

Teaching Strategies

See copy of 'General Introductory Notes' (appendix B to this chapter)

Are the paragraphs headed 'Aims' and 'Discussion' in need of amendment?

The paragraph headed 'Discussion' suggests forms of intervention that a tutor might make. Are these acceptable, incomplete?

Are the 'Notes' as a whole an adequate guide to students for the structuring of their discussions, in the absence of a tutor?

Is it agreed that it might be important for the tutor *not* to be present for the whole of a discussion session?

Assessment Criteria

Does each task need a separate set of criteria?

Would a copy of the 'General Introductory Notes' be useful to examiners as further guidance as to criteria?

PART THREE: FINDING A FOCUS

'The mind has mountains'

Gerard Manley Hopkins

Chapter 10

Research Topics and Personal Interests: Fictional-Critical Writing

Introduction: Finding a Focus

It was argued in chapter one that there currently exists a host of topics on which practitioner action-research would be valuable and even necessary. It might therefore seem that there could hardly be a *problem* about 'finding a focus'. On the contrary, we might say, at any one time we are likely to be aware of countless 'problems' to which our current practices are only questionable and provisional solutions; and every day brings new issues, in the shape of official 'policy statements', 'directives', and 'guidelines'. But in another way this *does* create a difficulty: which of these many 'problems' (or aspects of a problem) to select for the sustained attention which an action-research project requires.

It is as a means to this end — the selection of one focus for inquiry from among a number of possible concerns — that a procedure termed 'Fictional-Critical Writing' is proposed. It consists of writing a short piece of fiction about one's professional life and then analyzing the story to elucidate what professional themes it presents. This process has been used as part of the introductory phase of the Anglia part-time MEd in Educational Research; the theory behind it is presented in Winter (1986) and Winter (1987) pp. 139–45. The following presentation has four stages: (1) The need to make explicit our implicit professional interests, (2) how fictions can be seen as statements about the meaning of experience, (3) how the analysis of a fiction (the 'critical' half of 'fictional-critical writing') makes explicit the significance of the fiction's implicit meanings, and (4) some examples of teachers' stories together with commentaries on the stories which show how they are related to the specific research topic chosen.

The Problem: Making Implicit Interests Explicit

Clearly, some aspects of this process of selecting a focus for an investigation are dictated by relatively straightforward considerations. There are certain things for which our job description holds us responsible, and certain matters are given priority by staff meetings, or through specific requests from our immediate superiors or groups of colleagues. Let us suppose, therefore, that we have narrowed the choice to two or three possible topics, for example, evaluating the staff appraisal scheme, implementing the National Curriculum in mathematics, or improving the school's links with parents. Even supposing that we have chosen just *one* of these topics: we are still hardly in a position to begin an investigation. The scope of each topic is potentially vast: where would we begin? Take 'staff appraisal': almost everything going on in the school *might* be relevant; there is a shelf full of books written specifically on the topic, and its various different aspects involve consideration of a wide range of general theories (sociology, social psychology, management, learning theory, observation methodology, etc.). Few of us will have the time to do a *comprehensive* review of all of this, so we will use our *existing* knowledge (as skilled, experienced, professionally educated practitioners) as a basic resource. We will therefore *select* which aspects of the life of the school are relevant, and we will only consider *some* of the literature relating to *one or two* aspects of the topic. So we still have the question: how do we make these selections?

The simple answer is: we decide what seems 'interesting'. But this merely serves to renew the question. What is the nature of our 'interest'? Although our own immediate understandings and concerns give us a rich and complex set of resources from which to start (and these must not be underestimated), they will necessarily be organized in a particular way which itself is problematic. In simple terms, our state of awareness of a given matter (our interests, knowledge, assumptions, sets of categories, etc.) is organized in such a way as to make it 'fit in' with all the other aspects of our experience. But the way it 'fits in' is not according to a neat logical pattern. In emphasizing the rich possibilities of our initial awareness, we are also emphasizing such things as emotions, motives, unconscious memories, ambitions, irrational anxieties, overarching beliefs, and half-glimpsed insights. This is not an orderly, coherent structure: it contains oddities, quirks, ambiguities, contradictions, and tensions.

Thus, when we feel 'particularly interested' in staff appraisal, or 'more interested' in one aspect of staff appraisal than another, this sense of interest has many different sources. Some of these concerns may be potentially at odds with each other — so that I may (for example) be very keen on improving the quality of teaching, but very hostile to the idea of measuring effectiveness. Some concerns, of which we are hardly aware, may be quite deeply buried, originating in half-forgotten experiences — for example, of being badly taught in a certain way during our own schooling, or of being continually compared unfavourably to others in early childhood.

Now, it is not possible to *rid* ourselves of these manifold and contradictory aspects of our interest in a topic. They are what our 'interest' consists of. But if we are to make use of the different dimensions of awareness with which we approach an area of our practice, it is important that we understand them as fully as possible. Otherwise, if left unrecognized, this complex structure of interests will — without our noticing — distort our decisions as to how we should interpret and evaluate the various accounts and events brought to light by our investigation. The result will not be that our conclusions are 'wrong', but that we may not succeed in gaining any insight that we didn't have before. In other words we may find that, subconsciously as it were, we make any 'new' insights 'fit in' with our current pattern of interests, so that the precious time invested in our inquiry may not — in the end — yield much substantial progress.

This, then, is the basic reason for trying to make explicit our concerns. We want to dig down to find the foundations of the interests we bring to a topic, to reveal the themes and beliefs on which our interest depends, to make explicit the contradictions and ambiguities which will be an important resource for developing our thinking. We want to move as quickly as possible beyond what is already familiar, and to find the points where we have genuine uncertainties, where time spent in an investigation may more quickly be rewarded with genuine progress. (For a different approach to a similar set of ideas, see the Postscript in this volume on 'ideology' and 'critique'.) It is to this process that the writing and subsequent analysis of fiction can contribute. Let us, then, in the next section, begin to explain this suggestion, which may strike some readers as somewhat unexpected in a book about methods of 'research'.

Fiction and the Meaning of Experience

Stories as Statements

By 'a story' what is meant is: a fictional narrative — of any length. The first point to be made, then, is to distinguish 'stories' from other forms of narrative — diaries, histories, and autobiographies, for example. Given this distinction, the next point to note is that a story does not simply recount events, and that our interest in a story is not simply that we want to know 'what happens next'. A 'story' (in contrast to other narratives) is a selection of events (some real, some imaginary, some half-way between the two) which have been organized into a pattern which has some sort of general significance. Hence: 'stories are statements'. They can be printed or acted or filmed, and even danced or set to music.

If the entertainment value of stories lay *merely* in our desire to know 'what happens', it would be difficult to explain why people often go to see the same play or film several times, and enjoy rereading favourite novels. It would also be difficult to explain the universal appeal of the 'crime thriller' TV series, because we always know in advance that the regular stars will survive whatever danger they may temporarily find themselves in. The 'thrill' is not a real uncertainty as to what will happen, but a form of playing with that uncertainty. Each episode thus expresses a general statement about the perpetual threat to moral order posed by the forces of evil, about the fragility of virtue combined with the necessity that virtue should triumph. It is the permanence of the threat which requires the eternal repetition of its overcoming. Different individuals require different moral heroes with whom to identify, ranging from Terry McCann (Arthur Daley's 'Minder') to Miss Marples.

Or consider a performance of *Hamlet*. We know very well the sequence of events. What we are interested in is the play as a statement about the relationship between action and analysis, or between confidence and despair. Similarly, *Othello* is a statement about jealousy, or about the relationship between heroism and cynicism. On the different scale, in Richmal Crompton's innumerable 'William' stories the statement might be said to concern the well-meaning rationality which lies behind boys' apparently wild and destructive behaviour. Of course, the generality of the statement underlying a story bears no relationship to its 'literary' worth. General statements concerning the endangering of the good and the punishment of the wicked are just as much the underlying message of *Noddy Goes to Toytown* as of *Paradise Lost* and of a story about 'a little girl called Jessica and a great big giant' made up on the spur of the moment by a parent attempting to lull a two-year old to sleep. But all this does raise the question of what we mean by 'a statement'.

Stories as Ambiguous Statements

In order to portray a fiction as a *simple* statement, as in the previous section, it was necessary to reduce the meaning of the story to an empty abstraction. As soon as one considers the details, statements about meaning become both complex and open to question. Thus, one interpretation of *Hamlet* is that it concerns a 'poetic' idealist refusing to tolerate sexual and political corruption. Alternatively he can be seen as a 'neurotic' adolescent failing to come to terms with the complex practicalities of the real world. *Othello* can be seen as a noble hero unfortunately and viciously betrayed, or as a naive soldier whose lack of human awareness renders him hopelessly and inevitably vulnerable. A 'William' story can be read as a somewhat sexist celebration of 'boys will be boys'. Alternatively it can be interpreted as a critical analysis of the way in which male children, excluded from participation in the adult male world, take refuge in fantasy adult role play, which continually brings them into conflict with the real adult authority of the world from which they have been excluded. In each of these cases the main point is that the fiction asserts *both* versions simultaneously, thereby creating not simply 'a statement' but the rich ambiguities of fiction. Stories, in other words, are interesting precisely because they are ambiguous — and they convey this ambiguity easily and naturally, in contrast to the highly convoluted statements that would have to be made in order to express a similar degree of complexity.

A fiction, then, selects characters, events, and situations in such a way as to bring out the ambiguities and contradictions of experience. In this sense they are like 'myths' — 'engendered by the inherent disparity of the world' (Levi-Strauss, 1981, p. 603) for example, by the inherent oppositions between power and weakness, youth and age, heroes and villains. But the oppositions are never simple: power has its vulnerability, and weakness its sources of strength; the hero may go to heaven, but 'the devil has all the best tunes'. Bertholt Brecht makes this into a point of principle. His plays 'treat social situations as processes, and trace out all their inconsistencies' (Brecht, 1974, p. 193). He elaborates:

> Each scene, with first an independent meaning, is discovered through its connection with other scenes to share in another meaning (quoted in Brooker, 1988, p. 81),

thereby demonstrating 'the instability of every circumstance, the joke of contradiction' (Brecht, 1974, p. 277). To grasp the overall sequence of different scenes is thus to be forced to stand back from each one individually and to appreciate the ambiguities and ironies of the story-as-a-whole.

In this way, since the *statements* made by a story are always ambiguous, it is perhaps more accurate to think of it as posing *questions*. Is this character admirable, or not? Is this situation regrettable, or not? The answer is always: 'Yes *and* No.' In this respect, stories vary: some are less ambiguous than others. But no story is *entirely* without ambiguity, and so no story fails entirely to pose the reader a question (see Belsey, 1980, pp. 90–3).

Different readers therefore can always respond in different ways. We can sympathize with Satan rather than with the angels, with the giant rather than with Jack and his 'poor mother', and with 'the naughty dog' rather than with Noddy. It is the underlying ambiguity of stories which makes them always open to a variety of approaches, by readers with differing concerns, values, or purposes. Even the author has no absolute privilege here: authors can learn more about their own stories from hearing readers' responses.

A Story is a Reflexive Statement

At its simplest, the ambiguity of a story is created by the fact that the reader may sympathize with the various characters it contains. In order to create them, the author must (in different ways) identify with each one. Consequently, the ambiguities of a fiction may be thought of as representing (in some sense) the ambiguities in the author's personal awareness. This is a complicated matter, of course, but we can begin by suggesting that an author *embodies a set of ideas* in a fictional form. A particularly clear example of this is Sylvia Ashton-Warner's novel *Spinster* (Ashton-Warner, 1985a). This contains within a fictionalized narrative an account of the author's theories of education, which she had previously tried unsuccessfully to publish directly. Five years later, following the success of the novel, she did publish the non-fiction form of these ideas, in *Teacher* (Ashton-Warner, 1985b), so that we can clearly see how she used the fictional form as a framework for her theories. For example, the same incidents are presented (in almost exactly the same words) in *Spinster* on pages 14, 197, and 200–1 and in *Teacher* on pages 106, 43, and 36–7. In the 'Letter to my American Publisher' which introduces *Teacher*, Sylvia Ashton-Warner identifies with the words of her own fictionalized 'self-portrait':

> I'm sending the Creative Teaching Scheme from my country to yours, Bob, because I believe it is important. As Anna Vorontosov said in *Spinster*, 'I must do what I believe and I believe in what I do; life is too short for anything else'. I believe it is universal. (p. 24)

But this example also raises questions about the *differences* between the fiction and the non-fiction. Why does Sylvia Ashton-Warner portray herself fictionally as an exiled foreigner and as an emotionally frustrated spinster, when she was born in New Zealand (where the events take place) and seems to have discussed her teaching regularly over lunch with her husband (see *Teacher*, pp. 107–8)? As an answer, we might suggest that this might be her way of representing symbolically the loneliness of her educational crusade and her sense of the erotic component of the teaching process: she is 'wedded' to her class of Maori infants. Moreover, to put it this way begins to suggest that a fiction does not simply 'contain' ideas that an author already knows, but is also a means whereby the implications of incompletely formed ideas can be explored. The lack of factual accuracy 'frees' the ideas so that they can be *played with*, in the play of inconsistency and analogy between different scenes, different characters, and different images.

The link between play and discovery is a familiar theme in learning theory. In fictions, authors play with ideas, images, events, people, and situations from their own life experiences, so that even where (as in the case of Sylvia Ashton-Warner) the fiction is in part a self-description, it is always a self-exploration as well. It is for this reason (because we know that writing is a process of self-discovery) that we encourage young children to write stories: the organization of words is the organization of our experience into meaning.

Another familiar notion here is that of 'imagination'. The play of imagination in constructing a fiction allows a wider range of our experiences to be drawn upon in constructing the text. It allows fantasies, fears, desires, and unconscious motives to be organized in relation to specific memories. In this way, organizing a fiction has something of the therapeutic quality of dreaming.

There is, finally, an even more precise sense in which writing is an act of self-exploration, namely as a struggle with the medium of expression itself. Experiences are always more complex than the words we have available, so that what we may intend as *descriptions* of an external reality always turn out to be accounts of the relationship between our own inner reality, the world we perceive, and the shared symbols and linguistic usage in which we try to link the two (see chapter four, on reflexivity).

It is possible to take this relationship for granted and write a fiction which *seems* to be simply descriptive of characters and events, but very often an element is included which acts as a sort of concealed confession: 'This is not *actual* reality; this is me, trying to make sense of reality.' So we have films made about film-makers and musicals about the staging of a musical. Shakespeare the playwright makes Hamlet stage a play as one of his attempts to find out what is 'really' going on. Indeed, one of the commonest story patterns is that of an investigation to find 'the truth', so that the events of the story describe the same process as the writer is engaged in through the writing of the story. In this sense all hero-investigators are indirectly representing their authors, as *seekers* in search of meaning. Thus in the film *The Third Man* we may remember mainly images of the corruptions of post-war Vienna — crumbling mansions, Orson Welles in the sewers — but the central figure in the *story* is Harry Lime's friend Holly, a writer of thrillers, who — like his creator and like us as we watch the film — is trying to find out the truth, about Harry and about his world.

What I have tried to argue in this section is that the writing of a fiction is a method of organizing personal experience in order to explore its possible meaning. As a 'method' it has certain advantages: it is able to present both the contradictions of experience and its general significance; it also suggests the reflexivity of any attempt to judge the meaning of events: all descriptions are (at some level and in some way) *self*-descriptions.

Analysis: Fictional-*Critical* Writing

But the meanings of fiction are only implicit. A further stage can thus take place, which clarifies the ambiguities and contradictions of the experiences represented in the fiction. This process has something in common with what is called 'criticism', but it is essential to note that — unlike a lot of 'literary criticism' — we are not concerned to make *value* judgments, but to *make explicit* the meanings (the purposes, the implications, etc.) which the story partly embodies and partly conceals. In a similar way, the contradictory reversals and combinations of dream symbolism are subjected to a rationalizing explanation by the psychoanalyst. The first stage of the therapy is the recollection of the dream, which brings together significant experiences in need of exploration; the second stage is to explore the significance of the experiences by analyzing the structure of the dream.

Freud has called the analysis of dreams 'the royal road' to the unconscious. The process described here is put forward, in an analogous but more cautious fashion, as 'one possible route' to a level of personal awareness of our professional concerns which we may otherwise not easily bring to mind. We start by elaborating a story which embodies the complexity of those concerns in a 'playful' and implicit form, and we then make explicit the structure and implication of those concerns by asking of the story: 'What sort of statements about our (your/my) concerns is this story trying to make?'. In order to answer the question, we consider how one detail relates to another in the light of the text as a whole, and notice points of ambiguity and contradiction, which are likely to be points where new themes might emerge (see chapter four — dialectics). It is at this point that the discussion begins to turn towards what professional themes and concerns might be an appropriate focus for an investigation. These are the themes which have emerged (from the story and its analysis) as being both important to the writer yet also somewhat unformed and ambiguous, and thereby seem to offer scope for clarification and fresh insight.

It is worth emphasizing that this sort of analysis is most easily carried out *in the first place* by someone other than the writer. This is not because someone else can see the *real* meaning which is hidden from the writer, but simply to engage in the collaborative process in which we learn with and from others (see chapter four). The analysis of a story provided by another is a step in a conversation, in which writer and reader compare interpretations. What makes the collaborative process particularly appropriate in this context is that, because the meanings of fiction are always ambiguous, different readers (of which the writer is one) will easily find alternative interpretations with which to question one another. In this way, the mutual exchange of stories and interpretations readily becomes a fruitful learning process for the exploration of complex professional issues. The next section provides examples of this process, showing in each case how the writing and discussion of a piece of fiction relates to the selection of a research topic.

Examples

This 'fictional-critical' process (of writing a story about one's professional life and exchanging interpretations as to the themes it reveals) has been carried out by groups of teachers at the Anglia Higher Education College. It takes place during the introductory phase of a part-time in-service course (the MEd) for which a topic for investigation has to be selected. The three examples included here are all from the first group of ten teachers. They have been selected to give a balance of length, style, and topic, and because the discussions — the 'critical' phase — were fully documented. Of the remainder of the group, one worked from a radio play, and two others produced non-fictional, autobiographical writing. The work of the other four has been excluded with great regret, due to lack of space.

Obviously, it is not possible to prove that the topics chosen or the form of the investigations would have been different had it not been for the writing of the stories. However, a number of matters can be reported which suggest the value of the process. One of the teachers wrote in her project proposal that she intended to carry out a detailed reanalysis of her story, in order to make explicit the ideology with which she was approaching her investigation. Another said, after the discussion of his story, that he intended to write another, more closely related to his current professional responsibilities, which seemed to indicate a sense of the *potential* value of the work. A third said that writing and discussing her story had clarified for her the total negativism of her feelings towards her current work, and played a crucial role in her decision to make an immediate change in her career direction (a decision which proved quite quickly to have been highly productive). Finally, I have used the process myself. My story and its analysis are to be found in Winter, 1986, and the decision as to the focus of inquiry which is described there (educators and authority) led directly to the two investigations included as chapters six and nine in this volume.

Special Needs Education:
'The Magi'

Ann Leontovitsch

(Ann Leontovitsch is Acting Head of a Special School for children with learning difficulties — both moderate and severe)

Peter looked at the blur of colours on the table. He picked up the wooden peg board and threw it onto the floor. It made a clunk and clatter as all the pegs flew under the desks and chairs. Peter smiled. He waited for the teacher to come to him. He liked it when she held his hands and made loud noises with her face close to his. But today she looked round and sighed and continued to rustle something shiny. Why didn't she come? Jane didn't come either. Peter liked her too. She was busy wrapping another child in a piece of striped material. A girl started to pick up the pegs and put them on the table in front of Peter. He threw them on the floor again. Miss Smith made some sharp noises and the pegs were taken away and a jigsaw put on the table. Peter threw it on the floor but it didn't make a nice noise only a dull sound and no-one came to him. He sat there watching the patterns of shadows on the window.

Someone was pulling at his jumper. He lifted his arms. He saw dark and smelt warmth then it was light again and Jane was talking quietly to him. Peter smiled. Jane pushed his arms into some stiff material which scratched him and smelt strange. Peter tried to move away but she held his arms firmly and pulled the material around him. She took his hands and pulled him to his feet, then pushed something onto his head. It hurt his ears. He shook his head but it wouldn't come off. Jane held his hands tightly. Peter was afraid. His arms hurt, his ears hurt and there was a strange smell. He started to cry. Jane heard the thin distressed wail and spoke softly to him. She wiped his face. Peter liked Jane, he didn't feel so frightened now. She pushed his tongue back into his mouth and pushed his chin to close his mouth. Peter tried to swallow but couldn't, he opened his mouth and allowed his tongue to feel free again. Jane put a shiny box into his hand. Peter liked the pattern on the box and held it up in front of his face.

Someone was pushing him in his back. He put his foot down carefully on the floor and moved forward to avoid the push but it happened again and again. At each step another push. Peter looked at the shiny patterns of his box. Someone snatched the box from him. Peter stood there. He had nothing to watch now. Jane pulled his arm and he walked with her. The piano started to play. Peter smiled. He liked the feelings the music made through his feet but Jane led him out of the door. He stopped. He wanted to stay with the music but Jane gripped firmly on his arm and pulled him back into the classroom.

Commentaries

1   [by R Winter — initially]
    A sense of irony is created by the gap between Peter's limited awareness of the Christmas play and the *scope* of what he is supposed to represent to others (one of the 'wise men'). So we are led to ask: is there perhaps a form of wisdom in the pure sensuousness of Peter's level of experience? Is this story, then, a plea that he also should be taken *seriously*?

2   [by Ann Leontovitsch, after discussion with other members of the group]
    The needs of the system — the need to aim at 'normality' — are posed against the needs of the child. Caring adults nevertheless don't know what the child's needs are, or rather, are not really sure what those needs are. Should 'education' be aimed at Peter's normality?

I was asked: who wanted the children to take part in this type of activity? In my mind was a mother, crying, saying how nice it was to see her child looking 'normal'.

What I've learned about my professional work: I felt that my thoughts on the failure of what we provide for our children with severe learning difficulties were similar to the ideas in other people's stories on the lack of *relevance* of the education system. What should we actually be doing with our children? How can we make education relate to the children's reality? Should we attempt to do so? What is reality? Teachers, educational managers, parents, and children all have different realities.

The Story in Relation to a Research Focus

My story was concerned with our lack of understanding of a severely handicapped child's perception of the world. Each child presents a new set of questions for the teacher. Also, my belief that much of what we do in the classroom has no relevance to such children. So my research topic is concerned with the ways in which teachers of special needs children could develop new skills to meet the needs of those children through in-service training. The connection is the difficulty teachers have in meeting the needs of children with severe learning difficulties.

Subsequently, in response to a strong recommendation from an LEA adviser, Ann changed the focus of her project from in-service education to the evaluation of a recent administrative and curriculum change: the integration of the secondary age children in her school with *severe* learning difficulties with the secondary children with *moderate* learning difficulties. However, Ann's summary of this new project still has echoes of the problem of Peter and the Christmas play, as in the following extracts from her introduction:

This piece of research will evaluate the changes that have taken place in the school, particularly the experiences of the pupils with severe learning difficulties. As such, it is a case study of the educational experiences of a group of pupils....The SLD children are now being offered a wider curriculum, but are they able to benefit from these areas and cope with the new demands being made upon them?....Are [they] enabled to adopt more 'normal' behaviour patterns by the example of the MLD children, or are they being bullied or laughed at?....I hope the study will help us to understand better the experiences of these pupils and to provide a better basis from which to plan any further changes.

Children's Writing
A Fable

Helen Thorne

[Helen Thorne is Deputy Head of a junior school]

'Mr Wilcox, telephone for you.'

'Who is it, Beryl? I'm up to my eyes right now. Sorry, Mary, I don't mean you, but that wretched phone hasn't stopped ringing today. You go ahead. It's not that important. I'll see you later. I'll catch you before you leave. O.K. Beryl, I'll take the call.'

Peter Wilcox sighed, rearranged his frown into that of the calm chief executive, and picked up the receiver.

'Hello.'

'Is that Mr Wilcox?'

'Yes, speaking.'

'Is that Mr Wilcox . . . . Sunnyglen School?'

'Yes . . . look, can I help you at all?'

'It's about the swimming pool.'

'Sorry, I didn't catch your name.'

'It's Mrs Willis . . . . I'm calling about the swimming pool. It's just not good enough, you know.'

'But, Mrs Willis, there must be some mistake. We haven't got a swimming pool.'

'You can't fob me off like this. My boy went swimming today, so I know what I'm talking about and I'm telling you it's just not good enough.'

'Look, Mrs Willis, I'm afraid I just can't help you. We haven't got a swimming pool, so whether it's good or not is hardly at issue. There's obviously been some sort of mistake here. Surely you need to speak to Mrs Thompson at Sunnyside. They have a swimming pool. Let me give you their number.'

'Yes, but I was sure . . . . He told me . . . .'

'Ah, here it is . . . 857445 . . . . Have you got that now? Glad to have been able to help you . . . . Bye.'

As Peter made his way to the staffroom to make himself a well deserved cup of coffee, he dedicated a moment of sympathy to Marjorie Thompson, head of Sunnyside. His parents were bad enough but at least they knew what school their child attended. Maybe there was something in this parental involvement business after all. Still, perhaps it was a bit unkind of him to actually give the woman their number. Chances were that she'd have cooled down before she'd have found the number for herself . . . .As it was . . . hard luck, Marjorie.

Mary was washing her coffee mug. Her bag and coat lay across a chair in anticipation of departure.

'Mary, you wanted to see me, didn't you?'

'I was going to tell you what happened at the pool today . . . .'

'The pool . . . ?'

'Yes, you know, we took the third year up to Brisco Park . . . .'

'I've been out all day at that seminar. It completely slipped my mind.'

'Ah, well, I was going to tell you about Dean Baker. Forewarned is forearmed, and his mother is bound to be on the phone before long.'

'What's he done this time?'

'He threw all his underwear into the pool after the lesson, so we brought him home in his trousers and anorak.'

'And his clothes?'

'Clogging up the Corporation's filter system by now . . . I'm surprised his mother hasn't been on, complaining about the cost of his thermals. Still, he's been difficult all term, since his mother remarried . . . .'

'Oh my God. What's her name? It's not Willis, is it?'

'Yes, I think it might be. I'll check his file.'

'Oh well, there's no point in worrying about it any more tonight. Let's leave it for now. No doubt I'll have to have it out with Mrs Willis tomorrow.'

'Well I can't see what she has to complain about. If her son behaved himself for five minutes there wouldn't be all this fuss!'

When Peter arrived at school the next morning, Mary was in the office reading Dean Baker's file. The green envelope was twice as full as most in the cabinet, bulging with reports and recommendations.

'Medical reports, educational psychologist's reports, social worker's reports, minutes of case meetings, correspondence, academic records, samples of work....Thank goodness they're not all like this. Anyway, there's a letter here from the social worker; Mrs Baker remarried last February and her name is now Willis, but Dean will still be Baker.'

'Thanks, Mary. Just leave it all there.'

The file sat on a shelf near his desk during the morning, a tangible reminder that not only was he going to have to explain to this mother that despite being in receipt of Family Income Supplement, they were not entitled to the replacement of underwear wilfully destroyed by their child, but also that her son's headmaster was not the sort of person who made mistakes about the pupils in his care.

The phone rang fifteen times that morning, but there was no call from Mrs Willis.

Towards the end of lunchtime there was a group of children outside his office. The dinner lady who accompanied them could barely control herself to speak. Her head nodding with righteous anger, she snapped, 'Fighting in the playground again' and stormed away.

Peter was not surprised that Dean Baker was one of the group. The boy eyed him sullenly.
'I spoke to you yesterday about fighting,' began Peter.

The boys shuffled and looked down.

'And here you are back again today. Why?'

Perhaps, Peter thought to himself later, he had lacked his usual energy in dealing with thugs this lunchtime. Probably still feeling a little uneasy about his mistake with Mrs Willis. Still, he spoke to Dean and his mates about their behaviour twice a week as it was, and he had not yet managed to find a strategy or angle that made much difference. Children like Dean took up so much time, and Peter found it increasingly hard to believe that it was not time wasted. Oh well, at least he hadn't had to speak to the boy's mother yet: with a bit of luck the silly woman believed him.

The large green file lay there on his desk. Quietly, Peter picked it up and put it in the wastepaper basket.

Beryl was answering the telephone. 'Good morning, Sunnyglen School. Educational Welfare Office? Just one moment while I look out the file.' She went over to the filing cabinet and returned to the telephone.

> 'I'm sorry but we do not have any records for a pupil of that name....Yes, well, Dean Baker...it does sound familiar....Look, do you think it's possible you've got the wrong school? Why not try Sunnyside; people are always getting us muddled...Any time, you're welcome. Bye.'

Dean Baker and many of his friends began, gradually, to fade until they were barely visible to the naked eye. If they ever turned up at Sunnyside, no-one ever mentioned it.

Peter Wilcox became the Headteacher of the innovatory primary magnet school. It was a tribute to his pioneering work in the County, and the publication of his article: 'The Management of Resources and the Child with Special Educational Needs'.

Commentaries

1 [by R Winter, initially]
Headteachers are highly thought of for their mastery of certain forms of paperwork (articles on themes dear to the DES, such as 'The Management of Resources'). But this is at the expense of the paperwork concerning *children*. Children *and* their files thus 'disappear' from the school-as-a-resource-management-problem. The only fable-like quality here is that in this story the 'disappearance' is literal, not a mere forgetting. With splendid irony, the annihilated child is given the name of 'Baker', so that he becomes the unrecognized offspring and real responsibility of Kenneth B, the government minister. Similarly, 'Peter' is perhaps the betrayer of the One who 'suffered the little children to come unto Him'.

2 [by Helen Thorne, after discussion with other members of the group]
Peter Wilcox was initially well-meaning, but had reached a point in his career where he felt he should be achieving some 'real' success. Although he was successful in terms of status, he was aware that his school, and ultimately he himself, was having no beneficial effect on certain pupils. Despite the best efforts of the

bureaucratic machine, he was failing with Dean Baker, and losing the confidence of Dean's mother and possibly other parents. He sacrifices his earlier ideals, and decides to succeed purely within the limits of the system he inhabits.

The story arose out of a staffroom joke — a way often used to dispel threat or criticism from outsiders. I thought it might be interesting to explore the feasibility of the joke. The effect of the story is clumsy: pupils cannot of course be 'lost'....However, I have tried to investigate the growth of the wish which is concealed behind the joke, and how this 'wish' — seen in individual situations — is gradually being reflected nationally in some of the ideas in Kenneth Baker's Education Act. What will happen to children who offer nobody 'credit'?

The Story in Relation to a Research Focus

Discussing her story, later, Helen said, 'It is about *guilt*. When I teach, it is *I* who learn — the children disappear, especially ones with difficulties'. In this way, she continued, Peter Wilcox also represents an aspect of her *own* person as an educator, and it is these two comments which most clearly link her story with what became her research focus.

Helen's original intention was to investigate strategies for parental involvement, and there are traces of this theme in the story, but she then moved school, and the project she eventually chose to undertake concerned methods for developing children's *confidence* in writing.

She begins her project proposal by expressing her dissatisfaction with the excessive dependence of children's writing upon their *teachers'* initiatives. Pupils' writing, she says, frequently shows the 'uniformity' of the set instructions, rather than the 'individuality' of the pupils. They 'need a great deal of support from the teacher...and...faced with a written assignment (do) not know how to proceed unaided.' In her summary, she writes:

> The strategies I propose to use are culled from the work of Donald Graves, Lucy McCormick Calkins etc, and include giving complete freedom of choice over subject matter, the provision of an audience, and a real context for written work, the occasional use of a 'scribe', and the publication of chosen completed work. Children will be encouraged to feel that their work belongs to them, not to the teacher.

In elaborating upon her document for the rest of the group, Helen said, 'In the teaching of English, the teacher aims to become passive: the teacher has to disappear.' Thus, in emphasizing the *reality* of the context and the audience for the children's work, and their relative autonomy in relation to their teachers, the focus of Helen's project can be seen as an attempt to reverse the situation described in her 'Fable': it is the *teacher* who disappears, not the pupil.

Educational Drama and the Teacher-Pupil Relationship: 'The Bronze Trumpet'

David Crosson

(David Crosson is Head of a junior school)

Long ago, and in a distant land, where there were not as many flat surfaces as there are today and here, there lived a race of small and nimble people. In many ways they lived small and nimble lives; avoiding trouble where they could, and finding what they needed where they were.

Of course, they had great difficulty in avoiding *all* the problems that threatened them, and if I were to tell you that they lived in a thick forest, you would see what I mean. So if they were scratched badly by long thorns while collecting fruit; if they were worried by or about their neighbour's children, or if they wanted to be able to fly among the trees without being seen, they would make a visit to a hut in a clearing just outside their village.

In this hut there lived an old man who never spoke unless he were spoken to; who never laughed unless he found something funny; who never failed to cry at others' misfortunes. And with him lived a little girl who tried to behave in the same way and sometimes did. The old man, as you will suppose, knew many things which others did not, and was unsurprised, therefore, at the problems he had in teaching them to the little girl.

Now one day, when the sun shone strongly in sharp patches on the leafy floor (which was no surprise to anyone except, perhaps, the old man), the little girl turned from her game with the glass beads to find that her friend had gone. He was no longer sitting in the shade listening to the birds (which was a surprise to her). So she left her beads and went to see, and took a long time about it because the old man was in none of his usual places.

It was only by chance, or so it seemed, that the little girl should finally come to the place of the Great Trees and should see the old man crouched down with a bent, brown back, at the ribbed foot of the greatest tree of all. Still and quiet, he leant against the brown, bent trunk as if he were staring at its clutching roots (although the girl could see that his eyes were closed). Still and quiet, the girl waited without breathing, for she *had* learned quite a few things although she was little.

She waited and stared for so long that what she saw, or she herself, seemed to come and go, and wobble in and out. So it was a shock to find that the old man was looking straight at her and as if he had been doing so for some time. He was speaking too, and this is what she heard:

'and because of that I suppose it's time for you to learn how to do it before it's too late; although I don't know if you know enough yet (although I *don't* know how anybody knows what anybody knows about). So you ought to start and here it is.'

And he held out towards her a fine wand of bronze, hollow, with one end flared and a stem the thickness of what *you* would call a pencil and the little girl would not. (If I know what she knew about.)

The little girl hesitated to take it, for she knew what she didn't know about. She did ask him what it was, however, and the old man tried not to tell her that he'd just told her. He wasn't perfect, so he told her that and then he told her this:

'It is a special thing, and the most difficult to use. How old it is, I do not know, but I am not the first to use it, and may not be the last.' (With a smile at her.) 'It is no more than a hollow tube, yet with it we can hear the voices of the trees.'

And he smiled again as if she understood him. While she watched, he twisted the narrow end of the wand between two thick ribs of the tree's trunk. Then he put an ear to the trumpet end, crouching in the way she had seen him before. Then he stood up and held the wand out again.

'Find out how to use it,' he said. 'I'm going to feed the tortoises.' And off he went.

Now the little girl took the wand, although she was rather worried, as I suppose you or I might have been. For the tree was very big and very old and was very fierce-looking for a plant and to a little girl. But she did as she had been told and shown. She tried and tried and tried to hear the voice of the tree, but heard only her own little heart beating in her ear, and she knew that wasn't it.

She tried twisting the tube into different places on the trunk. She tried listening with either ear, and even turned the wand around and pushed the small end of it into her ear as far as she dared, despite the warnings she had had from the old man when she was smaller and had first played with her beads. (And if you don't know what those warnings were, I fear you didn't listen properly when you were younger than you are now.) She tried turning the tube in different ways. But she did not hear the voice of the tree. So with a heavy heart and a sore ear and aching back she returned to the hut as the sun began to set. She had worked hard, you see.

On her return, it was beginning to grow dark and she saw the old man waiting for her in the soft air by the door. He handed her a bowl of food, without saying anything, and she said nothing back for a long time. When she did speak, it was to say:

'If you could show me again how you did it, then I could do it too.'

At which the old man shook his head and laughed gently:

'No, my dear. You have not understood your task. You will not hear the tree sing by copying me. You must not do what only looks right, as a hare or a golden beetle would see. It must be how it feels to you. If you can't make sense of it, you won't hear it. I'll come with you tomorrow if you'd like, for a short while.'

And in a short while they both fell asleep.

The very next day they set off, with the trumpet, to the place of the Great Trees and the little girl tried again and the old man sat beside her in the leaf-litter and watched her. While she worked, she watched him too, very closely but slyly, from time to time. She saw him frown and she saw him smile; she saw him tracing patterns in the loose leaves and gazing up into the knotted forks and blue sky. She heard him sigh and she heard him chuckle but she didn't hear the tree sing to her at all. Yet in what *he* did there seemed to be a pattern. So more and more, and perhaps without knowing even what she did, she trimmed the tube and changed her position so that he smiled more often and seemed more contented. But still she did not hear.

She grew tired, of course, and was so eager to please his old face, and she did grow ashamed of herself and thought she would never do it. So, at last, when he seemed to be smiling and nodding more often than before, she cried:

'I think I've done it. I can hear the tree.'

At which the old face frowned as deeply as the tree was ribbed and the old voice asked:

'And what do you hear?'

'A roaring sound, like a lion!' (But she was rather red-faced.)

Then the man grew angry and muttered and stood up painfully and started to go, until she called him back.

'You mistake me,' he said. 'I was only smiling because I did the same thing as you when I learned, although I don't think I lied. Your job is not to please me. You will only do so when you really understand (Although of course you please me when you sing and dance.) Do not think, my dearest child that you will find the way by watching my face. You must listen only: to yourself inside and the tree outside.'

Watching her, and her crumpled flower-face, he smiled once more, and patted her head and left her.

So the girl was alone to listen. And she did listen and heard less and less as time went by. The voice of the birds faded; the soft whisper of the wind took its leave; even the sound of her constant heart shrank away. And by and by in the small silence there grew a tinier sound. It grew in a swell; a rush; a solid echo: wave after wave filled the trumpet and her head. She listened and listened and then ran home.

'And what did you hear this time? For I see you have had some success.'

'It was a sound like the sea, where I have been once, if you remember. I never knew a tree could hold the sea.'

'Well my dear,' he said, 'It can't, you know, not in that way. What you have heard is only what we hear all the time but seldom listen to. It is nothing but the sound of our own ears talking to us. Listen now and you shall hear it still.'

So, in quiet tears, the little girl listened and heard it still, although much gentler.

'Now,' he said, 'you have made a beginning. Until you hear yourself you cannot understand anything. If you know how to listen you may have more success tomorrow.'

In this way the second day ended and the girl heard the sea in her head, until she saw it in her dreams.

On the third day she made her way alone to the Great Trees and listened once more for their voice. She did indeed hear the sea again but now she knew it was herself she paid it no more attention than her heart or her breath. And by and by she grew aware of something else: a deep sighing it seemed, and a soft flutter too, that rocked her gently. So she lay against the body of the tree and listened. When she awoke she remembered what she had heard and ran to the hut.

The old man was not outside on her return. So she went inside and did not see him at first, for he lay on his bed in the corner as if he were asleep, although it was the middle of the day. In her excitement she took his arm and told him what she had heard.

Slowly he listened and slowly smiled.

'Yesterday,' he said, 'you heard what was inside you. Today you have heard outside. The tree moves, you see, in the wind and with its growing, for even though it is creased and huge it is still young. The branches sigh against each other and the leaves flutter against the air. Although it soothes it is not the sound of its voice.

No, it speaks with voices that alarm and disturb and tell me what I need for those who come with questions. You must learn, and quickly now. You have to listen both in and out. I will come with you this afternoon but first I must sleep.'

The girl left him and played with her beads again, though now they seemed no more than babies' toys and she left them in the dust.

When the old man had settled himself at the foot of the tree (which he did slowly, for you must remember that he was very old), he sat for a long time, staring at the sky, watching the black slash of a vulture floating high above. When he did look again at the girl, she could not look back, but stared in her turn at the brown of a withered leaf.

'Sometimes, they say,' he said, 'that people learn most easily when they are afraid. Perhaps most quickly, rather. So this afternoon we must try such a thing, for time presses. Take the wand and try again. And do not be frightened, for I shall frighten you.'

Then the young girl took the trumpet, even though she did not want to, and the old man frightened her. While she tried to listen he was a lion, who roared and spat at her back. While she tried, he was a crow who perched on the lowest branch and laughed at her. He was a red baboon who reminded her, with a wagging finger, of lost parents. He was a black spider who spun a web around her until she knelt alone with no world that was hers.

Then he was a small maggot with her own face upon its

head, and she could bear it no longer, but flung the trumpet into the bush and wept. And at the last he was a soft pigeon who settled on her shoulder and wept, too, into her ear until she became quiet and soothed its feathers. Home they went, and if they held hands they did not talk.

But in the morning they did, and although the old man looked very frail, they laughed at the game they had played the day before, and could not agree who had been the more stupid. Yet there was something to be told to her, and there is something that I must tell you. For on the other side of the mountains there lived a race of giants who lived large and complicated lives in a land that they had made entirely flat. And in the way of giants who think they know everything they had a special purpose to make everyone else know it too. Or so it seemed to the old man, and to the girl when he told her.

> 'You see now why we have no time left,' he said. 'For it is only the fear of what I know that keeps them on the other side. And they must know that I will not be here much longer, as you would know if you had been listening on that first day by the trees. So you must take my part today and they will be in fear of what you know and stay where they are. All that you need more is, of course, the voices of the trees. It must be today, for that silly game yesterday took too much of my strength.'

As she left alone that morning, the young girl felt as if she had never walked the path before. You can, of course, imagine some of what she felt, and yet not all, unless you had known the old man for as long as she. And when she found the tube under the leaves it was to her, for the first time, her own hand that held it. And it was to her, for the first time, her own ear that listened. So for the first time she heard the voices of the tree that morning. Many voices, high and low; young and old; some singing and some in a whisper. It was a tinkling rush of urgency that filled her with excitement and alarm; that tore up and down the sap veins of that tree that had listened for so many years to all round it.

She could not have told how long she listened, for the voices changed constantly and there was always some new note to take her anxious fancy. When she did leave she flew back to the hut with long legs and the braids in her hair fell loose.

The old man lay in his bed with his face to the wall, but he knew she had heard, he knew. So she did not have to tell him. She could not have done.

'Then you have heard at last,' he whispered, still to the

wall. 'Then you are ready for the black shapes on the mountain top, and I can sleep.'

'But no,' she cried, 'oh, no. How can I be ready yet? How can I be like you?' And her secret tore from her: 'I have heard, yes, I have heard indeed, but *I do not understand what they say to me*. I asked them so much and they replied, but I do not know what they answered.'

Then he turned slowly to face her and whether his look was of laughter or sadness she could not tell.

'Well now, there's a thing,' he said, looking quite at her. 'It would surely take my years and yours and more to *understand* what is said. I don't think it could ever be done, you know. I've never done it and never thought it was important, although it would be interesting.'

'Then how can it be of help to me?' She shouted angrily in her loneliness. 'What have we been about these last days? Why was I frightened so much and so badly yesterday. Tell me.'

He turned back to the wall, with an apology and great effort, and answered quietly.

'The trees are bigger than anything else on either side of the mountain, you see.'

In the long silence, she knew she had to go. She thought of the mountain tops. She could imagine the flying feet coming towards the hut from the village. So she went to meet them, shutting the door quietly after her with the hand that did not hold the trumpet.

Commentaries

1   [by R Winter — initially]
    This is an elaborate story of the educational process, where the learner must learn (in order): independence of the teacher, honesty, self-knowledge, and only then — finally — knowledge of the outside world. The whole process takes a long time and yet it is very urgent: the vulnerable young must be protected against the threats of the adult ('giant') world. This tempts the teacher to take short-cuts, and thus to use fear as a motive. Similarly children expect, impatiently, not only to *know* the world but to *understand* it as well. But perhaps to 'know' the world is sufficient. An

interesting distinction: is this an argument against premature conceptualization, a plea that 'experience' itself be allowed time to develop? The trees are the *natural* world; so perhaps we have here a Rousseau-esque view of the child's naturalness threatened by the giant's *culture*.

2 [by David Crosson, after discussion with other members of the group]

The ability to hear the trees was intended, in some respects, to represent a goal that was, for the old man, sufficient *in itself* — the mastery of knowledge was valuable as an act in itself. This gave him status and confidence, but it was also a *betrayal* of the young girl, whose sense of learning required something else, and who was going to find herself, finally, adrift in the outside world without help to confront it (the giants).

I was concerned, when writing, merely with the interesting mismatch of purpose, but on reflection I find this question of betrayal more worrying — for what is the ultimate purpose of our aims for children? Since we know more than they do, we have to take certain things for granted — suppositions, predicted into their futures, about the value of either the knowledge or the skills they will require. Are these suppositions adequate, and are they understood by the child at the time of learning, or later on?

Looking back on the story, it took shape as an allegory, but it was not finally as simple a one as I had intended, for the characters grew and destroyed what was meant to be a light-hearted and humorous thing. What I now realize is that I sense some violence being perpetrated on the girl, leaving aside the 'frightening' scene. For, from the start, the old man is thrusting *his* purpose upon the girl. Although he seems to know a lot about the process of learning, he seems to know little about the girl herself — her sense of the world other than as a *learner*. The process is *student*-centred rather than *child*-centred. She is, after all, an *apprentice*, and he does not fulfil her requirements as an independent person, although he insists on her learning independently as far as possible. Is there a way out of this for the teacher? Is not even the question 'What do you want to do today?' loaded with implications that undercut the 'child-centred' desire?

The fairy-tale tone of the narrative was initially nothing more than a device for telling the story, but its hectoring tone at times is perhaps a further reflection of [the points in the previous paragraph]; for the story-teller is in the same predicament as the teacher: he holds all the meanings, at least at the beginning . . . .

With the giants of the National Curriculum coming over the mountain, can the teacher find a mode of teaching, or a language, which allows the child to make her own sense of things from her own purposes (as perhaps the trees have done) or is this indeed a liberal and Rousseau-esque fantasy?

So was the old man right after all?

The Story in Relation to a Research Focus

David later described his story as 'a critique of the conventional teacher-pupil interaction'. His research project will focus on educational *drama* as a possible point within the curriculum where a more acceptable basis for this interaction might begin to be developed. He introduces his project proposal as follows:

> In educational drama the teacher (and pupils) can manipulate the social environment in the classroom by restructuring, through a consensus of the imagination, the relationship between the participants in a process of learning. 'Dramatic' techniques (such as establishing dramatic roles, achieving flexibility within the relative status of those roles, teaching in role, finding a focus for the action, locating a feeling response, building dramatic tension, etc.) can be used to free teachers and pupils from the constraints of the 'real' time and place. More importantly, perhaps, teachers and pupils may find, through their restructured relationship, a new 'easiness' with each other, a way of working which can avoid many of the interpersonal and professional problems that occur within more conventional and perhaps institutionally derived relationships. As a result, children often *seem* to understand and communicate more readily.
>
> This has been my experience, from time to time, in using educational drama in the classroom. It is an experience which has provided insights into processes of learning — demanding reflection upon the nature of those processes as well as the role and purpose of the teacher.

Postscript

Some Notes on 'Ideology' and 'Critique'

Ideology

One of the most important and awkward questions for social research is: how can researchers claim to be any less 'biased' than those they are researching? One approach is to say that the researcher makes 'a critique' of the 'ideology' of those she or he is investigating[1]. However, these two concepts ('ideology' and 'critique') — although indeed potentially very useful in clarifying the nature and the purposes of social research — are complex and often controversial. In particular: how (or in what sense) is it possible to be 'outside' ideology, in order to make a critique of it? The nature of this debate and its links with the approach to practitioner action-research presented in this book are outlined below. (For a more detailed exposition and explicit reference to the academic tradition for theories of ideology, see Winter, 1987, pp. 60–87).

We may start with the general idea that 'ideology' refers to a set of ideas which interpret the world according to the point of view (the interests, values, and assumptions) of a particular social group. These ideas may be expressed directly in books, pamphlets, and slogans, but also *indirectly* in specific roles (with their special sets of expectations) in symbolic objects, and in ritualized practices. One conclusion we may be tempted to draw from this general description is that whereas ideology presents the world from a 'skewed' point of view, 'science' can (by means of 'research') present the world 'as it really is' — objectively, impartially.

But the problem begins when we notice that according to the original statement, it must be the case that *all* social groups have an ideology, so that sharing an ideology is one of the ways in which *any* social group exists. For example:

> Ideology is not an aberration . . . it is a structure essential to the life of societies. (Althusser, 1977, p. 232).

Ricoeur (1981) agrees (although in other respects he writes from a very different standpoint). The origin of ideology, he says, lies in 'the necessity for a social group to give itself an image of itself' (p. 225). Ricoeur goes on to suggest that as part of 'an image of itself' any social group will create:

A   a set of justifications for its regular activities,
B   a set of practices which are taken for granted and thus do not need to be analyzed,
C   a simplified schema which makes the ideas of the group clear-cut and effective,
D   an orthodox standpoint from which unwelcome alternatives and innovations can be rejected (*ibid*, pp. 225–8).

However, if *all* social groups necessarily create a self-justificatory ideology, then it must follow that social researchers cannot be free of ideology either, since they also necessarily belong to a social group. They will at the very least belong to the group of 'social science research workers'. Furthermore, we have seen throughout the arguments of this book that 'research workers', as a separate group share a range of orthodox assumptions, routine practices, self-justificatory claims, and special role expectations, which we have tried to oppose, in the name of practitioner action-research. Together, these constitute the ideology of that small specialized group who make a living by 'doing research'. In a different way, this is also part of a general and widespread ideology concerning 'science', as part of a belief in progress, a reliance upon technology, and a yearning for certainty and control. So the problem is: ideology is interpreted as 'not-the-truth'; but if all social groups have an ideology, and since we are all members of various social groups, then the thinking of each of us is ideologically influenced. What resources, then, do we have for discovering a 'truth' beyond ideology?

Before attempting to deal with the problem, let us see how it could affect us as professional workers attempting to engage in an action-research project. I argued earlier, at the beginning of chapter two, that one of the defining characteristics of knowledge in the professional areas concerned with understanding people is that it is *not* a system of accumulated certainties, but always a matter of interpretation. In order to take professional decisions, we are forced to *choose* one interpretation or another. Thus, concerning any given educational situation, there will be competing ideologies with differing interpretations as to how that type of situation 'ought' to be dealt with. (Should the head be 'a forceful leader' or 'a skilful delegator'? Should grammatical rules be taught as such to a whole class, or only as they arise in individuals' work?) Each particular opinion will be surrounded by an ideology consisting of general attitudes, moral and political values, and accumulated 'knowledge' supporting that opinion. Now, when we choose to investigate an area of professional decision-making, we are bound to choose an area in which we have strong concerns and commitments. Otherwise we wouldn't be 'interested'. The pun here is revealing. It serves to warn us that we could easily find that we have set up our investigation so that it confronts one ideology (which we oppose) from the standpoint of another (which we share). In the end we may have to accept that this is inevitable, but the immediate problem is that we risk not learning anything new. Instead, we may simply *rehearse* (once more) a familiar debate, armed with 'fresh' evidence within well-worn categories. In contrast, if research is to be worth the effort involved, it needs to offer (in some sense at least) the prospect of going *beyond* competing ideologies, to offer the possibility of *changes* in our thinking and in our practices. So we return to our problem. Is this possible? And if so, what *sort* of procedures and changes are we concerned with?

In working towards a positive response to this question, the first point to note is that the statement, 'All thinking merely represents the self-justifying interests of some social group or other' is self-cancelling. If it is true of 'all thinking' then it is true of the statement, 'All thinking merely represents . . . etc.' because that statement itself must also represent the self-justifying interests of a social group. Thus, by warning us against 'all thinking', the statement also warns us not to accept the validity of the warning! Arguments of this type, therefore, do *not* succeed in excluding the possibility that there *might* be certain forms of thinking by means of which we can go beyond the ideologies by and in which we normally live. So we can continue optimistically in our search.

The second point, closely linked with the first, is that ideologies — although powerful influences — are not totally engulfing and overwhelming. One of the reasons for this is that each of us belongs simultaneously to many different groups — a family, a profession, a specialized role within that profession, a gender, a social class, an ethnic group, a political state, an age group, etc. Furthermore, we *identify* with an even wider range of groups, based on political views, religious beliefs, cultural activities, and so on. If, as has been argued, *all* groups generate an ideology, then the thinking of any one person at any one time will be influenced by many *different* ideologies. The total effect of 'ideology-as-a-whole' is *not*, therefore, to create a simple and unified set of meanings; instead it leaves our thinking full of contradictions and ambiguities.

Thirdly, the ambiguities and contradictions of ideological representations created by the structure of ideology (as noted above) are further increased by the complexity of the way in which we respond to them. Take for example the never-ending sequence of police serials on TV. Superficially, of course, they assert the ideology of 'law-and-order', the need for Us ('decent people') to be vigilant against Them ('deviants', 'criminals'). But in order to show the threat posed by deviants, they have to be shown as very nearly 'getting away with it'. This creates excitement and entertainment, but it also makes the actions of the deviant seem glamorous, and amidst the exitement of the chase we almost *want* them to 'get away with it'. Similarly, by exposing 'corruption in high places' the adventures of the crime-busters give us grounds for doubting the decency of the very institutions they seem to be protecting. In the same way, returning to educational ideologies, to hear the assertion 'You've always got to be tough with kids in the first few weeks' is — momentarily at least — to renew the thought that possibly one might *not* be tough, to wonder why the point is being made at this particular time, and thus even to wonder whether it really is such a good strategy as the speaker suggests. The point is that the relationship between a statement and our response to that statement is always complex: we respond at many levels, drawing on irrational, contradictory, and partly submerged emotions and motives. Hence, the reason why ideological representations are so widespread and so endlessly repeated is that their impact is ambiguous and confused, and thus *in need of* continual reinforcement.

Altogether, then, we can conclude that ideology is not like a hammer which beats our thoughts into a simplified unity, nor like a prison wall which confines our understanding within clearly defined limits. Instead, one might imagine it as a sort of loose mesh, which indeed entangles parts of our thinking, but through which certain types of reflection can (with effort) struggle to freedom. It now remains to consider what types of reflection these might be.

Let us begin by making a distinction between two types of thinking:

1 the act of *interpreting* experience in terms of a set of categories;
2 the act of *questioning* the categories in which interpretations are presented.

What we might conclude from the previous arguments is that all *interpretations* of experience must fall within ideology: we do not have the means to stand outside *all* ideologies and view the world 'as it really is' (although this is the implicit claim made by positivist social 'science' — see chapter three). On the other hand, the ambiguities and contradictions of ideology mean that we *do* have resources for *questioning* any given set of categories. Since ideology is not unified, we always have access to alternatives. This is the reason why the method of 'opposing' ideology presented below is not called 'science' but 'critique'.

Critique

The following brief suggestions concerning methods for 'critique' are derived from the principles presented in chapter four. As such, they offer an overall perspective on the critique of ideology which corresponds to the model of practitioner action-research offered in this book.

1 *Reflexive Critique*
   Ideology presents accounts of situations in the form of apparently objective judgments which are supposed to correspond accurately

to an external reality. It thereby creates certainties which can be taken for granted.

Critical analysis, in contrast, questions these judgments by making explicit the way in which they inevitably depend on interpretations which are based in the speaker-writer's general system of values, assumptions, and interpretations. (For an example, see chapter four, pp. 44–6.)

2   *Dialectical Critique*

a   **Ideology** presents phenomena as unified and stable. It thereby creates a sense of the world as straightforward, comprehensible, and familiar.

Critical analysis, in contrast, questions the unity and stability of phenomena by searching for their inherent contradictions, which render them unstable and thus likely to change, to become *un*familiar. (For example, see chapter four, pp. 49–50, 54–5.)

b   **Ideology** presents phenomena as clearly distinct and separated from each other. It thereby creates a set of easily used category distinctions. Similarly, it creates a series of apparently isolated issues, each of which on its own seems relatively easy to grasp.

Critical analysis, in contrast, questions this distinctness and separateness, by searching for the concealed links between apparently distinct phenomena, and also for the ways in which individual events and issues are given significance by the context of their relationships with others. (For an example, see chapter four, pp. 52–3.)

3   *Collaboration and Risk*

Ideology presents us with interpretations of our experiences which explain our existing interests, concerns, and assumptions and thereby justify them as reasonable and well-founded.

Critical analysis, in contrast, questions those interpretations by seeing them as only *one* set of possibilities *alongside* (and no longer necessarily preferable to) the interpretations of others taking part in the investigation as our collaborators. Others, in that they play different roles in the situation, will be members of different social groups and will thus have differing interpretations in the light of their own interests, concerns, and assumptions. (For an example, see chapter four, pp. 57–8, 61–2.)

The risk here is twofold. Firstly, the analysis will question the conventional (ideological) 'hierarchy of credibility' between different accounts of the situation, and will thereby bring into focus the rationality of groups whose point of view is usually dismissed as irrational, uninformed, or unimportant (Becker, 1971b). Secondly, the analysis will question the process by which we treat our own interpretations of events as preferable to those of others, especially when we define ourselves as 'doing research'. In this sense, by exposing our own interpretations as *only* one possibility among several (those of our collaborators) we question the self-justifying ideology of the researcher's privilege.

4   *Theory, Practice, Transformation*

Ideology presents theories of situations which claim to be valid generalizations based on accurate descriptions of how things are. Armed with the claim to an authority derived from 'the facts', ideology asserts the timeless validity of one interpretation, as a well-founded orthodoxy ('true'), and opposes the claims of other interpretations as mistaken or incomplete ('false'). Ideology confronts the validity claims of one interpretive theory with the validity claims of another interpretive theory.

Critical analysis, in contrast, questions the authority of all theories, by treating them as always open to question (see 1, 2b, 3 above) and thus likely to change (see 2a above). Theories are not, therefore, valid in themselves (as accurate generalizations) but are merely possible strategies which will be tested through practice and particularly through changes in practice. In other words, critical analysis questions the claims of all interpretive theories in the light of the principle that theories and practices are part of an unending process of transforming each other. *Any* 'theory' is therefore only a transitory moment in a cycle of alternations between practice and reflection upon practice, i.e., in the process of developmental change.

Some Examples of Educational Ideology

The previous section offers a general reinterpretation (in terms of the vocabulary of ideology and critique) of some of the previously proposed methods and approaches for action-research. Let us now consider some more specific suggestions that have been made. How might certain aspects of our professional knowledge as educators be seen within a theory of ideology, and thereby exposed to critique?

1   Ideology presents the attitudes and activities of *individuals* as the primary reality, leading to the neglect of social, historical, and political forces[2]. Thus we tend to explain the behaviour of learners as due to varieties of 'personality', levels of 'motivation', or amounts of 'ability'. Similarly, we explain the effectiveness of educational situations as due to the personal charisma of individual teachers or managerial heads, and educational progress as the achievement of individual innovators. By the same token, when things go wrong we can blame the impact of individual 'disruptive' pupils or students, or (when the scope of the problem is

wider) the inadequacies of individual teachers or heads of establishments. In each case the importance of the social, historical, and political *context* is ignored, and this is the ideological appeal: by focusing on individuals we concentrate on issues and processes which seem clear cut and manageable. If the problem is an individual, then she or he can perhaps be 're-educated' (which once more reaffirms the value of our own profession), and at the same responsibility for the existence of the problem is comfortingly circumscribed.

2　Ideology presents the outcomes of socially and politically negotiated *judgments of value* as though they were objects whose value could be established by the operation of a market, i.e., as though they were economic commodities[3]. The basic argument here is that the *price* of something has little connection with its own essentially *worthy qualities*. A small, leaky flat in a fashionable area costs as much as a solid and spacious house in a non-fashionable area; a highly advertised perfume costs ten times as much as a 'Boots Own Brand' version that many would say 'smells just as nice'. In educational terms, a market in knowledge as a commodity is created by a system of examinations and graded certificates, so that the goal of education is displaced from its *essential* concern with the development of understanding towards the acquiring 'currency' or 'capital' in the form of diplomas. (See Becker (1968), and Dore (1976).) This in turn affects many other aspects of the way we come to think about our work, e.g., our conceptions of 'ability', 'intelligence', 'knowledge', 'levels of work', 'appropriate curricula', etc.

　　The ideological appeal of this lies in the ways it creates straightforward technical goals and criteria as a basis for our decision-making. The process of critique would entail noting how the categories in which we interpret a given event or issue depend on our taking for granted the 'market model' of education and would raise the question: how are these categories related to those other formulations of education as 'the development of understanding'? The tension between these two is a permanent feature of attempts to understand educational realities. In wider, more directly political terms, the operation of a market in educational goods (diplomas) appears to justify existing power relations as being based on 'merit' ('intelligence', 'ability', 'qualifications') in the same way as the market in economic goods justifies existing power relations by making it seem as though they are based on 'free' consumer choices and 'free' contracts between employers and employees.

3　Both the above examples are translations into the context of professional life of ideas which originated in the critique of structures of thought concerning politics and economics. In contrast, Becker's widely influential theory of 'the ideal client' arise directly from the study of professional work (Becker, 1971c). Professional work is usually not carried out *entirely* for money: professionals also expect to obtain some degree of personal satisfaction and fulfilment from their work. Hence, in conceptualizing our various 'clients' we will be strongly (but not necessarily consciously) aware that some clients afford us more fulfilment than others. Such clients will present us with just that type of problem that our professional training and level of resourcing allows us to solve, and to know that we have solved. In this way, there arises among teachers and lecturers a set of ideas concerning, for example, 'educable' learners, 'well-motivated students', 'supportive' home backgrounds, and 'positive' peer-group influences, accompanied by their opposites. These ideas add an ideological dimension to our knowledge, in that they provide a set of categories for describing clients' characteristics in terms of professional workers' needs. Such categories will *always* be present, but they can always be questioned, because we can always ask: what categories would we use in order to understand our pupils or students in terms of their *own* needs?

Conclusion

Theories of 'ideology' indicate the ways in which the motives and pressures of practical life influence our perceptions of events and how our practices are affected by those perceptions. The term itself 'ideology' draws attention to the *difficulties* we can expect to experience when we investigate and reflect upon our practices in such a way that we attempt to gain *new* insights and to *change* our practices. Consequently, understanding the structure of ideology helps us towards those forms of analytical reflection by means of which we can question our taken-for-granted ideas. These are the forms of reflection that enable us to explore to their fullest extent the limits of our professional autonomy, and thus to assert our control over events and over the interpretation of events.

We necessarily live within a web of ideologies. Our practices, and our interpretations of those practices are inevitably influenced by the ideologies which shape our awareness of the world in which we live. Our investigations will thus necessarily both begin *and end* in ideology. But that brief, intervening moment of critique (of questioning practices and interpretations — our own along with others) allows us to have confidence that ideology need not, finally and completely, entrap our awareness, that we *can* learn to interpret our experience in new ways, and to shift our practices in directions that — within limits — we choose.

To deny the very existence of ideology is to claim an absolute freedom of thought which is belied by our common experience of regular patterns in the actions and attitudes of people we know, and in our own. At the other extreme lies the claim that we are *forced* to interpret the world in a particular way, because ideology completely determines our thinking and yet so cunningly disguises itself that we are wholly convinced that the world *really* is as we normally (for our practical purposes) interpret it. This represents a degree of despair which again does not square with our experience: we tend to see *other* people's opinions and actions as constrained by influences of which they are unaware, but we then characterize our own opinions as based on a rational appraisal of 'the evidence'. Such a discrepancy suggests that expressions of generalized despair at the overwhelming power of ideology may perhaps have their own concealed motives. More consistent, therefore, and in between these two extremes, lies the claim that we possess the intellectual resources for conducting a critique of ideology. This expresses a fundamental optimism, that in the end we are free to question the structures of our thought, (in spite of the power with which they urge themselves upon us) through momentary acts of radical doubt which are a necessary prelude to real and possible progress.

Notes

1 See Carr and Kemmis, (1986), chapter five.
2 This aspect of the theory of ideology will be found fully expounded in Althusser, (1972).
3 The underlying argument here is presented in more detail in Geras, (1972).

Bibliography

ADORNO, T. (1973) *Negative Dialectics*, London, Routledge and Kegan Paul.

ALTHUSSER, L. (1972) 'Ideology and ideological state apparatuses', in COSIN, B. (Ed) *Education, Structure, and Society*, Harmondsworth, Penguin.

ALTHUSSER, L. (1977) *For Marx*, London, New Left Books.

ASHTON-WARNER, S. (1985a) *Spinster*, London, Virago Press.

ASHTON-WARNER, S. (1985b) *Teacher*, London, Virago Press.

AUGARDE, T. (1984) *The Oxford Guide to Word Games*, Oxford, University Press.

BARTHES, R. (1977) *Image, Music, Text*, Glasgow, Fontana.

BARTHOLOMEW, J. (1972) 'The teacher as researcher', *Hard Cheese* No. 1, Goldsmiths College, University of London.

BECKER, H. (1968) *Making The Grade*, New York, John Wiley.

BECKER, H. (1971a) 'On methodology', in *Sociological Work*, London, Allen Lane.

BECKER, H. (1971b) 'Whose side are we on?', in *Sociological Work*, London, Allen Lane.

BECKER, H. (1971c) 'Social class variations in the teacher-pupil relationship', in COSIN, B. *et al.* (Eds) *School and Society*, London, Routledge.

BELSEY, C. (1980) *Critical Practice*, London, Methuen.

BENNETT, N. (1976) *Teaching Styles and Pupil Progress*, London, Open Books.

BENNETT, N. (1978) 'Educational research and the media', *Westminster Studies in Education*, Vol. 1.

BLUM, A. (1974) *Theorizing*, London, Heinemann.

BRECHT, B. (1974) *Brecht on Theatre*, London, Methuen.

BROOKER, P. (1988) *Bertholt Brecht: Dialectics, Poetry, Politics*, Beckenham, Croom Helm.

BROWN, L. *et al.* (1982) 'Action-research: Notes on the national seminar', *Classroom Action-Research Network Bulletin*, No. 5, Norwich, University of East Anglia.

BURROUGHS, S. (1984) 'The role of the peripatetic remedial teacher', unpublished Teacher Fellowship Report, Brentwood, Anglia Higher Education College.

CARR, W. and KEMMIS, S. (1986) *Becoming Critical*, Lewes, Falmer Press.

CLASSROOM ACTION-RESEARCH NETWORK BULLETINS, 1–10, obtainable from Cambridge Institute of Education of CARE, University of East Anglia, Norwich.

CICOUREL, A. (1964) *Method and Measurement in Sociology*, New York, Free Press.

CROUCH, H. (1988) Unpublished MEd Dissertation, Brentwood, Anglia Higher Education College.

DERRIDA, J. (1978) *Writing and Difference*, London, Routledge and Kegan Paul.

DORE, R. (1976) *The Diploma Disease*, London, Allen and Unwin.

ELLIOT, J. (1980) 'Action-research in schools: Some guidelines', *Classroom Action-Research Network Bulletin* No. 4, Norwich, University of East Anglia.

ELLIOT, J. (1982) 'Action-research: A framework for self-evaluation in schools', Working Paper No. 1, *Teacher-Pupil Interaction and the Quality of Learning*, London, Schools Council (mimeo).

ELLIOTT, J. and ADELMAN, C. (1974) 'Classroom action-research', *Ford Teaching Project*, Norwich, University of East Anglia.

ENRIGHT, L. (1981) 'Diary of a classroom', in NIXON J. (Ed) *A Teachers' Guide to Action-Research*, London, Grant McIntyre.

FISK, M. (1979) 'Dialectic and ontology', in MEPHAM, J. *et al.* (Eds) *Issues in Marxist Philosophy, Vol. I: Dialectics and Method*, Brighton, Harvester Press.

FULLAN, M. (1982) *The Meaning of Educational Change*, New York, Columbia University Press.

GARFINKEL, H. (1967) *Studies in Ethnomethodology*, Englewood Cliffs, Prentice Hall.

GERAS, N. (1972) 'Marx and the critique of political economy', in BLACKBURN, R. (Ed) *Ideology in Social Science*, Glasgow, Fontana.

GRAVES, D. (1983) *Writing: Teachers and Children at Work*, London, Heinemann.

HABERMAS, J. (1970) 'Towards a theory of communicative competence', in DREITZEL, H. (Ed) *Recent Sociology*, No. 2, New York, Macmillan.

HABERMAS, J. (1972) *Knowledge and Human Interests*, London, Heinemann.

HAVES, J. (1988) Unpublished MEd Dissertation, Brentwood, Anglia Higher Education College.

HEGEL, G. (1969) *The Science of Logic*, London, Unwin.

HEGEL, G. (1977) *Phenomenology of Spirit*, Oxford, University Press.

HEIDEGGER, M. (1968) *What is Called Thinking?*, New York, Harper and Row.

HOPKINS, D. (1985) *A Teacher's Guide to Classroom Research*, Milton Keynes, Open University Press.

ISRAEL, J. (1979) *The Language of Dialectics and the Dialectics of Language*, Brighton, Harvester Press.

JACKSON, D. (1981) 'Food for thought', in NIXON, J. (Ed) *A Teachers' Guide to Action-Research*, London, Grant McIntyre.

KEMMIS, S. *et al.* (1982) *The Action-Research Planner*, 2nd ed., Victoria, Deakin University Press.

KITWOOD, T. and MACEY, M. (1976) 'Teaching styles or research styles? The implications of the Bennett report', *Education for Teaching*, No. 101.

LAWSON, H. (1985) *Reflexivity*, London, Hutchinson.

LENIN, V. (1972) *Collected Works*, Vol. 38, London, Lawrence and Wishart.

LEVI-STRAUSS, C. (1981) *The Naked Man*, London, Jonathan Cape.

LEWIN, K. (1946) 'Action-research and minority problems', *Journal of Social Issues*, Vol. 2.

MACDONALD, B. (1980) 'Letters from a headmaster', in SIMONS, H. (Ed) *Towards a Science of the Singular*, Norwich, University of East Anglia.

MACDONALD, B. and WALKER, R. (1975) 'Case Study and the social philosophy of educational research', *Cambridge Journal of Education*, 5, 1.

MARKOVIC, M. (1984) *Dialectical Theory of Meaning*, Dordrecht, Reidel Publishing Co.

MCHUGH, P. *et al.* (1974) *On the Beginning of Social Inquiry*, London, Routledge and Kegan Paul.

MIDWINTER, E. (1972) *Priority Education*, Harmondsworth, Penguin.

NIXON, J. (Ed) (1981) *A Teachers' Guide to Action-Research*, London, Grant McIntyre.

PAYNE, J. (1988) Unpublished MEd Dissertation, Brentwood, Anglia Higher Education College.

POLYANI, M. (1962) *Personal Knowledge*, London, Routledge.

PRISK, T. (1987) 'Letting them get on with it: A study of unsupervised group talk in an infant school', in POLLARD, A. (Ed) *Children and Their Primary Schools*, Lewes, Falmer Press.

RICOEUR, P. (1981) 'Science and ideology', in *Hermeneutics and the Social Sciences*, Cambridge, Cambridge University Press.

ROTH, J. (1966) 'Hired hand research', *The American Sociologist*, 1, 4.

RUSSELL, B. (1946) *A History of Western Philosophy*, London, Allen and Unwin.

SLOMAN, P. (1980) 'A quango for all seasons', *Times Educational Supplement*, April 20.

SOMEKH, B. (1989) 'The role of action-research in collaborative enquiry and school improvement', *Classroom Action-Research Bulletin* No. 9a, Norwich, University of East Anglia.

STEEDMAN, C. (1986) *Landscape for a Good Woman*, London, Virago Press.

THOMPSON, K. and TUNSTALL, J. (Eds) (1971) *Sociological Perspectives*, Harmondsworth, Penguin.

WALKER, R. (1985) *Doing Research*, London, Methuen.

WERTHMAN, C. (1971) 'Delinquents in schools', in COSIN, B. *et al.* (Eds) *Schools and Society*, London, Routledge.

WHITTY, G. (1974) 'Sociology and the problem of radical educational change', in FLUDE, M. and AHIER, J. (Eds) *Educability, Schools, and Ideology*, London, Croom Helm.

WILKINSON, J. (1982) 'Head first into the deep end', *Classroom Action-Research Network Bulletin*, No. 5, Norwich, University of East Anglia.

WINTER, R. (1980) 'Institutional research and institutional relationships: The methodological problem', *Classroom Action-Research Network Bulletin* No. 4, Norwich, University of East Anglia.

WINTER, R. (1981) 'Social research as emancipatory discourse' (mimeo) reprinted (1984) in *Classroom Action-Research Network Bulletin* No. 6, Norwich, University of East Anglia.

WINTER, R. (1982) 'Dilemma analysis: A contribution to methodology for action-research', *Cambridge Journal of Education*, 12, 3.

WINTER, R. (1986) 'Fictional-critical writing', *Cambridge Journal of Education*, 16, 3; reprinted (1988) in NIAS, J. *et al.* (Eds) *The Enquiring Teacher*, Lewes, Falmer Press.

WINTER, R. (1987) *Action-Research and the Nature of Social Inquiry*, Aldershot, Gower Publishing Co.

WINTER, R. (1990) 'Teacher appraisal and the development of professional knowledge', in CARR, W. (Ed) *Quality in Teaching: Arguments for a Reflective Profession*, Lewes, Falmer Press.

WOLF, C. (1989) *Accident*, London, Virago Press.

ZAMORSKI, B. (1987) 'A case study of an invisible child', *Classroom Action-Research Network Bulletin* No. 8, Norwich, University of East Anglia.

Subject Index

Access courses (accreditation of prior learning): 7, 76, 124–157

Action-research –
accessibility of methods: 8–9, 14, 26, 35–6, 38
cyclical format: 11–14, 31, 67, 112
definition of: 3, 8, 10–14
examples of: 15–19, 78–95, 97–111, 124–157
facilitators in: 11, 60
and improvisation: 7, 8
and innovatory practice: 5–7, 13, 54–5, 77n, 112–3
and interpersonal ethics: 23–5, 61, 117–8, 120–2
and learning: ix, 4, 6, 8, 14, 18, 25, 60, 75, 120
need for (value of): 4–5, 7, 28–9, 36, 67
political ideal of: 4
and professional work (professional development): ix, 4, 5–8, 14, 18, 28–30, 34–7, 45, 67, 74–6, 122, 171
and risk: 38, 60–2, 120, 190
time constraints upon: 9, 34–5
see Positivism

Assessment issues: 5, 39–41, 54, 78–95, 142–153, 192

Authority –
of 'factual' accounts: 43, 63, 66, 191
through knowledge ('science'): ix, 28, 30, 43–5, 63, 67, 72, 191
and modes of writing: 62, 72, 74
through status: 56–7, 72, 74
teachers, learners, and: 6–7, 15, 17, 78, 85, 88–92, 125, 133–6, 139, 142, 153, 169, 183

Classroom interaction issues: 15–17, 53, 61–2, 136, 185

Collaboration: 11, 60, 74–5, 114, 168

process of: 24, 56–9, 61, 97, 117–8, 120–2, 168, 190–1
rationale for: 4, 55–6, 61, 62, 190–1

Common-sense –
and action-research: 25, 31–3
and ideology: 193–4
and positivism: 30–5
see Generalization

Common culture as an intellectual resource: 40, 42, 67n, 163–4

Contradiction: *see* Reflection

Critique (of ideology): 189–194
see Dialectical critique
see Reflexive critique

Curriculum issues: 5–6, 8, 52, 54–5, 61–2, 76, 125, 127, 130, 135–6, 138, 153, 176, 184–5

Data –
in conventional social research: 30, 34, 37n
gathering: 14, 20–3, 56, 75, 79, 121
and interpretation: 1, 25, 48, 57, 61, 63, 84, 115, 118
see Selectivity (problem of)

Descriptions: 20, 28, 63
and ideology: 191
and positivism: 42, 50
and the problem of interpretation: 29, 36, 44, 54, 65

Dialectics –
academic tradition for: 51, 68n
and the analysis of change: 49–50, 54, 190–1
and common experience: 46, 48–9, 51
complexity: 48, 98
context of necessary relationships: 47, 52, 113, 115, 118–9, 125
explanation of: 46–51
and language: 46, 64, 68n, 72

198

Name Index

Adorno, T. 68n
Althusser, L. 186, 194n
Ashton-Warner, S. 166
Augarde, T. 67n
Barthes, R. 68n
Bartholomew, J. 3
Becker, H. 73, 190, 192–3
Belsey, C. 68n, 165
Bennett, N. 37n
Blum, A. 67n
Brecht, B. 68n, 165
Brooker, P. 165
Brown, L. 13
Burroughs, S. 76, 96
Carr, W. 4, 137
Cicourel, A. 67n
Comte, A. 29, 37
Crouch, H. 18
Derrida, J. 67n
Dore, R. 192
Elliott, J. 4, 9–14, 16, 20, 24–5, 31, 71, 73
Enright, L. 15
Fisk, M. 68n
Fullan, M. 69
Garfinkel, H. 67n
Geras, N. 194n
Graves, D. 78, 88, 94, 135, 176
Habermas, J. 23–4, 68n
Hart, S. x–xi
Haves, J. 18, 78
Hegel, G. 68n
Heidegger, M. 67n
Hopkins, D. 13–14, 25

Israel, J. 68n
Jackson, D. 15
Kemmis, S. 4, 9–14, 20, 24–5, 31, 71, 73
Kitwood, T. 37n
Larsson, Y. 136–8, 155–6
Lawson, H. 67n
Lenin, V. 68n
Levi-Strauss, C. 165
Lewin, K. 11, 31, 37n, 65
MacDonald, B. 3, 23
Macey, M. 37n
Markovic, M. 68n
McHugh, P. 67n
Midwinter, E. 23
Nixon, J. 4
Payne, J. 17
Polyani, M. 67n
Prisk, T. 16
Ricoeur, P. 186
Roth, J. 73
Russell, B. 68n
Sloman, P. 66
Somekh, B. 8
Steedman, C. 74
Walker, R. 3, 4
Werthman, C. 68n
Whitty, G. 30
Wilkinson, J. 15–6
Winter, R. x, 4, 9, 31, 34, 67n, 68n, 96, 98, 161, 169, 186
Wolf, C. 74
Zamorski, B. 17